Still Shining

Barclay College as a Lighthouse

Glenn Leppert, Ph.D.

Barclay College
PUBLISHERS

Barclay College Publishers

Still Shining: Barclay College as a Lighthouse
Copyright ©2025 by Glenn Leppert, Ph.D.

Requests for information should be addressed to:
Barclay College Publishers, 607 N. Kingman St, Haviland, KS 67059

Library of Congress Control Number: 2024945214
Paperback ISBN: 978-1-7354646-4-0

All rights reserved. Published by Barclay College Publishers. No part of this book may be reproduced or transmitted in any form or by any means, electronic or mechanical, including photocopying, recording, or by an information storage and retrieval system, other than for "fair use" as brief quotations embodied in articles and reviews, without written permission from the publisher.

First Printing March 2025
Printed in the United States of America

ENDORSEMENTS

Still Shining: Barclay College as a Lighthouse is at once a story of transformation and a picture of stability. Glenn Leppert picks up the history of Friends Bible College as it transitions to Barclay College. He makes a seamless transition from the work of Sheldon Jackson's *Barclay College: Lighthouse on the Prairie.* Telling the story of a college is a daunting task, since one must deal with academics, finances, governance, and athletics. Leppert pulls it off and makes the story interesting to all as he explores the impact of each presidential term. The reader almost feels that they are part of the college as Leppert chronicles the challenges, triumphs and transformation of the programs and finances of the college. At the same time, Leppert records the college's consistent commitment to its original purpose. *Still Shining* inspires the reader with a shining example of God's miracle that is open to those who remain faithful to him.

Mark Kelley, Doctor of Ministry, Small Groups and Senior Ministry Pastor and former Barclay College Academic Dean

Dr. Leppert captures a compelling argument that the mission of Barclay College has not changed even though the college changed its name. Nor has the mission statement changed over the years of operation. Focused on the mission of a Bible Centered Education the author proves how it has remained true to the founding purposes.

The author describes how persons and personalities have changed, but all have a historic value for what makes up the college's baseline. An old saying, "things may change, but the story stays the same" is front and center throughout this book.

The author tells the storied goal of accreditation and the argued path to fruition. The plateaus of success are proved through time and many years of energy, as displayed in this book. The years prove that sticking to the goal can pay off.

In my opinion, the book shows how every person named throughout the book engaged in the intellectual battle for the past and future of Barclay College. Captured in this book are the many individuals past and present who have made it the "light on the prairie."

    Dr. James L. Day, Educator and Barclay College Board member.

Exodus 17:14 says "The Lord told Moses to write this on a scroll as something to be remembered." Being mindful of this imperative from God's Word, Dr. Glenn Leppert has meticulously compiled a documentation of the continuing history of Barclay College in Haviland, KS, depicting the journey from 1990-2023. In recording the events and happenings of these years, he conveys the college's struggles and accomplishments from factual accounts, and communicates God's provision and leading for the college. Lover of history and gifted, diligent researcher, he authors *"Still Shining, Barclay College as a Lighthouse"* from one who was there and lived it.

The historic narrative not only confirms that Barclay College has remained true to its founding purpose and mission, to prepare students in a Bible centered environment for effective life, service, and leadership, but also tells of the faithfulness of the Lord to the work of this endeavor. Dr. Leppert has steadfastly fulfilled Ps. 145:4 that "one generation commends His work to another, and tells of His mighty acts." I am grateful that Dr. Leppert has written these accounts "on a scroll", for it IS something to be remembered!

    Marjorie Thompson former Barclay College Board President

DEDICATION

I dedicate this volume to the many students who have made my time at Barclay College a truly wonderful experience. Students, Board members, faculty and administration have been a very rewarding part of my journey at this lighthouse on the prairie.

PREFACE

Sheldon Jackson's 1992 book, *Barclay College: Lighthouse on the Prairies*, tells the story of the college from 1917 to 1992. In 1990 the name of the college changed from Friends Bible College to Barclay College. This history takes up the story of the college in 1990 and traces the many changes that happened from then to the present. I hope that I have captured the events and personalities from these years of change and have given a reliable account of this important era.

Glenn W. Leppert, Barclay College, February, 2024.

CONTENTS

1	From the Beginning (1917-1990)	1
2	What is in a Name? (1989-1990)	5
3	Following the Call (1990-1995)	11
4	Advantage (1996-1998)	23
5	Regional Accreditation (1998-2003)	33
6	An Attempt to Expand (2003-2005)	53
7	The Great Miracle (2005-2010)	67
8	Moving Online (2008-2023)	101
9	Graduate Studies (2011-2023)	137
10	The Best Kind of Drama (1990-2023)	143
11	Symposiums and Colloquiums (2016-2023)	147
12	The Future (2023-)	151
Appendix 1: Campus Faculty 1990-2023		153
Appendix 2: *ADVANTAGE!* Faculty 1996-2023		159
Appendix 3: Online Faculty 2008-2023		161
Appendix 4: Graduate Faculty 2011-2023		163
Appendix 5: Graduates 1990-2023		165
Index		199

CHAPTER ONE
FROM THE BEGINNING
1917-1990

Barclay College began in 1917 as the Friends Kansas Central Bible Training School with a specific purpose. The reason for the school's establishment was published as an opening statement in the *First Annual Catalog* that set out the classes and schedule for the 1917-1918 academic year. That purpose was to teach the Bible and to train workers for the Lord's vineyard.[1]

While the college has changed its name twice, it has never changed its focus.[2] The school immediately upon its founding became a training center for pastors and missionaries with classes offered in a two-year course of study beyond high school.[3] A third year was added in 1920 and in 1925, a two-year junior college department was added. In 1930, the name of the college was changed to Friends Bible College, and the curriculum and vision of the college were expanded to better train men and women to serve where God directed. The purpose for the college stated in the 1930 catalog at the time of the first name change remained the same as the statement of purpose in each of the earlier catalogs and contained the same language—"to train the mind but also to build character," to provide

---

[1] *First Annual Catalog of Friends Kansas Central Bible Training School 1917*, 5.
[2] *The Progress*, Volume 60, No. 1, Spring 1990, 2.
[3] *Crimsayvista*; "Into the Nineties" Yearbook for 1990-1991, 3.

a place "where the Word of God might be studied and sound orthodox teaching of the Bible maintained," to train "church workers, missionaries, and ministers," to "help prepare for service those who feel a definite call of the Lord for special service," and to secure "the best Christian experience for each student."[4]

In 1990 the college was rebranded as Barclay College in order to attract additional students, to raise the thinking of the public that it was an institution of higher education, to make it more open to students other than Friends, and to diminish the frequent confusion with Friends University. This name change did not change the purpose of the college.

The mission statement has been restated over the years in an attempt to make it clearer and more focused. The 1966 College Catalog used these words to give the mission of the College, "The purpose . . . to train the whole man so that he can intelligently assume a place of leadership, or support those who do assume the leadership of the church." Additionally: "To provide a Bible College course of proper instruction and training for effectual service and assist those students who are answering the Lord's Great Commission."[5]

This mission statement was reworded in 1975 with the renewal of the Articles of Incorporation:

> The purpose of this corporation is to establish and maintain a Bible college to educate young men and women of all races on a nondiscriminatory basis for Christian ministries on the collegiate level through a program of Biblical and theological studies, general education in the arts and sciences and professional studies in Christian Education, the pastoral ministry, world missions, and church vocational areas deemed desirable and to confer academic or honorary degrees for the satisfactory completion of a course of study or

---

[4] Fourteenth Annual Catalog of Friends Bible College, 1930, 5.
[5] *Friends Bible College Catalog*, Volume 36, 1966, 17.

endeavor. Basic in the philosophy of education of [Barclay College] is the conviction that Christian higher education should be oriented to the divine Scriptures, the Bible, finding in it its frame of reference and basis for the integration of all knowledge.[6]

An additional statement was prepared in the 1980's: "The purpose . . . is to prepare students for effective Christian life, service, and leadership." This involves:

Training the life in moral and spiritual values concurrently with the education of the mind in knowledge of the arts and sciences, our cultural heritage, and in constructive, critical, and creative thinking; producing in the student a realization of his/her accountability to God, a concern for his/her society, and a sense of responsibility to his/her own generation; and producing in the student a recognition that God is the author of all true wisdom, that spiritual forces are operative in all of life, and that life is lived to its fullest when brought into a right relationship with God's will as revealed in the Scriptures."[7]

The current statement of mission for Barclay College is the same: "The mission of Barclay College is to prepare students in a Bible-centered environment for effective Christian life, service, and leadership." The statement "Prepare students in a Bible-centered environment" indicates that the primary undertaking of the College is education with an integrated biblical perspective. Barclay College strives for academic and spiritual excellence by providing an environment that encourages higher levels of inquiry and learning. Bible instruction, the integration of biblical principles across the

---

[6] "Certificate of Amendment to Articles of Incorporation for Friends Bible College Association," February 13, 1975, attachment.
[7] *Faculty Staff Handbook*, Barclay College, 1980, 6; *Barclay College Faculty Staff Handbook*, 1995, 1.5.

curriculum, general education, and professional preparation are emphasized to ensure that the College accomplishes the first major goal: assisting each student in developing a Christian worldview and a collegiate level of knowledge appropriate to college graduates generally and to their chosen field specifically.[8]

"Effective Christian life, service, and leadership" means that Barclay College views its mission as broader than simple preparation for a career or helping students acquire knowledge. Rather, the college desires to assist students in knowing God, and from that relationship constructing meaning and understanding that will inform all of life's endeavors. The second major goal of the College, then, is to graduate men and women from the Haviland campus and online who can be generally characterized as biblically literate, prayerful, mission minded, servant-oriented, evangelical Christians, who are able to provide leadership to the church at large and in various professional fields.[9]

Barclay College identifies as an evangelical Friends (Quaker) college with this statement by the Barclay College Board of Trustees:

> Barclay College bases its existence in a rich history of evangelical Friends tradition. Barclay College is an evangelical Friends school which accepts and embraces persons with evangelical Christian beliefs from a variety of denominational backgrounds.[10]

The story of Barclay College from its beginning in 1917 to the changes in 1990 is told admirably in Sheldon Jackson's *Barclay College Lighthouse on the Prairies* published in 1992. *Still Shining, Barclay College as a Lighthouse* continues the story of the growth and development of the college from 1990 to 2023.

---

[8] This statement is drawn from the current *Barclay College Catalog*. It was composed as a part of the Self Study for the 1996 accreditation visit for ABHE. The statement is also found in the *Faculty Handbook*.
[9] *Ibid*.
[10] https://www.barclaycollege.edu/academics/campus/bible-and-theology/.

CHAPTER TWO
WHAT'S IN A NAME?
1989-1990

The, *Progress* for Fall 1989 was sent out with an insert prepared by the Executive Committee of the Friends Bible College Board with the question "What's in a Name?" Quoting an old Chinese proverb that the beginning of wisdom is to call things by their right names, they asked, "What does the name, Friends Bible College, convey to you?" and they explained that to them the name conveyed that the college was a four-year baccalaureate degree-granting Quaker institution associated with the Bible College movement. They saw the name as an excellent one for those who knew the college well.[11]

However, they also understood the name did not communicate the same thing to all people. They admitted that most of the secular colleges and a majority of people in evangelical Christianity had a wrong perception of what a Bible college was. Instead of

---

[11] Much of the wording in this chapter comes from the "What's in a Name" insert in *The Progress*, Volume 59, No. 3, Fall 1989.

seeing Friends Bible College as a viable, accredited college, it was seen as little more than a glorified Sunday school. Many believed that only classes on Bible and some ministry-related courses were taught.

A majority of secular universities and many Christian liberal arts colleges did not know the college required a solid grounding in liberal arts courses in all majors. And unfortunately, many prospective students did not consider FBC to be a "real college." [12] This was partly true because at the time there were over five hundred Bible colleges in the United States and only a very few had any kind of accreditation. Only eighty-eight Bible Colleges were accredited by the American Association of Bible Colleges (AABC).

And furthermore, although AABC was a member of the Council on Post-secondary Accreditation, a council with the sole purpose of assuring equality of assessment by all of its accrediting agencies, this was often disregarded. Even though the state universities were judged by the very same criteria as the accredited Bible colleges, most generally it made no difference.

That posed a great problem for the continuation and growth of the college. The moment the word Bible was mentioned to many prospective students or to other colleges in regard to transferring credits, a wall of resistance was erected. Explanations regarding full accreditation fell on deaf ears. This greatly hindered the mission of the college.

---

[12] Jackson, 135; "What's in a Name," Insert, 1989.

Friends Bible College was not alone in facing that dilemma. Fort Wayne Bible College changed its name in 1989 to Summit Christian College. Other AABC colleges at the rate of about four a year were asking permission to change their names. In 1989 about one-third of the AABC accredited colleges no longer had Bible as part of their name. Even AABC was asked to change its name by member colleges.

Earlier in 1986 or 1987 an alumnus mentioned that the college would do well to change its name. The very thought was rather galling, but after constantly bumping up against a serious image problem (even though unjustified), the college began to consider a name change. And it was not just an image problem, there were some very practical issues as well.

The misconceptions concerning the college impacted donations for the Public Affairs Office. It made the work of the Admissions Office extremely difficult. It created considerable work for the Academic Office trying to get student credits to transfer. It cut students off from receiving certain state funds and some scholarships. Having two Quaker colleges within one hundred miles of each other both having the word Friends in their name also caused confusion. More than once transcript requests meant for one college were sent to the other.

So, the insert included in the mailing asked alumni and friends of the college to prayerfully consider the need for a name change, and if they believed it would be good to do so, to suggest an appropriate new name. The administration did not want to have a contest but truly sought valid suggestions. The alumni responded with comments that encouraged a name change and several, although not many, gave suggested names. The most popular name received was Crossroads College, based on the college's location. The name which was selected after much careful deliberation and prayer was Barclay College.

Robert Barclay was an early theologian for Friends. After finding Christ, he became one of the outstanding figures in the history of the Friends Movement. Using the Bible as his textbook, Barclay wrote several significant theological works. The most noted of these was his *Apology For the True Christian Divinity*, which has become the classic, systematic statement of the Quaker faith. His theology was grounded in the written Word and his ministry was devoted to introducing people to the living Word. Barclay served his Lord with an intense devotion and made a lasting impact on the world, and his life modeled the purpose and goal of the college—biblically grounded academics, evangelism, and obedience to the Spirit. At the center of all that Robert Barclay wrote were the intertwined concepts of the Holy Spirit, learning, and ministry—three concepts combined today in the purpose for Barclay College. Like Barclay College, Robert Barclay believed: "No amount of education . . . can make up for the lack of the Spirit." Predominate through the process of seeking a new name was the determination that in no way was the mission of the college changing. Two points were made plain in all the articles and mailings related to the process: First, that changing the name would not mean that the college would no longer be a Bible college. There was a strong commitment to remain as a member of AABC. Second, changing the name would in no way change the purpose and mission of the college.

On Saturday evening, March 31, 1990, the Friends Bible College Association voted to change the name to Barclay College. Chairman of the FBC Board, Joe Schoonover, announced the name change, effective as of April 2, 1990. On Saturday evening, May 5, an official ceremony of the birth of Barclay College was held. It was a typical Kansas day with the bright sun and a brisk breeze as a large crowd gathered west of Hockett Auditorium for the "sign razing/raising" celebration. The old black and white Friends Bible College sign came down and a new crimson and gray Barclay College sign, painted by Gene Wineland, art instructor at

Pratt Community College, took its place. President Robin Johnston read a blessing prayer written by Vivian Thornburg, after which praise to the Lord and cheers went up from the crowd for the beginning of a new era at the college.[13]

Dr. Robin Johnston, President of the newly named Barclay College, explained,

> The new name will in no way change our purpose. It is still 'to prepare students for effective Christian life, service and leadership.' We will continue equipping ambassadors to spread the same 2,000-year-old message that Jesus Christ is the Way, the Truth, and the Life. We have been a constant source of Friends' pastors, missionaries, and ministers throughout the world, and in recent years a source for many other denominations as well, and we intend to continue.
>
> Since 1917, Barclay has unwaveringly rested on the one and only unshakable foundation, God, and His Word. Many colleges teach students to analyze, criticize and synthesize everything from Adam to atoms. Barclay is unflinching in its goal of reaching beyond just academics to improve the whole person.
>
> In a day when morality, industry, and honesty are being continually held up to ridicule, Barclay College is consistently and pointedly providing for its students, education that inculcates value as well as knowledge, character as well as concepts and service

---

[13] *The Progress*, Volume 60, No. 1, Spring 1990, 1, 2.

as well as success.[14]

---

[14] *The Progress*, Volume 60, No. 1, Spring 1990, 2.

CHAPTER THREE
FOLLOWING THE CALL
1985-1995

"Following the Call," the theme of the 1991 Yearbook, *Crimsayvista*, was appropriate as the college moved into the nineties[15] and began a "Decade of Development" under the new name Barclay College. The change of name happened in the middle of Robin Johnston's tenure as president (1985-1995).

When Robin Johnston assumed the role of president in 1985, the college was in debt from the need to borrow operating funds. The new president adopted a policy that disallowed all borrowing to meet operating expenses. This sometimes meant the college was several months behind in paying salaries but by 1990, the debt was mostly gone, and the operating expenses were steady. A matching grant and major volunteer labor had also refurbished the campus buildings that had been heavily damaged by hailstorms.[16]

---

[15] *"Into the Nineties"* was the theme selected for the 1990 edition of *Crimsayvista*.
[16] *The Progress*, Volume 60, No, 1, Spring 1990, 12, and *The Progress*, Volume 60, No. 2, Fall 1990, 2.

At the 1990 board meeting, the first board meeting under the new name Barclay College, the board adopted a fundraising campaign, "Decade of Development" to "assure a strong and fruitful future" for the college that would strengthen its place as part of the Christian community.[17]

The first phase of the developmental plan was the possibility of a new building that would provide expanded administrative space and a chapel/auditorium to replace the crowded chapel space in Founders Hall. The second phase was to have additional facilities to be added to the gym for physical fitness rooms, a swimming pool, handball courts and dressing rooms along with refurbishing Phillips Hall as residential space. The third phase was to create "mini residents" to serve as a retreat center for seminars, camps, and family reunions during the summer.[18]

For the first phase, the new building was to have sat west of Phillips Hall directly south of Hockett Auditorium. An increasing number of dreams were added to the discussions and the project eventually became too large and impossible to accomplish. Instead, additional space was created by refiguring the basement of Phillips Hall and leaving chapel in Founders Hall. With the creation of Lemmons Hall some years later, Phillips Hall was refurbished but into administrative offices rather than residential space.

The 1990 fall semester began with several new additions to the faculty. Mark Kelley replaced Gary Wright as the head of the Pastoral Ministry major as Gary moved into full-time evangelism. Before Gary and his wife Carol left Haviland to move to Indiana, Gary, who was an experienced stone mason, designed and constructed a beautiful twenty foot by five-foot three-inch Silverdale limestone sign to enhance the southwest corner of the campus. The structure, which includes flower boxes on each end, has the name of the college boldly stated in large letters on its face.

---

[17] Sheldon G. Jackson. *Barclay College Lighthouse on the Prairies*, Barclay College, 1992, 136.
[18] *The Progress*, Volume 60, No. 1, Spring 1990, 2.

That same semester Kathy Jay began as an adjunct professor in missions, and Ron Ginther assumed the role as English professor filling the vacancy left by Dr. Jo Lewis' accepting a position at George Fox University. Royce Frazier also joined the faculty as an instructor for Youth Ministry classes. Earlier in the fall of 1989 Del Huff, who had worked with the Janz Team in Europe, took on the role as chair of the Music Department and held that position until he left the college after the Spring 1992 semester, and Del Covington brought a new look to the Christian Education major as the major head.

Other additions occurred regularly from 1991 to 1995. In the Fall 1991 semester Jon Sarver from Southern California joined the faculty as the head of a brand-new Youth Ministry major. That fall Jim Rahenkamp assumed the role as head of the Elementary Education major to replace Dr. Fred Johnson who had joined the faculty in 1965 but resigned in 1991. Pam Roe began teaching piano and a new administrator, Doug Kunsman, the Business Manager for the college, became an adjunct to teach business classes. In the fall of 1992, Dorothy Hicks joined the adjunct staff for education classes. Sherry Covington began as English instructor in 1993 and Dr. Sheldon Jackson returned to the college as an adjunct. The Spring 1994 semester was the last semester as librarian for Roberta Leininger who along with her husband, Jim Leininger, had begun at the college in 1972. Spring 1994 was also the last semester as science and math instructor for Jim Leininger. Sarah Patterson began as librarian and Dr. Gene Pickard returned to the college (after 1982-1986) as professor of missions.

Students in 1990 were active well past the end of the semester. First, during the mini term (May 13-29) seven students and sponsor Del Covington went to Mexico to fulfil a practicum for their degree. They worked on buildings at a camp and held church services. They also spent five days at the Friends mission in Rough Rock, Arizona. Several groups of students kept up the tradition of ministering across the country presenting the gospel in music and drama. The choir along with the Barclay Singers and the Jubilee Singers had a highly successful tour of the Northwest completing thirty-five concerts in churches and schools. These were in addition to twenty-seven concerts given prior and just after the tour. Del Huff directed the choir and Brenda Choate led the two groups of singers. During the summer, the Barclay College Singers under the direction of Brenda Choate sang and counseled at four different Quaker camps and gave concerts in six states—Idaho, Wyoming, Colorado, Nebraska, Iowa, and Kansas. The Barclay College Drama Troupe working with Del Covington visited a number of camps and churches in Indiana, Michigan, Ohio, Virginia, North Carolina, and Tennessee.

Three Barclay College students had the opportunity to minster internationally. Sophomore Diego Chuyma, from Bolivia, travelled with the Christian Sports Outreach International to play soccer and to distribute Christian literature in Holland, Belgium, Germany, and Austria. Colleen Bontrager, a first-year student from Kansas, spent the summer in Hungary under the auspices of Music Works International—Summer Ministries, a project sponsored by the college under the direction of Del Huff. Pat Neifert, also a first-year student from Kansas, spent the summer in the same program but in Russia singing with a group that included Russians.[19]

A highlight of the 1990 spring semester was the establishment of the Merle Roe Preaching Award. The Merle Roe award was established to encourage the development of quality preaching. Merle Roe was a student at the college in the depression years and a former Friends superintendent recognized for his preaching style.

Sports in the 1990/1991 season came off very well. In a basketball game with Central Bible College on February 2 the Barclay Bears set not one but five new records. Thad Roher set a school record with 55 points. "Other records broken were field goal percentage—70 percent, 15 assists by Geoff Robinson, tied a school record for an individual, set by Randy VandenHoek, and a margin of victory record, which was 72 points." Other sports honors for the year include

---

[19] *The Progress*, Volume 60, No. 1, Spring 1990, 7-8.

the soccer team coached by Del Covington placing second in the Midwest Christian College Conference Tournament (MCCC), Logan Kendall being selected as a second team all-conference player in volleyball and the Barclay Bears Basketball team capturing first place at the Oklahoma Baptist College Invitational Tournament. The MCCC basketball tournament for 1991 was hosted by Barclay College.[20]

The Lady Bears 1995 volleyball team ended their season on a positive note as they were crowned champions of the National Bible Collegiate Athletic Association in the tournament in Oklahoma City. Deb Durham and Tammy Sorensen received the honor of being named members of the All-Tournament Team.[21] The 1995 soccer team also ended their season with two members, Jeff Carpenter, and Stephen Rader, named to the All-Conference Team for the Midwest Christian College Conference.

From 1990 to 1995, a number of enhancements were added to the college programs. In the fall of 1991, an all-school Day of Prayer was scheduled (2nd Wednesday after the retreat). A day of prayer was part of the schedule for several years. In 1992, taking advantage of fiber cable laid across Haviland by the telephone company and a new system installed at the high school, a college class, Church Growth Principles, was offered over the fiber-optic A+ Interactive Television System. Other classes followed in the next two years. The studio was housed at the high school. The Fall 1993 semester was followed by a January term which ran from January 3-January 27, 1994. January terms were offered in Spring 1994, 1995, and 1996. The board decided in March 1995 to close this short semester. When the January term was active, students could take up to 17 hours in the fall and up to 4 hours in January. In Fall 1993 a "reading day" was added to the schedule as preparation for finals. This was on the calendar through the spring of 1997 but not again until Fall 2005 and then it was added back as Exam Preparation Day.

---

[20] *The Progress*, Volume 61, No. 1, Spring 1991, 14.
[21] *The Progress*, Volume 65, No. 4, Fall 1995, 8.

A new building was constructed south of the library and classes moved from West Hall to the new building, dubbed the Education Center, in the spring of 1994. That fall the new building became known as Jackson Hall and Jeanie Fitch began as science instructor by moving items from West Hall to the new science lab. Jackson Hall featured three good sized classrooms and the science lab. All but the basement ceramic lab classes left West Hall.

From the fall of 1984 through the spring of 1995 each fall and spring semester began with an all-day in-service that featured presentations by faculty members and outside speakers. These met in various places including the Library Classroom, a retreat center at a farm near Pratt, in the student center, and at the Ross home near Haviland. The in-service meetings from 1990 to 1995 were especially academic with presentations on academic advising, social studies in ministry, learning paradigms, integration of truth and learning, accreditation, and assessment.[22]

In the fall of 1994, the College Level Examination Program (CLEP) exams that had been given on campus through the Registrar's office changed from paper-based exams to computer-based exams. Since the college had computers, it became a national CLEP test center.[23]

The Registrar's office had implemented the very first computer on the college campus in 1986 utilizing a simple open spreadsheet to create a database for registration and records. In the fall of 1996, this simple program was replaced with an actual Student Information System (SIS), FX-Scholar. This greatly improved registration, reporting, and record maintenance in the Registrar's office.

Five major things impacted the college in the fall of 1992 and during the 1994/1995 academic year. The first significant item was the closure of the joint Elementary Education program that had been created in 1978 as a joint program with Saint Mary of the Plains

---

[22] *1995 Self Study*, C5.
[23] Barclay College Faculty Meeting Minutes, May 10, 1994.

College of Dodge City. Elementary education classes were offered on the Barclay College campus by Barclay professors, but the student teaching and all licensing matters were managed through Saint Mary of the Plains. Saint Mary closed abruptly in August 1992 leaving the Barclay College program in the lurch. Talks were immediately arranged with Tabor College and a joint program was worked out similar to that with Saint Mary. However, the Kansas Department of Education did not at first accept this second program. An arrangement was made that would allow all students able to complete their programs within a short timeframe to be accepted by the state. With those students graduated, the Barclay education major changed to one with a focus on private Christian school teaching. Full state approval and accreditation through the Association for Christian Schools International (ACSI) happened later.

The second item was the celebration of 100 years of Christian education throughout the Fall 1992 semester but specifically on October 2, 1992. That day the college and community celebrated the centennial anniversary of the founding of Friends Haviland Academy as well as the college in 1917 when the academy was expanded with the creation of the college. *The Progress* asked in its Spring 1992 edition "What if Barclay College did not exist?" The following answer was given: "More than 800 graduates would not have entered the fields of ministry and service. Nearly 100 cross-cultural ministers would not have taken the Gospel to more than thirty-five countries around the world. Many pastors in at least ten Friends Yearly Meetings around the world may not have entered the ministry. Hundreds of schoolteachers, church workers, youth ministers, church musicians, businesspeople and leaders may not bring the influence of Christ to bear upon the needy world."[24]

The celebration (Centennial Spectacular) on October 2, 1992, was indeed spectacular with more than 800 in attendance to rejoice and reminisce over the 100 years of education begun with the academy in 1892 and continued with the college in 1992. The evening began

---

[24] *The Progress*, Volume 62, No. 2, Spring 1992, 8.

with numbers from the Haviland Brass, then an introduction of past presidents by Robin Johnson—Sheldon Jackson (1946-1964), Stanley Brown (1964-1967), Wanda Mitchell (1971-1976), and Norman Bridges (1976-1985). Several reunion choirs led by Roy Clark and Bob Ham took turns in presenting past favorite pieces. The music was followed by an auction of academy and Bible college memorabilia before Brenda Choate led the current 1992 choir in concert. In addition, a record was set on October 3rd at the 61st Ladies Auxiliary Auction. The goal of $100,000 for 100 years of Christian education was exceeded with a total of a little over $118,000. There were over 1200 people present.[25]

The third thing that impacted the college was the approval of new programs for the college. In addition to the four-year degree Barclay was approved to offer two different two-year associate degrees. One was an associate degree in arts and sciences; the other an associate degree in biblical Studies. These two degrees made it possible for students wishing to attend the college to take Bible classes to do so and then transfer to another college to complete another major.

A third associate degree was formulated and a year later came into being. This was a degree in youth ministry in conjunction with Youth For Christ International. YFC chose Barclay College to be their mid-west training center. Classes and a certificate program were added to the curriculum in 1996. At this same time the college was working with Houston Graduate School of Theology to create an extension of Barclay in Texas. State and accreditation issues prevented this from becoming a reality.

The fourth significant item was that in the fall of 1992 the college began working on the preliminary steps for obtaining regional accreditation through the Accrediting Commission of the North Central Association (NCA). Accreditation through the

---

[25] *The Progress*, Volume 62, No. 4, Fall 1992, 2 & 4.

Accrediting Association of Biblical Colleges (AABC, now the Association for Biblical Higher Education, ABHE) was secured in 1975 and a successful ten-year review was accomplished in 1985. A second review would also be completed successfully in the Fall 1995 semester, but the AABC/ABHE accreditation was not always accepted by other colleges, problems with transfer credits were constant, and funds available in Kansas were not available to colleges without regional accreditation. Thus, the college began the process of seeking regional accreditation.

Preparation for the self-study for NCA began during the Fall 1992 semester as the college worked through the Preliminary Information Form (PIF) preparing a final document in November 1992. Although this document, in the end, was never submitted formally to the accrediting commission, the process set the college in place to begin preparing the self-study for the ten-year review for the Accrediting Association for Bible Colleges which was scheduled for the Spring 1995 semester. The Registrar was given Wednesday afternoons to focus entirely on the Preliminary Information Form which was a basic document required by NCA.[26]

In April (April 3 to 7) 1993 Glenn Leppert carried a copy of a preliminary self-study to Chicago as he attended an annual NCA convention. The study was presented to the self-study committee and discussed with them, and comments, requirements, and necessary procedures were carried back to Haviland. The faculty was introduced to the self-study process in the Fall 1993 in-service. Each faculty member was assigned to a "Faculty Plus" committee the plus being selected board members and community people; and each committee was given the responsibility for a certain area of the criterion. After work on the study was begun, President Johnston made the decision not to pursue it further. However, in the Fall 1994 board meetings the board moved to engage again in seeking regional accreditation. Their decision led to Robin Johnston's resignation as president that following spring. The suspension of the regional self-

---

[26] Faculty Meeting Minutes September 14, 1993.

study was due partially because of the need to do a study for the State of Kansas as the college sought State approval of the Elementary Education program in the summer and fall of 1993 and the spring of 1994. While completing that study, there was also the need to complete the self-study for the ten-year renewal from AABC.

The fifth event was that Robin Johnston stepped down after ten years as president following the Spring 1995 semester. His resignation was reported to the faculty in February 1995.[27] The Board concluded its search for a new president by appointing Art Fowler, an evangelist from Castle Rock, Colorado (Art Fowler Ministries) as the new president. Mr. Fowler began to plan for the transition by appointing Glenn Leppert as the Academic Dean and by sending a consultant to study the college in order to formulate a plan for his first year. When he realized that being president of the college would require him to relocate to Haviland and could restrict his worldwide evangelistic work, he declined the position in mid-July. Glenn Leppert accepted the role of acting president as well as Dean and Registrar and served in all three positions until a new president assumed office in January 1996.

Fall 1995 was a unique semester. As the self-study for AABC and the preliminary information for NCA was written in 1993/1994 the college noted that one indicator of stability was the relatively little turnover in faculty and administration. However, a number of changes took place in the spring of 1994 and the spring of 1995 which contradicted this.

In May 1994, Dr. Bruce Hicks, who had been Academic Dean since 1984, resigned as Dean. Teaching loads were adjusted for the 94/95 academic year, and he was kept on as a full-time professor with plans to retire at the end of the academic year. Because her husband was leaving and because the Elementary Education Program was laid down during the Spring 1994 semester, and the last of the graduates who were permitted to complete the program were graduated in

---

[27] Barclay College Faculty Minutes Spring 1995, minute number 94/95-118.

May, Dorothy Hicks, the head of the Elementary Education major also planned to leave.

Robin Johnston, president since July 1985, resigned in February. He was rehired by the Board at their February Board meeting to serve as Director of Alumni and Church Relations contingent upon approval of the new president. Del Covington, Christian Ministries professor from 1987, resigned in late May to accept an offered position at Letourneau University. His leaving made vacant the General Education English position, held since 1993, by his wife, Sherry. Also, Chad Gates, Vice President for Development since December 1988, resigned in order to take a position with a Bible Ministry in Nebraska. His resignation vacated the Book Store Manager position held since January 1989 by his wife, Julie.

Sheryl White of Oklahoma City was offered a contract for a combined position to teach some of the Christian Ministry classes and to cover some of the music hours as well as to serve as the Christian Service Director. Dr. John Steiner, of Conway, New Hampshire, was hired to teach the balance of the Christian Ministry courses and to cover some of the English classes. Heidi Longstroth replaced Sarah Patterson as librarian and Keith King began adjunct teaching in Christian Education. For the Academic Dean's position, Glenn Leppert, Registrar since July 1985, signed a contract for the 95/96 academic year combining the two positions of Academic Dean and Registrar (the same as for the 94/95 academic year). He was, also, the acting president that fall. In an article in the Summer 1995 *Progress* he joked whether he was to be the "acting president" or just "to act like a president."[28]

Also, in the fall of 1995 Pamela Steiner became the bookstore manager and yearbook advisor, Jeff Gillingham returned to the college as Athletic Director, and Carmen Velazquez assumed the role as secretary for admissions. Other changes included Lisa Kuzak joining the maintenance department, Arden Sanders, Kathleen Kellum,

---

[28] *The Progress*, Volume 65, No. 3, Summer 1995, 1.

Keith King, and Amy Brokar taking on adjunct positions to teach linguistics, junior high ministry, and women's' basketball. Gene Pickard moved from part-time to full-time as chair of the Missions Major while Jan Kelley took on a new role as administrative secretary.

The ten-year review for AABC had been scheduled for the Spring 1995 semester, but scheduling changes by AABC placed it in the Fall 1995 from September 24 through September 26. The faculty had created a great study and the AABC team visit to the campus came off successfully. During the fall, arrangements were being finalized to form a cooperative program with Youth for Christ International and as a part of this arrangement a third associate degree. Considerations were also in progress with Houston Graduate School of Theology with the possibility of a branch campus of Barclay College in Houston. Thus, with a number of personnel changes, a presidential search under way, a new SIS being initiated, explorations for new programs, and an accrediting visit, Fall 1995 was a full semester.

CHAPTER FOUR
ADVANTAGE
1996-1998

Under the leadership of Glenn Leppert as acting president, the college thrived in the fall of 1995. The AABC visit went extremely well, new programs such as the joint program with Youth For Christ International were initiated, and the college waited in anticipation for a new president.

The Barclay College Board named Dr. Walter Moody as president when they concluded their presidential search late in the fall of 1995. Dr. Moody had experience as a pastor, a licensed therapist, administrator, and professor. He, with his wife Patricia, had lived in South-Central Kansas from 1982 to 1989 and served as a school psychologist and the director of the Westside School at the Larned State Hospital. His son was a student at Barclay College and Moody served the college several years as an adjunct professor. He moved to Haviland to assume the role of president early in January 1996.[29]

Dr. Moody came with a number of goals for the college. He wanted to see the college acquire regional accreditation and he restarted the process for doing so. He hoped to enlarge the curriculum to include additional vocations and entered into discussion with Pratt

---

[29] *The Progress*, Volume 65, No. 4, Fall 1995, 1.

Community College for a joint program.[30] He was also interested in creating off campus teaching points,[31] and he established a distance education program known at first as LEAP (Leadership Education for Adult Professionals) which became the remarkably successful *ADVANTAGE!* program. When the program was fully developed *ADVANTAGE!* students were able to take classes not only in Dodge City, Great Bend, Larned, Pratt, and Wichita in Kansas, but also in Denver and Colorado Springs in Colorado, Easley South Carolina, and Brandywine, Indiana. The college schedule was changed to allow more time for students to minister off campus, and Dr. Moody was able to have the college purchase a 47-passenger bus.

While these were great goals for the college and were accomplished, Dr. Moody made other changes that were not well received. He dismissed every one of the female instructors and made numerous changes in office personnel hiring some office help who did not exhibit the values held by the college. Faculty meetings became briefings rather than times of discussion and prayer. Conflicts between the president and students happened and a rather harsh Christmas chapel (the last chapel of the fall 1997 semester) resulted in a decrease in enrollment that following spring.

As early as March 1996, Dr. Moody restarted the application process with North Central Association that had been set aside in 1994.[32] Even though the board at their Fall 1994 meeting had declared their intention to achieve regional accreditation nothing had happened in 1995 with the change of leadership and the focus on the accreditation through AABC. In 1996 faculty, staff, and others were assigned to various committees to consider portions of the criteria, and work began once again on the Preliminary Information Form which called now for considerably more to answer. The process from 1996 to 2002 was successful and the college in April 2002

---

[30] *The Progress*, Volume 66, No. 2, Fall 1996, 1.
[31] *Crimsayvista*, 1996, 39 and *The Progress*, Volume 66, No. 1, Summer 1996, 2.
[32] March 18, 1996, memo from Mark Kelley to Walter Moody discussing the restarting of the process for seeking accreditation.

gained candidacy status with NCA.[33]

Arrangements were made with Pratt Community College not only to provide space for the *ADVANTAGE!* classes to meet but for a joint program in which students could earn an associate degree through Pratt Community College in auto mechanics or nursing, or electrical engineering (or several other vocational areas) and have that associate degree become an integral component of a mission's degree at Barclay. The student would earn their AA from Pratt but also a BS from Barclay.

The *ADVANTAGE!* program began in July 1996 with a major in Business, with the first cohort actually beginning classes in October. A second major, Psychology, was added in May 1997. Christian Ministries (Theology in Colorado) became a third major in 1998. In 1998 the name was changed from LEAP to *ADVANTAGE!*.

Detailed modules were created for each class that contained the syllabus, readings, and assignments. Students worked through the readings and assignments and then came to class once a week to meet with a professor. Projects were sometimes assigned that would require students to meet with each other during the week or weekend. Some classes included an extended meeting period on a weekend.

ADVANTAGE! was a cohort system with students beginning together and working through the program as a cohort. Altogether there were sixty-nine cohorts in the years from 1996 to 2015 with four hundred ninety-nine students enrolled. Two hundred and nineteen students graduated from the program before it joined the online program in 2015.

In the spring of 1996, Registrar Glenn Leppert developed a correspondence program that made it possible for students to take classes for college credit at a distance from the College. Called Home

---

[33] See additional material in chapter 5.

College, the program began with thirty-two courses available in Bible, Theology, Ministry, and general education. These were courses purchased from a college in Canada and from a mission organization (International Correspondence Institute, ICI) that prepared courses for missionaries and indigenous church leaders. These courses provided both a way to cover needed independent studies on campus but also a means for *ADVANTAGE!* students and others to complete college level classes needed for graduation on their own schedule. Hundreds of courses were taken by campus, *ADVANTAGE!*, and online students between 1996 and 2017. Eight students actually completed associate degrees solely with transfer and Home College classes.

During the spring of 1996, a program that offered short-term mission opportunities was put in place. Volunteers were invited to apply for three-to-twelve-month assignments in various college offices, as assistants to instructors, and to help in the library. The volunteers were not paid but given room and board. Two volunteers applied to work in the library. One was Phyllis McCracken, who took a leave of absence from her thirty-year library position with the Salem, Oregon, public library to assist in completing a number of projects in the library. She had a wonderful experience the six months she was at the college, not only helping the college well, but also learning about students and their commitment to Christ and their acceptance of her. She also had an influence on many. Following her, Dorothy Teter from Baker City, Oregon, also helped in the library for five weeks.[34]

During the 96/97 year the first courses to support the Youth For Christ certificate that was created in 1995 were offered with the YM317 YFC Ministries class. In partnership with Western Kansas Youth For Christ, under the direction of Jon Sarver, who was also the chair of the Youth Ministry major at the college, Barclay College conducted YFC training opportunities that could be added to a

---

[34] *The Progress*, Volume 66, No. 2, Fall 1996, 1 and *Crimsayvista* 1996, 38.

Youth Ministries major, and used to obtain ministry credentials from Youth for Christ. The program in conjunction with Youth For Christ included a two-week summer institute to assist students to pass the YFC credentialling examination.

In the fall of 1997 first semester drama students worked on a variety of skits for chapel and local church services. They also presented a major production, "Jonah and the German Whale" a tale of Jonah and his disobedience. In the spring semester another major production, "Book Mark" was given. The play was about how the Gospel of Mark was written.[35]

The first weekend of May 1997 was extremely busy. The college choir gave a concert on Friday evening. On Saturday Dr. Walter Moody was inaugurated as the 12th president of the college, and that evening at the annual alumni banquet a number of special awards were given. Then on Sunday honorary degrees were awarded to Paul Thornburg, missionary, and pastor from the Evangelical Friends Church, and to Jack W. Wease, general superintendent of the Evangelical Methodist Church, and the status of president emeritus was bestowed on Sheldon Jackson and Robin Johnston. Seventeen students graduated.

Several notable changes took place in the campus academic program in the years 1996 to 1998. In the fall of 1996 the campus schedule was changed to have classes meet twice a week, either on Monday and Wednesday or Tuesday and Thursday. This allowed Friday to be set aside for meetings or to be used for ministry and sports teams to leave campus for a longer ministry experience. The "reading day" that had been part of the finals week for many years was removed for the Spring 1998 semester. (It would return in the Fall 2008 semester.) A new major, Psychology, replaced the older Christian Ministries major.

---

[35] *Crimsayvista*, 1998, 7.

There were a number of personnel changes from January 1996 to May 1998 when Dr. Moody stepped down from the presidential position and became an adjunct instructor teaching *ADVANTAGE!* classes in South Carolina. In the Fall 1996 semester, Erik Ritschard assumed the position as Academic Dean and Sylvia Morley took on the role of English professor. In the fall of 1997 Chris Anderson became the Youth Ministry professor, Scott Svoboda became chair of the Music department, and Drs. Sheila Knepper, and Donald Stimpson joined the college as adjunct science and math instructors. Donald and Sheila, husband and wife, university professors from Chicago, having purchased the Haviland-Brenham meteorite properties came to Haviland to create a meteorite study center and museum. Dan Scott joined the faculty as an adjunct for business in *ADVANTAGE! and* Catherine Westerhaus became an adjunct for psychology. Neil Thompson joined the college as Vice President for Institutional Advancement in the summer of 1996. And, Janet Wiley joined the college as cook; her Jell-O salads with insertions did not prove favorable with most students.

In the summer of 1996 air conditioning was installed in the men's dorm, and the chapel and the wall outside the chapel were painted. The old house on the corner of Kingman and Elm was painted gray and trimmed in crimson and became the admissions office. A storm just before the fall semester began removed a number of trees that had been around Phillips Hall making that building look different. And, the college purchased a bus which was re-painted with the college name and was a very welcome addition to the sports and music programs.[36]

A Barclay College Athletic association was formed in the fall of 1996 to support the college's sports program. Another new feature for athletics was that the college joined a new conference—the National Christian College Athletic Association (NCCAA). The

---

[36] Carla Wankum, *Crimsayvista*, 1997, 56.

1996 Barclay Bears soccer team went undefeated at home, beat Manhattan Christian College for the first time in seven years, and finished third in the MCCC tournament. Two players were honored; Jeff Carpenter was named conference MVP and Tony Southammavong was elected to the all-conference team.

A number of adjuncts joined the faculty in the fall of 1997. On campus, Herb Flinkman as Bible professor and Everett Jantz for philosophy. For *ADVANTAGE!* James Lund, Billy Manning, and Stephen Talley as professors of psychology. Becky Towne became the Christian Ministries adjunct for *ADVANTAGE!* and, later, the director for the program in Colorado. Also in Fall 1997 Tom Hinderliter, who came to Barclay in 1988 as Dean of Students, took on the role as a primary instructor for the restart of the education major as a Christian School Education major. While the major did not lead to state certification it was certified later by the Association of Christian Schools International (ACSI).[37] In the spring of 1998 several staff members were added or promoted. Brenda Johnston became the Vice President for Business, Winona Urban joined the staff as bookkeeper, and Madeleine Coconis took the position as Development Assistant. Andrea Hallett became the Food Service Director starting January 1998. Two new secretaries that semester were added: Christine Becker and Tricia Sirkel. Debra Durham was promoted from Assistant Director of Admissions to Director and Ryan Haase began as an admissions Counselor.[38]

During the Fall 1997 semester the college's 80 years were celebrated by a bus tour of historical sites, a music festival, alumni soccer game, and the annual auxiliary auction.[39] The Ladies Auxiliary Auction which began back in 1932 to raise needed funds for the college continued to be a major source of income for the college through the years. The Fall 1996 and the Fall 1997, the 65th and 66th annual sales, were no exceptions, in fact both were quite successful—each

---

[37] *The Progress*, Volume 68, No. 1, Spring 1998, 4.
[38] *The Progress*, Volume 68, No. 1, Spring 1998, 3.
[39] *Crimsayvista*, 1998, 22.

raised over $60,000. A new feature was introduced to the 1996 sale that continued each year after. Sheryl White arranged for the Introduction to Youth Ministry and the Introduction to Christian Education classes to host a "Carnival of Praise." The carnival was designed for the kids of the parents at the sale and kept them busy all day with music, stories, games, and even that first year a petting zoo.[40] The 1997 Missions Emphasis Week gave students the opportunity to attend workshops from various mission organizations among which were the Oriental Mission Society (OMS), Evangelical Friends Mission (EFM), and New Tribe Missions. The speakers for the week, Carolyn Coons, from Azusa Pacific University and Kemp Edwards from OMS, inspired students to consider missions and reminded them of the immediacy of missions. One does not have to travel overseas to be a missionary.[41]

The annual Christmas chapel, the last chapel of the Fall 1997 semester, had always been an upbeat positive event. In the decade before Christmas 1997, President Johnston had always done this chapel and in addition to speaking about the Christmas story always encouraged students to do their best and to represent both Christ and the college well as they went home. The Christmas chapel 1997 came off quite differently. The president used it to reprimand students and to elaborate on unrealistic expectations. The result of this discouraging chapel was that numbers of students did not return for the Spring 1998 semester. The FTE in Fall 1997 was 125. The FTE for Spring 1998 was 115. There had been tensions throughout the five semesters that Dr. Moody was with the college. Changes to the commencement program that had been approved in the fall before he came angered students, firing staff had created unpleasantness, dismissing faculty prayer times, and beginning faculty meetings with just a moment of silence along with turning faculty meetings into briefings, changing data on proposals for substantive changes

---

[40] Tony Factor, *Crimsayvista*, 1997, 10; 1998, 22.
[41] Elkie Frans, *Crimsayvista*, 1997, 24.

submitted to the accrediting agency, and tense relations with students engendered his resignation in the Spring 1998 semester. That semester did, however, end with a high note.

Beginning sometime in the spring of 1997 a certain student, Rick Johnson, gained the attention of the Registrar. Rick was the first to enroll each semester. He submitted all required paperwork, whatever it was, in a timely fashion. He volunteered for student government positions and had his name on the intermural lists. He was a model student; except that he was not a student at all. He was the figment of the imagination of a couple of students who believed that they were "pulling a fast one" on the administration. It was the awards chapel, the last chapel of the spring semester, and all of the awards were given out when the Registrar announced one more award. He introduced it as the "Most Unique Student Award" and announced the recipient as Rick Johnson. After a stunned moment of silence the student body went wild. The secret that they had thought was well hidden from the administration's knowing had been known all along! Tony Factor and Bruce Becker formally accepted the award on behalf of Johnson. The 1998 edition of the yearbook captioned the photograph of their acceptance of the award with these words: "Rick, a fictional student, received this award because he was the first to register for classes each semester and was a willing participant at every activity." Another positive highlight of the Spring 1998 semester was the graduation of the first ever *ADVANTAGE!* graduates.

The *ADVANTAGE!* program began in 1996 and by Spring 1998 when Dr. Moody left Kansas and set up a new cohort in Easley, South Carolina, there were five cohorts finished or in process. There would be sixty-nine cohorts altogether before the *ADVANTAGE!* classes began to be listed as part of the regular semester. In 2015 the *ADVANTAGE!* program was folded into the Online program. The first cohort was a business management cohort that began in Larned on October 8, 1996, and finished the first of the three semesters on March 20, 1997. There were fourteen students enrolled in six regular classes and eight independent studies. The last *ADVANTAGE!* classes finished in December 2015. There were two hundred ninety-eight *ADVANTAGE!* graduates twenty-five of which went on to complete a master's degree with the college.

CHAPTER FIVE
REGIONAL ACCREDITATION
1998-2003

On February 21, 1998, the college launched a comprehensive campaign; the first in more than thirty years. It officially began with a crowd of more than 150 people meeting on campus for a banquet to learn that more than $1.15 million had already been raised or pledged. The stated goal was to raise $3.75 million over a three-year period. David Smitherman, a former chair of the Board of Trustees, served as the chair of the campaign which was titled "A Heritage to Remember – A Future to Claim." Smitherman in promoting the campaign referenced the modest growth in enrollment in 1996 and 1997, the expansion of college programs off campus, tent making ministries available through the college, new majors, and the possibility of a cooperative arrangement for a graduate program with a major university as the reasons for the campaign. Chandler & Newville Inc. were hired to manage the campaign and the Chandler & Newville consultant to the college was Maurice Chandler.[42] He began his consultation in the silent phase of the campaign arriving first on campus in 1997.

---

[42] *Barclay Progress*, Volume 68, No. 1, Spring 1998, 1.

Maurice was a former vice president of development at George Fox University in Newberg, Oregon. Now serving as a campaign consultant he planned to retire when the Barclay campaign was completed. Instead, he responded favorably to the request of the Barclay College presidential search committee to consider the position of president of Barclay College. He explained that his decision was due to the leading of the Lord as he and his wife, Ellouise, prayed about this and determined that if the Lord opened the door they could do no less than to answer the call.[43]

Chandler assumed the role of President July 1, 1998, and set out a number of goals for the college. The top three were admissions, curriculum, and the completion of the comprehensive campaign. He hoped soon to have 150 students on campus and later at least 300. He wished to make certain that the curriculum was up to date. And, of course, he desired that the campaign would succeed in raising its goal. The Summer 1998 *Barclay Progress* reported that the campaign had raised $1.7 million by mid-July.[44] The Fall 1998 *Barclay Progress* reported that more than $2 million dollars had been donated toward the $3.75 million goal and that extensive improvements had already been made to college facilities, especially to the men's dorm.[45] By early summer, 1999, the campaign had exceeded $3 million.[46] The Winter 1999 *Barclay Progress* reported the total at $3.3 million when the publication went to press.[47] The conclusion of the campaign came in June 2000 with the final total exceeding the goal by $200,000. The overall total came in at $3,952,009.[48]

Asked what he wanted to do most for the college Maurice answered:

---

[43] *Barclay Progress*, Volume 68, No. 2, Summer 1998, 1.
[44] *Barclay Progress*, Volume 68, No. 2, Summer 1998, 4.
[45] *Barclay Progress*, Volume 68, No. 3, Fall 1998, 6.
[46] *Barclay Progress*, Volume 69, No. 2, Summer 1999, 7.
[47] *Barclay Progress*, Volume 69, No. 4, Winter 1999, 6.
[48] *Barclay Progress*, Volume 70, No. 3, Fall 2000, 4.

> I'd like to leave Barclay with the sense that young people going into Christian service will look at Barclay College as the place to attend. I want to assure that they receive a quality education, a deep sense of service orientation and a high degree of Bible training to prepare them for Christian service.[49]

Chandler, as president, began immediately healing the rifts that the departing president had left behind. A number of new faculty and staff soon joined him. Michael Landon began that fall as missions professor. Margaret Pent, a former opera singer, became the music professor, replacing Scott Svoboda. Elizabeth Griffin, a May 1998 graduate of the *ADVANTAGE!* program, assumed the role as director of *ADVANTAGE!* and Michelle Arbelaez joined the faculty as an adjunct for psychology in the *ADVANTAGE!* program.

Changes and additions to the faculty and staff were few for the rest of the tenure of Maurice Chandler. In the fall of 1999 Lois Kendall, who had served as faculty secretary for many years having completed a degree, joined the campus faculty as a professor in psychology. In the fall of 2000 David Williams became the professor for pastoral ministry, Jared Ross became an adjunct instructor in music, and Ruth Ann Wedel joined the adjunct faculty for Elementary Education teaching instructional media and computer applications. She also became the director of computer services, a position that Glenn Leppert had filled as Academic Dean. Steve Elmore assumed the music professor's position with Margaret Pent's leaving after completion of two years and Jeanette Parker began as interim director of the library. That same fall new staff members were added: Paul Till began as the *ADVANTAGE!* Kansas Regional Coordinator, Priscilla Schlichting assumed the role as Executive Secretary, and Michelle Morford joined the admissions staff as Enrollment Secretary. In 2001 Tim Garrett, a former youth pastor and missionary to Ireland, joined the faculty as an instructor for Youth Ministry. Following the

---

[49] *Barclay Progress*, Volume 68, No. 2, Sumer 1998, 1.

Spring 2002 semester Tim became the Dean of Students.[50] Spring 2000 Elkie Frans (Burnside) took on the role as adjunct to do yearbook. In Fall 2002, Michael Burns was added to the adjunct faculty to teach anthropology and Dr. Jeremie Frazier to teach biology while Mark Newland started as an adjunct for computer and math. He continued to teach math classes until Spring 2008.

Spring 2002 was the last semester for Jim Beeler who had served three years as Dean of Students. Jim left to be the pastor of a church in Indiana. Fall 2003 was the last semester for Elkie Frans (Burnside). It was the first year for Tricia Oren to join the faculty as an adjunct teaching the English Fundamentals class.

Academically the joint program with Youth For Christ International was well under way in 1999 and that fall YM419 YFC Summer Institute was offered for the first time. It met several subsequent years for credit and then for a while as a noncredit class. In the Fall 2001 semester the schedule for campus classes reverted back to MWF and TR classes.

In 2002 the college received candidacy status with the North Central Association. Dr. Moody had restarted the process of seeking regional accreditation through the North Central Association of Colleges and Schools before he left the college at the conclusion of the Spring 1998 semester. The first step in the process was an extended discussion and training session in the August faculty in-service at the beginning of the Fall 1996 semester. That was followed by appointing faculty members, staff, board members, and members of the community to various committees which began to meet regularly. Coordination and oversight for the self-study fell to Dr. Mark Kelley. In addition, groups such as the Committee for Assessment and Planning (CAP) were commissioned and began working on the college's assessment program and on a long-range plan. Erik Ritschard, who joined the college in 1996 as Director of the *ADVANTAGE!* program and then became Academic Dean in 1997, took charge of keeping CAP active.

---

[50] *Barclay Progress*, Volume 72, No. 1, Spring 2002, 3.

The first official step with NCA was the submission of the Preliminary Information Form (PIF) early in the summer of 1998. The PIF contained forty narrative pages and over four hundred pages of supporting documents.[51] In January 1999, the North Central Association responded to the PIF giving the college several new requirements to be met. These were met and the college was given permission to begin the required self-study in July 2000. A formal self-study was submitted in 2001. A comprehensive evaluation visit from the North Central Association took place January 28-30, 2002, and the final word that the college received candidacy status for regional accreditation came in May 2002.[52]

While CAP and the faculty were busy creating portions of the self-study the college engaged in preparing a long-term campus plan. One of the new president's top ten priorities was to produce a long-range planning committee to create a campus facility plan to guide the growth of the campus in the coming decades. He urged the Board to envision what the campus would look like in 2010. Accordingly, he asked the Board of Trustees at the October 1999 board meeting to hire Paul Cavanaugh of Places Architects of Wichita, Kansas, to facilitate a committee to develop a plan. The Board did so. The facility plan would focus on needs to accomplish regional accreditation and project a campus to accommodate 150 students in the near future and 300 farther out. Along with the long-range committee would be a "Blue Ribbon" Advisory Committee to assist.

A preliminary plan was presented to the Board by Paul Cavanaugh at their March 1999 meeting. It was a master plan designating use of space for renovation and improvement of campus buildings and grounds. Projected in the plan were "a new Student Activity Complex/Women's Dormitory, a chapel to replace Founders Hall, and renovation of Phillips Hall to include additional administrative offices."[53] The final plan along with a conceptual map showing existing

---

[51] *Barclay Progress*, Volume 68, No. 2, Summer 1998, 2.
[52] *Barclay Progress*, Volume 72, No. 1, Spring 2002, 2 and Volume 72, No. 2, Summer 2002, 1.
[53] *Barclay Progress*, Volume 69, No. 2, Summer 1999, 6.

and proposed buildings was accepted by the Board in August 1999.[54] Immediately upon acceptance the Board launched a physical plant and campus improvement fund program to implement it. The estimated need was for $500,000.

The faithful working of the plan dramatically changed the face of the campus between 1999 and 2003 when Chandler stepped down as president. First a new maintenance building was built on the northwest corner of the campus. Items stored in West Hall, which had been denied use for classes by the Fire Marshall, were moved to the new facility and West Hall which had been used by the college since 1953 was torn down. Before the building was razed items from it, the old women's dorm in Phillips Hall, and the old maintenance building were sold at auction, April 1, 2000.

The March 25 and 26 meeting of the Barclay College Board was one that significantly impacted the college. At that meeting, the Trustees directed that all use of both Founders Hall and West Hall be discontinued at the conclusion of the 98/99 school year. Negative reports from the state Fire Marshall and a structural engineer sealed the fate of Founders Hall which had been built for the opening of the 1917 school year. The building was not structurally safe and was to be demolished as soon as possible. West Hall, an eighty-four or so year old building, which had been purchased from the local school district in 1953 had been condemned earlier by the Fire Marshall. Once everything was out of the building it was torn down slowly over several months so that the bricks could be recycled.

To offset the removal of the two oldest buildings the Board authorized the administration to proceed with constructing a new Student Complex/Women's Dormitory. While originally conceived as a separate building with two functions a beautiful dormitory now known as Lemmons Hall was built onto the Broadhurst Student Center and the dining facilities were greatly enlarged. Student Government

---

[54] *Barclay Progress*, Volume 69, No. 4, Winter 1999, 1.

offices and a health room were included. The groundbreaking for the new dormitory took place on July 26, 1999. In addition the Board reviewed the preliminary version of the long-range campus facilities plan.

Alumni and friends of the college gathered on May 1, 1999, to say goodbye to Founders Hall. From 1917 until 1949 when Phillips Hall was dedicated Founders Hall *was* the college campus. In it were whatever offices there were, all classrooms including the choir room, the study hall, and the chapel, library, and gymnasium. In the words of Sheldon Jackson,

> it served more than 80 years as a center for training ministers, missionaries, and Christian workers and sending them all over the world as representatives of our Lord Jesus Christ . . . [leaving] sacred memories to hundreds of students who found inspiration, help and spiritual guidance there.[55]

Demolition began soon after the semester closed. During demolition, a gas line that was inadvertently left open exploded catching the corner of the building on fire. The flames from the fire reached as high as the telephone wires leading into Phillips Hall and left the college with no phone service for a while.

The physical plant and campus improvement fund launched in August 1999 resulted in sufficient funds to build the new maintenance building, remove two of the existing maintenance buildings, upgrade the parking lot east of Phillips Hall where Founders Hall had stood, and to fill in the street in front of Phillips Hall. A parking lot north of the men's dorm and east of Phillips Hall was constructed and lined with trees. It served both the dorm and the administration building. The hill on which Founders Hall sat and the land south of Phillips Hall were shaved down to form a gentle slope to Cherry

---

[55] *Barclay Progress*, Volume 69, No. 2, Summer 1999, 1 and 4.

Street, and the soil was used to fill in one block of Kingman Street making a gentle grade west of Phillips Hall to the area east of the library. This created a wonderful green area and was furnished with a wide sidewalk with benches and flower beds, increasing the beauty of the campus tremendously.

Two year-long celebrations were held while Maurice Chandler was president. The year 1999 was set aside as the "Year of the Alumni" and the year 2000 as the "Year of the Church." The year of the Alumni was designed to recognize and honor Barclay alumni. The celebration was kicked off in February with an elaborate Barclay College Homecoming Weekend that included concerts, special meals, alumni basketball games, and tours of the campus. A special edition of the alumni newsletter profiled alumni accomplishments. Throughout the year stories about alumni were in each edition of *the Barclay Progress*. One interesting feature that was found through the year was a series of articles, "Who's the Oldest Living Alum?"

Alumni were invited to come to campus to speak in classes and at chapel. One such alumni was Kevin Mortimer, Iowa Yearly Meeting Superintendent, who gave the Fall 1999 convocation address. During the 2000 "Year of the Church" the college recognized alumni serving in local churches. One alum who visited the college was Alan Weinacht, Indiana Yearly Meeting superintendent. College administrators, faculty, and musical groups visited churches and youth leaders, pastors, and others were invited to the college for seminars.[56]

Sports at Barclay was active in the years 1998 to 2003. Amy Fleener replaced Curt Cloud as Athletic Director for the Fall 1998. The Barclay College soccer team went to the NCCAA nationals in Florida for the second year in a row and came out fifth. Two players, Jeff

---

[56] *Barclay Progress*, Volume 68, No. 3, Fall 1998, 1; Volume 69, No. 2, Summer 1999, 7; Volume 69, No. 3, Fall 1999, 1; Volume 69, No. 4, Winter 1999, 2; Volume 70, No. 4 Winter 2000-2001, 1.

Carpenter, and Chris Hinderliter were named coach and assistant for the 1999/2000 year. The same year Jeremy Anderson, who was the assistant coach for the Barclay Men's Basketball team which also went to nationals was named as head basketball coach.

The Winter 1999 issue of the *Barclay Progress* reported that the college approved forming both a men's baseball team and a women's softball team. Professor Chris Anderson was selected as coach. That same issue emphasized the soccer team which ended the season 18-5 and finished second in the conference and won the conference tournament. Jason Pickard was named the conference's most valuable player and Eric Crain and Tony Southammavong received all conference honors. At the regional tournament, the team placed third and Pickard and Crain were named to the all-region team. One player highlighted was Eric Crain an All-American soccer player who excelled at the game while at Barclay. He achieved a number of honors and awards while playing soccer at the college: all-conference most valuable player and second team All-American in 1997 and 1998, all-conference and all-region team in 1999, soccer team captain in 1998 and 1999, and soccer team MVP in 1998. Crain said of this, "I got to use the ability that God has given me to be a witness for Him."[57]

The music program at Barclay was enriched by hiring Margaret Pent as the chair of the music department beginning the Fall 1998 semester. Margaret was "a professional opera singer, voice professor in Europe and the United States, and creator, producer and director of performances, choirs, festivals and competitions."[58] She came to Barclay with a number of goals for the music department one of which was to provide concert choirs and music ensembles to represent the college at churches within a wide radius of Haviland. She began with a Barclay College Christmas Festival in December 1998 that featured a gala reception hosted by Barclay College President and Mrs. Chandler, a festive Christmas dinner, and concert with

---

[57] *Barclay Progress*, Volume 69, No. 4 Winter 1999, 8.
[58] *Barclay Progress*, Volume 68, No. 3 Fall 1998, 3.

the Barclay College choir. This was followed by a series of local concerts and a concert tour through the Pacific Northwest May 3 through 16. In March 2000 Barclay College co-sponsored a concert in Pratt, Kansas, by the Bohemian Chamber Philharmonic from the Czech Republic with Margret Pent as a featured soloist.[59]

The Barclay College Singers and the Drama Team visited six nations in Europe. The trip was part of a credit class, "European Music Ministry and Cultural Practicum." The trip involved Germany, Austria, Hungary, Czech Republic, Bulgaria, and Slovakia. The singers performed in selected locations including some churches, received opportunities for musical and cultural development and were able to visit museums and historical sites. [60] To fund the trip the Singers and the Drama Team presented a dinner theatre on May 5, 2000. The production was titled "Salt and Light."

The music major had been suspended for a short while but was reinstated in the fall of 2000. Two instructors were hired to advance the program. Steve Elmore, music instructor at Wichita State University and at Newman College, came from Wichita to be the chair of the music program and Jared Ross, a Barclay alum who had taught music at Satanta, Kansas came as choir director. Both Elmore and Ross hoped to build up a quality program that would attract students with gifts of music wanting to minister. The program was hoped to be one that "would serve the church through preparing quality music leaders and sending out ministry teams."[61]

At the annual accrediting conference in Spring 2000, the college received the AABC Enrollment Growth Award for the 98/99 academic year. The award, sponsored by Christianity Today, Inc., was for 52% increase in one year.[62] Because of increased attendance, the college was preparing additional dormitory space and a high point of the Spring 2000 semester was the opening of Lemmons

---

[59] *Barclay Progress*, Volume 70, No. 2 Summer 2000, 3.
[60] *Barclay Progress*, Volume 70, No. 2 Summer 2000, 3.
[61] *Barclay Progress*, Volume 70, No. 3, Fall 2000, 1.
[62] *Barclay Progress*, Volume 70, No. 1, Spring 2000, 1, 3.

Hall on February 4. After a ribbon cutting ceremony women students housed in Phillips Hall trekked across campus to the new facility. The building was named for college supporter John Lemmons. Rather than a stand-alone building Lemmons Hall was a $1.875 million addition to the existing Broadhurst Student Center. The new dorm had the capacity to house sixty-four women and included an office and conference room for Student Council, a health clinic and greatly expanded cafeteria space.[63] A formal dedication for the new facility took place March 31, 2000.

The college was growing, and additional space was required for the maintenance department which had been squeezed into a portion of the old men's dorm that had been brought to campus from the Pratt Army Air Base back in 1947. Plans were drawn up for a new building to sit on the far northwest corner of the campus that would have bays for plumbing, electrical, carpentry and grounds. It would be large enough to house the bus and other college vehicles. The college had raised more than $70,000 which was a bit more than half of what was needed when the Mabee Foundation of Tulsa, Oklahoma proposed a dollar-for-dollar match to enable construction. The college was given until January 1, 2001, to raise $35,000 which the foundation would then match. The funds were raised, the match was made, and the new facility was completed in 2002.[64]

This grant from the Mabee Foundation was one of three substantial grants received in 2000. In March, a grant of $2,000 was received from the South-Central Community Foundation to purchase tables and chairs for the expanded dining space in Broadhurst. In May, a grant of $20,000 was received from the Crowell Trust to expand the college's campus computer network to Jackson Hall.[65] After the students moved out of the upper floors of Phillips Hall the space was converted into administrative offices. Volunteers on Wheels (VOW) a volunteer group from Northwest Yearly Meeting were

---

[63] *Barclay Progress*, Volume 70, No. 1, Spring 2000, 3.
[64] *Barclay Progress*, Volume 70, No. 2, Summer 2000, 1, 2; *Barclay Progress*, Volume 73, No. 1, 2.
[65] *Barclay Progress*, Volume 70, No. 2, Summer 2000, 2.

part of the crews and individuals who accomplished this task. The VOW group came to campus three summers in a row (1999, 2000, and 2001) and completed numerous projects for the college. The summer of 2001 was by far the busiest, and the Summer Fall 2001 *Progress* describes the great work they accomplished:

> The work included renovating a conference room; building and installing risers in the choir room; pouring concrete for a sidewalk and outdoor basketball court; artwork in the music department; lettering on the soccer scoreboard; building shelves in several offices and the bookstore; painting and caulking the entire interior of the library, faculty wing, gymnasium lobby, student center snack bar and game room, and several offices; removing carpet from the computer laboratory, digging an outdoor volleyball sand pit and conducting inventory in the library.
>
> On one project alone, VOW and local volunteers saved the college more than $12,000. The roof of the gymnasium had rusted through and had experienced a number of leaks during recent rainstorms. The cost of roof repair had been estimated at $13,375. VOW and the local volunteers accomplished the project at a cost of about $1,000.[66]

Two significant upgrades to the college programs were made in 2000. The academic program was re-organized in the spring, and beginning in July an office of External Studies became responsible for the distance education programs. A new position, Associate Dean of External Studies, was created. Elizabeth Griffin was the first to be appointed to this position. The new External Studies division took ownership of both the *ADVANTAGE!* degree completion program and the Home College program which had been created back in 1996 to provide correspondence studies for

---

[66] *Barclay College Progress*, Volume 71, No. 2, Summer Fall 2001, 7.

students at a distance from the college. As part of the reorganization, Registrar Glenn Leppert, who coordinated the Home College program from its inception was made the director of institutional research to assist in the college; assessment needs.[67] The other upgrade was to the college computer network. Phase one of the project to raise the level of technology across the campus was complete. Using fiber optic cable donated by former board member, David Chitwood, the library, and faculty offices were joined to the college network. The computer lab was also updated in the library. In addition the library catalog was put online via the internet.[68]

A number of highlights for the years 2000 to 2003 may be noted. In the Fall of 2000 the college changed its address. From the beginning, the mailing address had always been POB 219 at the local post office. In 2000 the post office changed the college from a post office box to campus delivery and the new address was made known to the college constituency—607 North Kingman Avenue. The first Christian School Elementary Education (CSEE) graduates were graduated in the Spring 2001 commencement. The cooperative elementary education major with Saint Mary of the Plains College and then briefly with Tabor College had to be shut down after the last state certified students graduated in 1993. In 1998 the college created a major in connection with the Association of Christian School International (ACHI) to prepare students to teach in private Christian schools.[69] Each of the first three graduates obtained positions in Christian Schools. The largest graduating class on record for the college after becoming a four-year college was the class that graduated May 5, 2002. Thirty-eight of the forty-nine graduates were present for the commencement exercises in Haviland.[70]

---

[67] *Barclay Progress*, Volume 70, No. 2, Summer 2000, 2.
[68] *Barclay Progress*, Volume 70, No. 2, Summer 2000, 2.
[69] *Barclay College Progress*, Volume 71, No. 1, Spring 2001, 1.
[70] *Barclay College Progress*, Volume 72, No. 2, Summer 2002, 1.

In May 2001, the first students to complete the *ADVANTAGE!* program in Colorado participated in the commencement exercises in Haviland. On December 21, 2001, the first commencement for Colorado *ADVANTAGE!* students was held at the Colorado Springs Friends Church.[71] December commencements followed until the *ADVANTAGE!* program became part of the online program in 2015. *ADVANTAGE!* students in Kansas completing their programs mid-year at times joined in the December commencements. On October 27, 2001, a comprehensive capital campaign was launched. Titled, "Building Solid Foundations" the goal was to raise $3.25 million to supplement the annual fund, to strengthen the college's endowment, and to add classroom space to Jackson Hall, and to fund the parking lot and landscaping for Phillips Hall. The resources from these foundations would enable Barclay College to "build upon the solid foundation of Biblical truth, Christian values and spiritual emphasis." The campaign was seen as a means to assure the college's entrance into the new millennium. President Chandler pointed out that the college was in the process of seeking regional accreditation, had made significant strides in technology, had updated the physical plant but that to attract and retain a quality student body these advances needed to continue.[72]

While the faculty remained basically the same during the years Chandler was president, 1998 to 2003, there were numerous additions to the support staff for the college. Jeremy Anderson, who had been the Kampus Bookstore manager joined the admissions staff as an admissions counselor in the spring of 2000. Jeremy transferred to Barclay from Indiana Wesleyan University and completed his degree through *ADVANTAGE!* He was the head coach of the men's basketball team. At the same time, Kristen Batten took over as manager of the bookstore, Rita Hart joined the business office team as payroll clerk, and Richard Sandstrom, a 1998 graduate, assumed the role as financial aid director.

---

[71] *Barclay College Progress*, Volume 72, No. 1, Spring 2001, 1. President's Cabinet minutes for August 29, 2001 approved the proposal to do this.
[72] *Barclay College Progress*, Volume 71, No. 3, Winter 2001-2002, 3.

In the spring of 2001 Gail Zook became the Kansas recruiter for *ADVANTAGE!*, and in the fall Ruth Cook, an alum of the college, replaced Brenda Johnston as Business Manager, while Tony Southammavong took on the role as accounts receivable clerk. Tony graduated in May 2001 with a degree in business administration. Also that fall, Herb Frazier, who had been Academic Dean from 1967-1975 and Admissions Director from 1978-1984 returned from teaching math at the public school to be the Development Officer. Annette Tucker joined the staff as dorm parent.[73] In sports, Travis Hodges was appointed as Athletic Director replacing Amy Fleener, and as an assistant to the admissions team. Nancy (Morley) Whiteman was named coach of women's volleyball and basketball. After graduation from Barclay in 1998, Nancy began as a full-time receptionist, and then was the faculty secretary.

Faculty emeritus, Fred Johnson and his wife, Esther, took on the role as directors of Alumni and Church Relations in the spring of 2001. The *Alumni Connector* was joined with the *Barclay Progress* and increased efforts were made to increase connections with alumni. Emily Leppert was hired to assist Heidi Longstroth as a library assistant in August of 2001.[74]

Three additions were made to the admissions staff in the Fall 2001. Paul Bryan as admissions counselor, Ron Wolfe as West Coast Representative, and Carlotta Clubb as enrollment secretary became part of the team of Jared Ross and Ryan Haase. Phillina Haselwood was added to the team as counselor in Fall 2002.

Other new staff joined in 2002 and 2003. In the spring of 2002 Melba Cook became the *ADVANTAGE!* Kansas Regional coordinator and in the fall Brad Lingafelter took on the role of Kansas *ADVANTAGE!* recruiter. Don Wolhlgemuth assumed the position as *ADVANTAGE!* recruiter in Denver. Dawn Brown became the academic secretary, and De Ann Garrett joined the college as an

---

[73] *Barclay College Progress*, Volume 71, No. 2 Summer-Fall 2001, 2.
[74] Presidential Cabinet minutes for August 28, 2001.

assistant to the Director of Marketing and Communications working with the college's website. Also the Spring 2002 Harlan Wheeler assumed the role of executive secretary in the President's office and Carol McKenna joined the team in the business office.

The Barclay College sports program remained active as the college entered the new millennium. In the spring of 2000 baseball was added to the sports options for the college. Chris Anderson was appointed as coach. The first season came off well and two players, Dusty Bauer and Isaiah Tetuan made the first-team all-region. Coach Chris Anderson was named Southwest Region Coach of the Year.[75]

In the spring a Barclay College Sports Hall of Fame was initiated with Jim "Bull" Bramlett, a former pro football player as the speaker for the opening banquet. Lynne Ann Ross Borchers and Thad Roher were the first two inductees into the hall. Borchers attended Barclay from 1978 to 1982 and excelled in both volleyball and basketball being chosen as an all-conference player in both sports and held the record for career points in basketball. Thad Roher played for the college from 1988 to 1991 was also an all-conference player for three years in basketball and held the men's basketball record for career points.[76]

In the summer of 2000, the college hosted a "church/industrial basketball team" tournament. The soccer team from the Fall 2000 season earned their third trip in four years to the national tournament in Florida. They completed the tournament in eighth place. Eric Crain and Brandon Weber came home with awards as MVP and first-team All-American for Eric and second-team All-American and all-region for Weber. Two other players, Mike Foster, and Nathan Williamson received honorable mention and were named for the all-region team.[77]

---

[75] *Barclay College Progress*, Volume 71, No. 2, Summer-Fall 2001.
[76] *Barclay College Progress*, Volume 70, No. 2, Summer 2000.
[77] *Barclay College Progress*, Volume 70, No. 4, Winter 2000/2001, 4.

A new scoreboard was installed in Hockett Auditorium early in 2001. In the Spring 2001 two additional members were inducted into the Barclay College Sports Hall of Fame. Former basketball players Rick Logan and Kayleen Stevens were honored as inductees. That same evening an All-Decade Soccer Team was named. Members of that team were: Jeff Carpenter, Eric Crain. Kevin Lee, Kris Sorensen, Jesus Cordova, Daniel Kerr, Brandon Cuevas, Jason Pickard, Ken Routon, Kurt Bashford, and Tony Southammavong. Honorable mentions were given to David Bond and James Pinkerton, Roger Powell, and Darby Hickman. Spring 2001 saw the inauguration of a women's softball program, a first for the college. Amy Fleener, the Athletic Director, took on the role of coach, and about a dozen games were scheduled for March and April with teams from Oklahoma and Texas in the National Christian College Athletic Association.[78] Also in 2001 Barclay hosted both the Southeast Regional Volleyball Tournament and the Midwest Christian College Conference Tournament.[79]

In Spring 2002 Nicole Ray Howard was named to the all-region women's basketball in the annual tournament. In preparation for the baseball season new coaches were named. Tim Garrett, Youth Ministry professor and Dean of Students, was assigned as the Women's Softball coach and a non-traditional student, Matt Kuffel, was named to be the men's baseball coach. The women's softball team was changed from a strictly college conference team to a club team to increase the possibility of games.[80] Not part of the college's sports program but none-the-less an athletic event which combined sports and fundraising was a "Great Commission Bike-A-Thon" that took place May 9-12, 2002. President Maurice Chandler, his wife Eloise, encouraged by David and Lynetta Chitwood in celebration of Chandler's 68th birthday rode bicycles from Riverton, Kansas to Fall City, Nebraska, a trip of around 250 miles. Friends of the college pledged various amounts per mile. Along the way the quartet met alumni and visited Friends Churches.

---

[78] *Barclay College Progress*, Volume 71, No. 1, Spring 2001, 8.
[79] *Barclay College Progress*, Volume 71, No. 3, Winter 2001-2002, 8.
[80] *Barclay College Progress*, Volume 72, No. 1, Spring 2002, 12.

The summer 2002 *Progress* announced that the Bike-A-Thon was successful with the announcement: "He did it! Leaving the Oklahoma-Kansas-Missouri border on May 8, President Maurice Chandler—joined enroute by several alumni and friends of the College—biked 261 miles in eastern Kansas to the Nebraska border." The trip was a success not only because of the funds raised but because of the friendships made and the awareness made of the college. Chandler stated: "I did something unique, raised awareness of Barclay College and raised fund support—currently more than $8,500, with more pledges coming in." [81] A second Bike-A-Thon trip was scheduled for March 2003. The route for this trip was from Denver to the Kansas border.

Beginning July 1, 2002, Ryan Kendall, a Barclay alum and a teacher and coach at Greensburg, Kansas, was appointed Athletic Director, replacing Travis Hodges in this position. Ryan started as Athletic Director but subsequently became coach of the basketball team, the Dean of Students and then later the head of the Sports and Recreation major as well as instructor for that major.

The Fall 2002 soccer team brought to the college the Team Sportsmanship All-Conference award at the conclusion of their season. A Barclay Athletic Booster Club was created by Ryan Kendall drawing supporters of sports at Barclay together with goals to improve the program and facilities. Fall 2002 Steve Davis, a former Barclay basketball player became the assistant men's basketball coach and Bryan Wachtel joined the staff as the assistant volleyball coach. Brad Lingafelter, the Kansas Regional *ADVANTAGE!* Coordinator joined the coaching staff in the Spring 2003 semester as coach for the men's baseball team.

Some interesting items from the years 1998 to 2003 may be added as a conclusion. The college had always provided its own food service through the years but for the 1999/2000 academic year experimented with a hired food service. Great Western Dining was

---

[81] *Barclay College Progress*, Volume 72, No. 2, Summer 2002, 4.

given a two-year contract for food service.[82] The experiment worked well but in later years the college returned to doing its own program to reduce costs. STUCO raised money from the student body, faculty, and staff in the Fall 2000 for a Christmas gift for a student from Mexico, Emilio Avila, in order that he might go home for Christmas.[83] Rick Johnson showed up in the yearbook for 2000 as a "secret" student and was given, for the second time, the special student award in the Spring 2001.[84] Two times in this period the Ladies Auxiliary sale exceeded all previous records. The 1999 auction raised over $70,000.00 which was more than any of the previous three years.[85] And the 2000 auction set a new high with $85,178.00.[86]

The Summer 2003 *Progress* summed up the period well:

> During President Chandler's five-year tenure there had been many improvements and significant developments at the college: Barclay achieved candidacy status with the regional accrediting body, established new academic majors and reinstated the church music major, added new full-time faculty positions, built new facilities including the women's dormitory and physical plant center, extensively renovated several buildings, received the AABC's Enrollment Growth Award, installed and expanded a computer network, and expanded the ADVANTAGE! Adult Degree Completion Program to several sites, including Colorado. The college's growth is reflected by the fact that more than 20 percent of all graduates from the college have taken place in the past five years.

---

[82] *Crimsayvista*, 2000, 7. See also President Cabinet minutes for October 10, 2001.
[83] *Crimsayvista*, 2000, 13.
[84] *Crimsayvista*, 2000, 47 and 2001, 67.
[85] *Crimsayvista*, 2000, 10.
[86] *Crimsayvista*, 2001, 12.

"Barclay College is a special place and has over the years made a positive impact on the world for God far beyond its size," President Chandler said. "Ellouise and I have been honored and blessed to have been associated with this institution, the Barclay family consisting of faculty, staff, alumni and friends of the college as well as the local community. We will carry many fond memories with us and look forward to continuing the wonderful friendships we have established here."[87]

Maurice Chandler had agreed to serve as president for five years and so resigned in the Spring 2003 and a presidential search committee began the task of finding a new president. Former Board member and chair, Paul Ross chaired the committee.

---

[87] *Barclay College Progress*, Volume 73, No.2, Summer 2003, 1.

CHAPTER SIX
AN ATTEMPT TO EXPAND
2003-2005

The presidential search committee that met throughout the Spring 2003 semester hoped to find a president who would continue the advances made in the Chandler years and would broaden the base for the college by enabling it to draw students from a wider pool. They hoped to find a president who had connections beyond the Friends movement who could draw students from those connections.

One candidate stood out from all those who responded to the announcements for the open position and submitted applications. This one had a Ph.D. in Adult and Continuing Education Administration and more than twenty-five years' experience in leadership, and in higher education. He authored numerous articles and books on leadership management of educational programs, and his dissertation focused on transformational learning. He had connections with the Free Lutheran church which it was hoped would draw students from that denomination to the college. Thus Dr. David Hietala was named to replace Maurice Chandler as president effective August 1, 2003.[88]

---

[88] *Barclay College Progress*, Volume 73, No. 2, Summer 2003, 1.

Upon accepting the position Dr. Hietala stated:

> I am excited about being part of a college that challenges tomorrow's leaders to think about the right things and to see their expanding world as a broad setting for ministry—with options only limited by time, attitude and the gifts provided by our Lord Jesus. I believe the opportunities for ministry, for promoting the Truth into every aspect of life and culture, are especially ripe and I look forward to watching Barclay College grow as we "go with God" to the place that He has set before us."[89]

At the Spring 2003 Board meeting, before the new president was named, the Barclay Board accepted a challenge that resulted in a "Go Ye Into All the World" campaign to raise funds to expand the college's missions major. From the beginning the college had had an impact around the world out of proportion to its size. This impact came partly through the many missionaries who were sent out from it. At least ninety-four missionaries had been sent to thirty-three nations over the years and in 2003 a ninety-fifth would soon be graduated. The college was in a building process to help provide workers for the "Great Commission" but had no full-time mission professor. The expansion of the college had brought some serious financial challenges that limited the hiring of new positions, yet the board was inspired to hire a full-time professor not only to provide leadership for missions but to satisfy the accreditation level recently received which demanded a full-time person for each major. Sheldon Carpenter, chair of the Academic Committee, agreed to chair the campaign and to lead in the effort to raise $40,000 so that a mission professor could be hired as soon as possible.[90] The campaign was successful, and the new professor began teaching classes in the Fall 2004 semester.

---

[89] *Barclay College Progress*, Volume 73, No. 2, Summer 2003, 1.
[90] *Barclay College Progress*, Volume 73, No. 2, Summer 2003, 1 and 3.

The new president began his role at the same time that several others joined the staff of the college. Justin Kendall joined the staff as the new Admissions counselor in June. Marcy Bunce, a 2003 graduate, became the secretary for the Vice President of Student Services and Dawn Brown, who had been part-time as academic secretary, became full-time and added the role of accounts receivable in the business office. That fall two adjuncts joined the faculty. Bernard Ashlock joined the *ADVANTAGE!* staff for psychology and Heather Sazama began as adjunct for Education on campus. Fall 2003 was the last semester for Ruth Ann Wedel who had managed the computer lab and helped students with computer issues and taught education classes.

A number of significant changes occurred in the summer of 2003. The State of Colorado approved Barclay's request to offer psychology and business programs in addition to the Bible/Theology and Christian Leadership programs that were operating through the *ADVANTAGE!* degree completion program. Demolition of West Hall, which had been built in 1913 and purchased by the college in 1953 was completed by the Hi Grade Sand Company of Harper, Kansas. In the Broadhurst Student Center the snack bar and the game room of the Bear's Den were joined together. The separating wall of wood and glass panels was removed, and the ceiling was taken down, giving the space an "industrial" look. The *Barclay Progress* invited everyone to the grand opening on August 18 stating "the Den was being totally remodeled this summer with new furniture, new activities, and a new look similar to a coffee house." Later the hallway on the east of the original snack bar was incorporated into the space and the whole received a new tile floor (summer 2006). When the hallway was added to the space a new counter was also constructed. Removing the partition between the two rooms and adding the hallway gave considerably more space and increased the usefulness for the student body. Volunteers on Wheels (VOW) returned to the campus also in the summer to complete projects of interior work in the new maintenance building and to do landscaping. They also helped in the Bear's Den renovation.[91]

President Hietala began in August by sending letters to Barclay supporters outlining the financial condition of the college. He followed this with an update in his first column in the *Barclay Progress* (Fall 2003). He noted the tremendous advances that the college had made, particularly with the new women's dorm. Yet he also shared that these advances came with a cost—$1.8 million borrowed for construction which would need to be repaid. He pointed out that shortly after the women's dorm was competed the nation was affected by 9/11 and the economy took some drastic hits which had impacted donations to the college. Although enrollment in the fall was up from previous years the years of inadequate enrollment left other debts that the college would need to address. In June 2003, the college eliminated a number of administrative and faculty positions to reduce expenses. However, a new Vice President for Business Services, David Brookman, was hired in October 2003 with the expectation that his expertise would be a great help. The Board in their fall meeting affirmed that they were all on board to support moving forward and agreed to increase tuition and to explore a fund development campaign. A series of meetings was arranged on campus involving faculty and staff in discussion of ways to structure work to support the task of teaching and learning.[92]

The 2003/2004 academic year was filled with activity. Early in August a dinner for Barclay College alumni and friends was held in Overland Park with approximately one hundred in attendance. Outgoing president, Maurice Chandler, encouraged the attendees to support the college and incoming president, David Hietala, was introduced. A similar dinner meeting happened in Tulsa, Oklahoma in January 2004. The Fall 2003 Ladies Auxiliary Auction contributed approximately $65,130 with $30,000 coming from quilts to the

---

[91] *Barclay College Progress,* Volume 73, No. 2, Summer 2003.
[92] *Barclay College Progress*, Volume 73, No. 3, Fall 2003, 2.

college. During the auction over one hundred children participated in the "Carnival of Praise." A one-time event at the auction was the presence of the Smokey Hills Public Broadcasting System's film crew to capture the presentation of the "Hero Next Door" award given to Hank Clark who had given over fifteen years of volunteer service to the college. Elizabeth Griffin, Associate Dean for External Studies, nominated Hank for this award as a way to say thanks and to celebrate his ninetieth birthday. From mid-November to the end of January ten new *ADVANTAGE!* cohorts began their educational journey in Wichita, Larned, Denver, and Colorado Springs. Several Colorado *ADVANTAGE!* students celebrated their graduation from college in graduation exercises held in Colorado Springs in December. The Admissions team began to meet every day from Monday to Friday in prayer for the college and for admission goals. A successful GAP (an admissions event that invited high school students to be on campus) was held in November to attract new students to the college.[93] In the fall of 2003, Glenn Leppert, Barclay College Registrar, and professor since 1985, received his Ph.D. degree from Kansas State University. His dissertation was a history of the "People to People Program" of Dwight D. Eisenhower. With the older 1978 MCI bus needing constant repairs a group of donors put up $30,000 and invited others to add to it to raise $60,000 to purchase a 1993 Van Hool forty-seven passenger bus. The monies were raised in time for the choir to use the new bus in their tour of the west coast in May.[94] Elizabeth Griffin left the college in April 2004 to take a position at the Larned State Hospital. She had been with the college since 1998. Former president Chandler and his wife Eloise planned another "Bike-A-Thon" this time to travel from Portland, Maine to San Diego, California in June. The trip was to raise funds for three private Christian colleges—George Fox University, Barclay College, and Azusa Pacific University.

---

[93] *Barclay College Progress*, Volume 73, No. 3, Fall 2003.
[94] *Barclay College Progress*, Volume 74, No. 1, Spring 2004.

The missions professor who began in Fall 2004 as a result of the "Go Ye Into All the World" campaign was Prosperly B. Lyngdoh a native of Northeast India. Prosperly had served as missionary, youth evangelist, and administrator in India and for several years was pastor of the Andheri Baptist Church, the first "self-supporting, self-governing, and self-propagating" church in western India. Realizing his need for education Prosperly was blessed with a scholarship to attend the Union Biblical Seminary of the Serampore University, and then in 1995 he had the opportunity to attend a Billy Graham seminar in the United States which resulted in enrollment at Gordon-Cromwell Seminary and his earning a master's degree in world missions and evangelism. Then he was accepted into the Billy Graham School of Missions, Evangelism, and Church Growth of the Southern Seminary in 2001 and graduated May 2004 and made connections with Barclay. Prosperly was a popular, yet challenging professor and his cross-cultural background and experience made a substantive impact on all students. He continued at the college until the end of the Spring 2010. Patsy, his wife, needed a change in her environment because of medical conditions.[95]

In the Fall 2004 semester there were other additions to the faculty and staff. Justin Carswell filled the position of Academic Dean and Executive Vice President which was vacated by the departure of Erik Ritschard who became the principal of a Christian School in Colorado. Justin assumed the position just in time to begin work on the ABHE self-study for the ten-year review and visit scheduled for 2006. Along with Justin new staff Louise Pelzl assumed the role of coordinator of the Business Office, Janet Horton became the clerk for accounts payable and payroll, Anita Cunningham began working in accounts receivable and human resources, while Carla Woods joined the college to support housekeeping. Two new *ADVANTAGE!* staff included Andrew Bennett a recruiter in Wichita, and John Fly a recruiter in Colorado Springs who also became an adjunct to teach in Colorado. In Haviland, three recent

---

[95] *Barclay College Progress*, Volume 74, No. 2, Fall 2004, 1.

graduates, Kaylan Jones, Shaleah Staats, and Susan Ostrowski came on board as admissions counselor, and coordinators in the academic department.[96] In the Spring 2005 semester Dr. Skip Payette joined the faculty as professor for Youth Ministry. Dr. Payette had completed a Doctor of Ministry degree and was almost finished with a Ph.D. in Christian Education and Church Ministry.[97] Other faculty additions included Delbert Regier an adjunct staff for Bible on campus, Viola Regier as adjunct for Education, and Jeff Starkey in *ADVANTAGE!* for Ministry.

A new addition to the facilities in Fall 2004 was the creation of a "Welcome Center" where guests to the college could be greeted. The former Financial Aid Office in Phillips Hall was given a facelift including an opening counter into the hallway. Harlan Wheeler was assigned to lead the work of the center.

Another welcome addition to the college program was the expansion of the prayer team for admissions. Under the leadership of Mary Nessler, former business manager for the college, alumni, community members, and others were invited to pray along at the same time the admissions team were at prayer. The Fall 2004 *Progress* reported that there were more than forty doing so.

Those prayers helped not only the admissions endeavors but had an impact on student life in general and especially an emphasis on missions. The "every fall" mission emphasis had the theme "On Mission With God" and featured Larry Walker, the Southwest Regional Director of ACMC (Advancing Churches in Mission Commitment). Several missionaries-in-residence" assisted in the week—Arden and Joy Sanders of Wycliffe Bible Translators; Willard and Doris Ferguson of EFM (Evangelical Friends Mission); Stacy Waddle, World Impact, and Dave and Mae Kellum of

---

[96] *Barclay College Progress*, Volume 74, No. 2, Fall 2004, 2.
[97] *Barclay College Progress*, Volume 75, No. 1, Spring 2005, 2.

EFM. During the Christmas break Dr. Skip Payette and three students (Tara Healy, Audrey Carlson, and Tyler Bousman) worked as College leaders at a Campus Crusade for Christ's Student Venture ministering to high school students and learning about the organization of these sorts of youth events. As the spring semester opened two students, Joshua Woodall, and Briley Deaton, out of their concern for the victims of the tsunami in Asia organized a drive to raise funds for relief. Working with the ministry organization of Gospel for Asia, they spear-headed a large-scale fundraiser that involved businesses from Greensburg to Wichita, Student Council and the student body, and an event that was well attended. The result was a donation of $3,000—enough to build a small building in some of the hardest hit areas of Asia. Along with this Youth Ministry students sponsored a talent show with a love offering and were able to donate $300 to the ABC Pregnancy Help Center in Pratt.

Student life was enhanced by two new features: a monthly Monday Study Break in which students were encouraged to take a break from study, to enjoy free food, and attend a one-hour seminar which covered such topics as conflict management, financial aid, healthy eating, and life after college. The second feature was an event that was scheduled for the third Thursday each month which was a lunchtime roundtable talk with faculty and administration.[98]

The sports teams for the college had a bland Fall 2003. No team lost every game; every team won some. The volleyball girls won their first three games, the soccer team won three games overall with women's basketball having eleven victories and the men's basketball with five wins. Fall 2004 turned out much better. The highest number of athletes turned out since Ryan Kendall became Athletic Director, and the excitement for the potential was very evident as the season began.[99]

---

[98] *Barclay College Progress*, Volume 75, No. 1, Spring 2005, 2.
[99] *Crimsayvista*, 2004, 16, 20, 22; *Barclay College Progress*, Volume 74, No. 2, Fall 2004, 4.

The potential turned out to be real and in the Spring 2005 looking back on the season it was reported:

> The men's soccer team this year improved a lot from last season. We had the best turnout of players in four years with up to eighteen players on the team resulting in our best record in four years. This year's team ended a long drought of scoring with five players doubling last year's high in goals scored. The team ended the year with a 6-13 record and four players receiving conference honors: Brad Carpenter, Josh Lofgren, Nathaniel Carlson, and Jared Haley... The men's basketball team had an exciting season starting off with a brutal schedule that included three NAIA schools and one NCAA Division II school. These games prepared the men for the season and helped them to be competitive throughout the season. Many games were tight with some wins and some losses. The team had a final record of 8-20 and a conference record of 3-7. Coach Ryan Kendall brought home the Association of Christian College Athletics (ACCA) Coach of the Year award while player Tommy Grace was named an ACCA Academic All-American.
>
> The women's basketball team experienced a thrilling season too. The ladies had to adjust to a new coach and did a fantastic job of learning a new system and working hard. Under the leadership of Coach Brad Lingafelter, this year's team will go down as one of the best in school history ending the season with an 11-11 overall record and a 5-3 conference record. Team member Sarah Williams led the conference in scoring and assists and together with teammate

Katrina Goering was named to the 2nd Team All-Conference. The entire Lady Bears basketball team greatly honored Barclay College by winning the Midwest Christian College Conference Sportsmanship Award. Peer athletes from other schools who felt the Barclay women best displayed Christ-like attitudes and sportsmanlike conduct throughout the season bestowed this award on our women. Coach Kendall's award was also bestowed upon him by his peer coaches in the association.[100]

The first *ADVANTAGE!* commencement held in Colorado was in December 2001. Commencements for Colorado *ADVANTAGE!* students as well as Kansas *ADVANTAGE!* students completing in December were held in 2002 and in 2003, but in 2004 when President Hietala learned that only blank diploma covers would be given out because no graduate had completed all requirements, he cancelled the graduation exercises. This, unfortunately, caused trouble. The leadership in Colorado proceeded with a ceremony and having no diploma covers to present created faux diplomas. Some graduates accepted these as final and consequently never completed the remaining requirements. Additional friction between the president and the *ADVANTAGE!* leadership came with adjustments that the president attempted to make in scheduling and in requirements.

The experiment for widening the base for recruiting students failed. Dr. Hietala did not generate contacts with his denomination that resulted in students enrolling. The administrators that Dr. Hietala gathered around him represented the Assemblies of God, the Salvation Army, and the Southern Baptist movement, and none of these made connections that resulted in additional students. Moreover, these administrators, although great at doing

---

[100] *Barclay College Progress*, Volume 75, No. 1, Spring 2005, 6.

their assigned tasks did not connect with Friends either. There was a great distance between the college leadership and the Friends movement that the college represented.

During this time, the Barclay College Board found itself repeatedly discussing whether they wanted to remain a Bible College or to attempt to become a Christian Liberal Arts college.[101] This took considerable energy from the decisions they should have been wrestling with. And, regrettably, there were issues primarily financial ones. Finances became problematic. The leadership proposed some unrealistic salaries for administrators citing the college had to look like other colleges to be successful. There was an unanticipated drop in enrollment. There was a substantial drop in giving to the college. And the costs of running a college continued to increase.

A memorandum from President Hietala dated May 25, 2005 indicated that the cash on-hand was less than what was needed to cover the payroll for May, that donor revenue was down as much as forty-five percent, that only thirty-eight of a projected sixty new students in Fall 2004 had enrolled, that the long-term debt was at $2.1 million, and that personnel cuts would be required as the budget would need to be drastically cut.[102]

Board actions to respond to these facts were varied. First, the decision to once again drop the process of seeking regional accreditation was made. The college exited the process with NCA on May 9, 2005.[103] Seven positions were eliminated (including that of President and Dean of Students). Salary and retirement benefits were reduced. Alumni were contacted and much prayer went up for the college.[104]

---

[101] Conversations with Board members at that time.
[102] May 25, 2005, memo to former presidents of Barclay College.
[103] May 9, 2005, Board minutes and letter to NCA.
[104] May 9, 2005, update from the Board Chair.

With tensions afloat in the distance education program, two further self-studies looming—one for the ten-year review for ABHE, the other for full accreditation with NCA—Dr. Hietala and his cabinet began preparing a document for ABHE, a document or plan which was required for closing any college. It was a plan to assure transfer of transcripts, payment arrangements for debts, disbursement of holdings, notifications to the entire clientele, and whatever else might be needed to assure a final closure of the institution. The document was not submitted to the accrediting agency. Instead, Dr. Hietala presented his resignation to the Board and David Brookman, Business Manager; Justin Carswell, Academic Dean and Executive Vice President; and Kim Pennington, Vice President of Community also resigned. The Board responded by issuing a "Now is the Time" Campaign.

A significant article appeared in the Spring 2005 *Barclay Progress*. It was written by DeWayne Bryan, a member of the Barclay Board. It was entitled, "A Future Depends on God." In the article Bryan compared the Exodus to the Boston Marathon and elaborated on how the obedient Israelites were given a future. The conclusion of the article is pertinent to the closing of this chapter:

> Barclay College is in a similar situation [as the Israelites who faced the Red Sea]. God's presence still graces the campus. Lives are changed, students are learning about the incredible grace of God, and many are called into ministry. Those who are not called into a ministry minister where preachers and missionaries cannot, in the workplace.
>
> The Egyptians for Barclay College have fallen in three categories. One was an unanticipated drop in students. Another was a substantial drop in giving. And still another was the rising cost of

personnel and running a college. There might be some spiritual warfare going on here too.

Barclay needs $750,000 to finish the year and "Now is the Time" for those of us who believe God will deliver us from this enemy to act. We need everyone who "believes" in God's work through Barclay to respond in faith. The race is on, and God is urging us to get ready to run with determination and endurance. So, with His help the "Now is the Time" campaign will provide this need by July 1st so we can look forward to another school year. If there is no faith, there will be no college.

The "Now is the Time" campaign is the first challenge Barclay faces. This money will allow the College to pay its bills and end the year in the black. We believe God desires that kind of stewardship from us. The second challenge is similar to the first. The College Board also believes that stewardship for next year is also necessary. An additional $750,000 needed to be cut from the budget in the 2005-2006 school year. Since the college depends on gifts and student enrollment for survival there are not many areas that can be cut. The Board of Trustees sorrowfully accepted this responsibility, and several positions were cut and/or reduced. If God blesses with a tremendous response to the "Now is the Time" campaign, staff will be rehired. There was no joy in this for the College Board and many have devoted a great deal of prayer to the situation. The Board does believe there is a future for Barclay College if people are obedient to God's direction in a generous way.[105]

---

[105] *Barclay College Progress*, Volume 75, No. 1, Spring 2005, 1 and 2

CHAPTER SEVEN
THE GREAT MIRACLE
2005-2010

While the issues were compounded at the conclusion of the Spring 2005 semester the feeling of being overwhelmed had been present all through the time that Dr. Hietala was president. The issues and pressures had begun before he accepted the position. In a report to the Board for the 2003/2004 academic year Registrar, Academic Dean, and full-time professor Glenn Leppert reported to the Board:

> The 2003/2004 academic year may, by all measures, have been the most intense year I have experienced at Barclay College. I began the year attempting to fill the roles that both Erik Ritschard and Ruth Ann Wedel had previously worked full-time at along with my usual role as Registrar, Professor, and "etc." This meant scrambling to find adjuncts to complete the teaching rosters and learning the network through "on-the-job" training ... A fair amount of time throughout both the fall and spring semesters has been the task of keeping up the correspondence and phone calls necessary to hire replacements for the

Missions and the Youth Ministries positions . . . I have been working on updating the college catalog. This has not been finished. I have been able to keep the curriculum guides current and have been able to create a number of reports that can be drawn from our database. I have worked with the company that we purchased our enrollment software from to make changes and enhancements of the program. The newest release of the program with these updates should be on campus soon. There have been significant changes in the *ADVANTAGE!* program, especially during the spring semester. Hoping to make the program more attractive to students, we have changed it from an 18-month to a 12-month program. This has meant rewriting all of the modules so that they will fit the new format. We have also rewritten one of the majors, the Christian Leadership major. This has meant some new classes have needed to be created. The problem is that we have had a tremendous change of personnel.

In addition, the college was gearing up for two major accreditation self-studies, one for the ten-year review for ABHE (AABC previous to July 2004) and an important self-study for the North Central Association and if the college chose to pursue the full state endorsed Elementary Education program a hosted visit within the next year would be necessary with the Kansas State Department of Education.[106]

Academic year 2004/2005 added additional concerns and by the end of the Spring 2005 the college faced a crisis. Funds were critical, $750,000.00 was needed just to complete the budget for the spring semester, leadership was needed since all the major administrative positions were now vacant with the resignations of the

---

[106] Glenn Leppert, "2003/2004 Report to the Board," May 2004.

President, Business Manager, Academic Dean and Executive Vice President, and Vice President of Community. The FTE for the college, which had been at one hundred sixty-nine for the Fall 2004 semester had dropped to one hundred seven for the Spring 2005 greatly impacting the budget. As wonderful as it was to have fifty students graduating that spring it meant that the majority of the off-site graduates would need to be replaced for the coming fall. (There were 50 graduated in Spring 2005—33 were *ADVANTAGE!* students and 17 were campus.)[107] As the Board met at their May 2005 meeting they were perplexed. None wanted to close the college. All knew that a real miracle would be needed if there was any way to keep the college going. There was no time nor funds to search for and hire a president. Likewise how to fill the missing vacancies and to make up for the shortfall in funds?

While the board prayed and pondered what to do, an employee of the college came forward and asked for the privilege to guide the college back to health. That person was Herb Frazier. Herb had first connected with the college back in 1943 when as a fourteen-year-old he came from Houston to be a sophomore student at the Friends Haviland Academy. After graduating from the Academy in 1946 he was gone for twenty years before returning in 1967 when he came as Academic Dean. He served in that capacity until 1975. He came back to the college in 1978 as Director of Admissions and filled that role until 1984. After teaching math for seventeen years at the local high school he again returned to the college as Alumni Coordinator in 2001. He knew the alumni and he had a passion for the college that inspired others around him.

Marjorie Thompson, the chair of the Barclay Board, introduced him to the alumni as president with these words:

> For over five decades, Mr. Frazier has been affiliated with Barclay College in many various aspects and endeavors. It was from this list of achievements

---

[107] *Barclay College Progress*, Volume 75, No. 1, Spring 2005, 5.

and his devotion to Barclay that the Board of Trustees chose to offer the presidential appointment to Herb last June. Because of his complete faithfulness and loyalty to Barclay, Mr. Frazier graciously accepted the challenge of becoming Barclay College's [15th] president.[108]

Over the years Mr. Frazier has served in development and alumni relations at Barclay, pioneered joint degree programs, and assisted in guiding the college through many of its accreditation reviews. Perhaps more importantly, Herb Frazier has the heart of a servant. No one is more persevering; no one is more tenacious. No one is more positive, and no one has more faith to believe and achieve. Herb's commitment to the Lord Jesus Christ is seen through his commitment to his family, his church, and his community. He and his wife Shirley are dedicated to serving God, to this college and its success, and to each member of the Barclay College student body, faculty and staff, the alumni, and the entire Barclay College Association.[109]

The Board did not just hand the college over to Herb to see what he could do but invested themselves heavily in the college sharing their talents, resources, and time. Prayerfully they "orchestrated" the affairs of the college and the Lord blessed. They prayed. They prayed for finances. They prayed for wisdom. They prayed for God's abiding presence on campus and with students in the distance education arm of the college. Their prayers brought financial and administrative rewards. The Board did not appeal to the alumni and friends of the college to give to the college but

---

[108] Article in the *Barclay College Progress* referred to Herb Frazier as the 17th president, but as Royce Frazier was inaugurated as the 16th, Herb was the 15th. The 17th for Herb is true only if the two interim presidents, Delbert Vaughn and Glenn Leppert are counted.
[109] *Barclay College Progress*, Fall 2005, 1.

rather to pray for the college and from that outpouring of prayer came an abundance of giving. The needed funds to close the semester were raised.[110]

In response, the college then launched a new campaign to secure additional resources to stabilize the college. They initiated a "Together We Succeed Campaign" with a goal to raise $1,200,000.00 to cover the portion of the budget not covered by student income, to pay off the line of credit at the local bank, and to reduce an outstanding loan. The college also praised the Lord that the 2005 Auxiliary Auction was an enormous success. With a tremendous crowd and much excitement the sale provided $82,577.50.

The board submitted a summary for the Fall 2005 *Progress* which was for the alumni and friends of the college. It stated, "Thank you for the support you have given the college. The financial status of the college has greatly improved. We are having a good year and the atmosphere on campus is wonderful."[111]

In the Winter 2005/2006 issue of the *Progress* DeWayne Bryan wrote on behalf of the Barclay Board:

> Barclay College is a "Miracle on the Plains" because God has blessed it throughout its history. When the world thought it was finished, God demonstrated His power by working another miracle.
>
> When we asked alumni and friends of the college to pray and be obedient, miraculous things happened. Everyone prayed and then responded. Barclay College received the mail, asked God to bless it and opened it. The college needed over $700,000 in a three-month period of time to open

---

[110] *Barclay College Progress*, Fall 2005, 2.
[111] *Barclay College Progress*, Fall 2005, 2.

their doors in August 2005. This is more money than they usually raise in an entire year. Yet God blessed the offerings of obedient Christians and performed a miracle. Barclay College received over $700,000 by the end of July.

Furthermore, Barclay College needed an entire administrative team. As people prayed about this need, God performed another miracle. A particularly good administrative team was in place before school began.

And now I must tell you the rest, but not the end, of the story. The initial need was not enough to sustain the college, so people have continued to pray and be obedient. More miracles continue to occur, and God continues to bless both those who give and Barclay College. One of those additional miracles was a Christmas Wreath response of over $100,000. We invite you to also praise God for what He has done and the gift of stability that Barclay College now enjoys.[112]

President Frazier said that when he accepted the challenge of being president there were three things he knew he had to do. Those were: to have confidence in the alumni and friends of the college, to find ways to attract more students to attend, and to trust the Lord with all his heart. The alumni and friends responded graciously, he did find a way to attract students, and his trust in the Lord was evident to everyone.

His first item of business was to create a president's cabinet filling the vacated positions. He approached three individuals each of whom responded positively. Lee Anders, the head of the business administration major agreed to add the role of business manager to

---

[112] *Barclay College Progress*, Winter 2005/2006, 1.

his duties taking on the task of teaching full-time and managing the finances for the college. Dr. Glenn Leppert, full-time Registrar, and instructor, agreed to take on the additional full-time role of Academic Dean, a position he had filled temporarily several times since he came to the college in 1985. Ryan Kendall, Athletic Director, and coach agreed to add the position of Vice President of Community (Dean of Students). The new president referred to their willingness to be his cabinet as "the first miracle the Lord provided."[113]

Along with a new cabinet that first fall were several fresh staff. Amber Vanderploeg, a 2005 graduate became the Accounts Payable/Payroll clerk. David Frazier, also a Spring 2005 graduate, joined the admissions team as a recruiter; Kim Sachs, a 1980 graduate, assumed the role as Women's Dorm Parent; Jason Van Meter, a 2004 graduate, took on the role as the Men's Dorm Parent along with his wife Jessica (Haley) and his daughter Eliana. Also Barbara Davis, who moved to Haviland in 2004 with her husband Ed, joined the staff in the Business Office as Accounts Receivable clerk. Robin Johnston, former president, began serving as Operations Manager, and Tricia Oren (Leppert) returned to the college as Academic Services Assistant. Ryan Haase, a 1997 graduate, who often volunteered with the maintenance department, became the Manager of the Bear's Den.

Joining the faculty were Ray Anderson who had taught history for thirty-three years at the high school level who took on the position of instructor for American History and James Pinkerton, a 1997 graduate, who came as an adjunct professor in the Bible division. Tim Garrett returned to the college, after doing missions in Scotland, as an adjunct teaching Youth Ministry and Christian Leadership courses. Everett Jantz, Heather Sazama, Viola and Del Regier returned to the faculty as adjuncts to teach philosophy, education, and Bible classes.

---

[113] *Barclay College Progress*, Spring 2006, 2.

For years, the college had sent students to various camps in the summer as counselors. In the Spring 2004 a change was made and in the summer of 2004 and again in Summer 2005 students were sent, not as counselors, but as worship leaders. In 2005 a group called Aria went to represent the college. The band consisted of Kris Smitherman on the bass guitar, Jared Haley on electric guitar and vocals, Andrew Happle on drums for the first half of the trip and Nathaniel Carlson on drums for the second half, Megan Frazier on vocals and David Frazier on acoustic guitar and vocals. The band was able to minister at six camps (five were Friends) and were exposed to youth in five Yearly Meetings.

Although enrollment was down in the Fall 2005, down to only 84 FTE on campus and 104 FTE overall, enthusiasm was high. Sixty percent of the students were Friends, although twenty-five denominations were represented. Mike Belasco was beginning his second year as soccer coach and started the season off well. James Pinkerton began his first-year coaching volleyball and looked forward to a great season. Their expectations were rewarded. Sarah Williams was selected as NCCAA Division II volleyball athlete of the week for September 19-23.[114]

Fall 2005 was the beginning of a new venture for several of the college faculty. David Robinson, Superintendent for the Evangelical Friends Church—Mid America, had a dream to provide training and mentoring for pastors to "rekindle reliable and effective leadership" in the local church. With the help of EFC-MAYM staff member, Dave Kingrey, an Institute for Pastoral Leadership Development was created. The Institute met for the first time in February, 2005. Meetings then took place each month with a much higher attendance than the founders had imagined. The first session had around forty students. The mailing list in April 2021 when the last session was held had three hundred and nineteen names. As an online program in its last several years the institute had students from

---

[114] *Barclay College Progress*, Fall 2005, 4 and *Barclay Progress*, Spring 2006, 7.

twenty different nationalities attend. Students represented three different Friends groups. There were students on every continent except for Australia and Antarctica. A dozen or more in the receiving countries translated the PowerPoints into native languages. Courses were offered in Worship Leadership, Theology and Church History, Old Testament, New Testament, Personal Life of the Pastor, Evangelism and Outreach, Church Leadership and Administration, Spiritual Formation and Spiritual Direction, Friends Faith and Practice, Family Building, Organizational Leadership, and Advancing the Church. There were individual classes within each of these categories; classes such as The Reformation and Preaching Through the Old Testament.

The institute was designed so that a pastor or student completing twelve courses over a period of three years would earn a Certificate of Excellence in Church Leadership. The first course was "Preaching, Teaching and Worship" taught by Barclay College professor David Williams. Glenn Leppert, Barclay College Registrar, and professor, taught the third course "Theology and Church History." The institute continued until 2021, with the last several years being fully online with classes broadcast to many locations. Over the sixteen years many of the Barclay faculty taught courses.

President Frazier's first year began with enthusiasm and ended the same way. Herb was able to report in the *Progress* at the end of the spring semester, "Prayers and financial gifts have been overwhelming. With all accounts paid in full, all designated funds in place, all loans paid off except the bond issue on the women's dorm, current monthly bills up to date and significant reserve funds, Barclay College continues to be the 'Miracle on the Prairie.' I am in the process of securing funds to stabilize the college's future."

One significant thing that happened in the month of April was the ten-year review for the accrediting association. The Spring 2006 *Progress* reported:

Barclay College has been accredited by the Association of Biblical Higher Education since 1979. Every 10 years the college conducts a self-study and is reviewed by ABHE for a 10-year renewal of accreditation.

The ABHE team visited the campus April 3-5, 2006 to conduct this routine evaluation. The team members were highly complimentary of the college's employees and student body. They commended the college on its internal assessment program, dedication and commitment of staff, well-organized and prepared documents, spiritual needs fulfillment, athletic program, and the many avenues for learning leadership.[115]

Members of the faculty were busy that spring. In relation to his doctoral dissertation, Dr. Glenn Leppert was invited to speak at the 50th Anniversary of the People-to-People and the Sister Cities Program at the University of the Pacific in Stockton, California, on April 29. Unfortunately, airport conditions did not allow him to personally make the trip as scheduled. He prepared a PowerPoint presentation in his stead. Dr. Leppert was also published. He wrote a chapter on the history of Barclay College for a book entitled, *Founded by Friends: The Quaker Heritage of Fifteen American Colleges and Universities*. Dr. Skip Payette, returning Youth Ministry Professor, also had a book published. *The Life and Legacy of Orange Scott and Luther: The Birth of The Wesleyan Church*. David Williams wrote a review for the book *Extreme Church Makeover* by Chuck Mylander and Neil Anderson.

At the annual Association Dinner, March 25, 2006, Marjorie Thompson presented a statement of identity for the Association to consider for approval. It read, "Barclay College bases its existence in a rich history of evangelical Friends tradition. Barclay College is an

---

[115] *Barclay College Progress*, Spring 2006, 2.

evangelical Friends school which accepts and embraces persons with evangelical Christian beliefs from a variety of denominational backgrounds." The statement was accepted unanimously.[116]

The 2005/2006 academic year concluded with several significant events. A personal evangelism seminar, March 24-25, held in Derby Kansas gave students intensive opportunity to "study, observe, and practice essential aspects of relational evangelism and discipleship."[117] Part of the experience included going door-to-door in Derby. A very successful Heartland Conference titled "Help for the Helper" was held April 7-8 on the Barclay campus with pastors, social workers, counselors, and students coming to hear four speakers. Royce Frazier, adjunct professor, and counselor, presented "What do People Want When Living Hurts" and "Are God and Freud on Speaking Terms?" Barclay alum Ruth Miller Kemper from DCCCA Family Preservation in Wichita, Kansas spoke on "The Legacy of Divorce," and "The Spirit of Wisdom and Revelation." Brian Mills, also a Barclay adjunct and Cornerstone Family Consultant, and Bernard Ashlock from Christian Counseling Associates of Garden City, Kansas, made presentations. The conference was designed to encourage and enlighten those who helped ones hurting in society. April 10-13 the Spiritual Life Emphasis focused on "Dynamics of an Authentic Christian Community" which was student led. One other event was the retirement of Sylvia Morley, English professor at Barclay for ten years beginning in 1996. Students and faculty saw her off with a retirement party on May 5 by sharing many memories of her classes and a poem written just for her retirement by Dr. Glenn Leppert.[118]

Even that first summer, usually a lean time for the college was blessed. President Frazier wrote:

---

[116] *Barclay College Progress*, Spring 2006, 4.
[117] *Barclay College Progress*, Spring 2006, 9.
[118] *Barclay College Progress*, Spring 2006, 7.

I am thankful for the Lord's provisions. The college has completed the months of June and July without incurring any indebtedness, with all bills paid and all funds in place. June and July are the most difficult months of the year financially and yet the Lord has provided. Thank you for supporting the college so the Lord's work can continue. Sixty percent of last year's on campus students were preparing for a church vocation. I expect the percentage will be higher for the 2006-2007 year. Know that your gifts are bearing great dividends for the Kingdom.[119]

Summer 2006 was busy as well. Volunteers on Wheels (VOW) who had been on campus several times previous were back on campus for two weeks in June. They completed a number of projects—they re-wired the Bear's Den and the gymnasium, added new siding on the front gable of Hockett Auditorium, did major "face lifts" in the dorms, and fixed doors. In addition to the work of VOW, college personnel laid ceramic tile in Broadhurst Student Center hallways, cafeteria, restrooms, and the Bear's Den. The most ambitious project was installing carpet in the library. The Academy class of 1956 gave $34,045.00 to accomplish this. Every book had to be removed from the library and stored elsewhere—Jackson Hall and Hockett Auditorium—and the shelves all dismantled before the carpet could be put down. Then, with the carpet in place, all the shelves were reassembled and books by the armfuls were carried back and put in place with great care to make certain they were in the correct place. In addition to these projects on campus the faculty was engaged in ministry. David Williams was guest speaker at Rocky Mountain Yearly Meeting. Glenn Leppert spoke at an area rally in Coyle, Oklahoma, several faculty members counseled at camps, and Skip Payette directed a summer camp.[120]

---

[119] *Barclay College Progress*, Summer 2006, 2.
[120] *Barclay College Progress*, Spring 2006, 4.

There were several who joined the staff and faculty in Spring 2006. Dr. Skip Payette returned to the faculty as the Youth Ministry professor after a year at the School of Urban Missions in San Diego, California. Emily Harkness (Leppert), a 2004 graduate, who had served as the Assistant Librarian began as the Director of Library Services. Three other Barclay alums joined the staff as well. Pam Fulbright (Roberts) came as the Christian School Elementary Education instructor and Josiah Williams after graduation accepted a position in Admissions. Holly Doggett (Unruh), a 1999 graduate became the Welcome Center Receptionist. Pam's husband, Dennis Fulbright joined the adjunct faculty staff along with Christa Zapfe and Judy West of Greensburg. Brian Hanneken came on board as the *ADVANTAGE!* Coordinator and Academic Services Assistant. Each of these joined the college in the semester just before the 2006/2007 academic year which would become a most unusual year.

The Fall 2006 semester began with several new faculty. Clarence Doelling was added as adjunct in business. Jerry Hodges joined the adjunct staff for Bible. Ryan Kendall assumed a new role as Sports Recreation and Ministry professor for a new major, Sports, Recreation, and Ministry, which began that fall. Gary Damron joined the adjunct staff for history. Hannah Kendall was engaged to teach an art class, and Kim Stewart began as piano instructor.

Fall 2006 was the 90th fall semester for the college. Like many semesters previous, Gospel teams and faculty were actively engaged in going to churches to share. One church, in fact, requested a college team one Sunday each month. The choir had a full schedule for the fall, the board met in their annual fall meeting to discuss ways to connect the Yearly Meetings with the college, and a great Ladies Auxiliary sale took place raising more than $80,000.00. Plans for classes to be called "College 101" were being arranged for late spring. These were classes to equip camp leaders and those who would be ministering in camps for the camp season. Other classes were set for those participating in the Saltshaker program. Courses were also being prepared to be offered at the annual Ministry Conference (Yearly Meeting). Each of these classes was taught by college professors.

Along with the College 101 classes, the board agreed to restart the *ADVANTAGE!* degree completion program with the name changed to *Barclay College Advantage!*. This program allowed students who had earned fifty or more college hours to complete their degree at educational sites distant from the college. The program had begun in 1996 but was closed in 2004 with the last classes finishing out in 2006. The restart, although approved in 2006, did not begin with new students until Fall 2009. Courses for the restart were offered in Bible, Theology, Ministry, and General Education.[121]

Spring 2007 was just as busy as the fall of 2006 had been. During the Spring Break (March 16-24) a group of students went to Lafitte, Louisiana, to help victims of Hurricane Katrina. In Louisiana they teamed with Friends Disaster Services to help rebuild five homes. The eleven students were part of a program put together by Barclay student Jon Harkness called "Operation John 13" based on John 13:34-35. They worked at raising funds for the trip and doing evangelism training before the trip. (The first Operation John 13 trip took place December 16-22, 2006 with a group of six going to New Orleans to assist the Samaritan's Purse Disaster Relief.)[122] Later in March Lieutenant Governor Mark Parkinson was on campus to view the college. He met with a number of students.[123] April 2-5, the college held its annual "Spiritual Life Emphasis Week" with Professor David Williams speaking throughout the week on "The Power of Vision." The week incorporated chapel services, special evening services and even a prayer meeting in Pratt, Kansas, which was a project for the Acts class. Many reported that they could especially feel the power of the Lord at work throughout the week.[124] Breakaway 2007 was held April 12-14 for potential Barclay students from around the country. Thirty-three students from eight states came to sit in on classes, meet the faculty and students, experience dorm life and be a part of chapel. Dr. Francis "Skip" Payette,

---

[121] This second *Advantage!* program was folded into the Barclay Online Program in 2015. Courses in business and psychology were also included.
[122] *Barclay College Progress*, Spring 2007, 7 and *Barclay Progress*, Winter 2007, 7.
[123] *Barclay College Progress*, Spring 2007, 2.
[124] *Barclay College Progress*, Spring 2007, 5.

Professor of Youth Ministry challenged the students to be listening for God's voice in their daily lives. Inpop Records artist Jimmy Needham and his wife Kelly performed in concert Friday night for a crowd of over one hundred and fifty.[125]

Later in April (20-21) in response to a recommendation by the Barclay Board as a means to address needs of the Mid-America Yearly Meeting the college organized and held a successful Church Planting Summit. Over one hundred attended the meetings and workshops and learned from experienced church planters Hubert Nolan, Mark Wright, and David Davenport and a number of others. Frank Penna and Barclay students led the services in worship and prayer.[126]

The 2006/2007 basketball season ended on a good note for both the men's and women's teams. Both teams ended with a win at the ACCA National tournament with the women placing 3rd with a 2-1 record and the men with 3-1 and bringing home the Consolation Championship trophy. The men also ended the season with the best record for a men's team in the past seven years. Several players received individual awards. Sarah Williams received 2nd team All-Conference for the third year in a row and was also named an ACCA All-American. Katrina Caldwell was an Academic All-American, and Shelby Williams was nominated to the all-tournament team at the National tournament. Jake Gere was an ACCA All-American Honorable Mention as well as being nominated to the all-tournament team at Nationals. Keith Reeser was an Academic All-American as well as a David Terry Award nominee which is the highest honor at the National tournament and is awarded to the athlete who not only displays athletic ability, but also is involved in Christian service and campus leadership. The college choir closed off the semester with a Midwest tour through four states—Missouri, Indiana, Illinois, and Ohio.[127]

---

[125] *Barclay College Progress*, Spring 2007, 6.
[126] *Barclay College Progress*, Spring 2007, 5.
[127] *Barclay College Progress*, Spring 2007, 6.

During the 2006/2007 academic year the faculty followed up on items identified in the recent self-study process as well as acting on issues raised by the ABHE visiting team who were on campus in April 2006. They worked the assessment plan that had been re-tooled previous to the accreditation visit. They reviewed the overall college objectives—the mission statement and the institutional goals, examined each of the divisional program objectives and how they were aligned with the specific courses within each major of the division, and studied the connection between the divisional objectives and the requirements built into the Student Learning Portfolio. They also reviewed the objectives and purposes for the Christian Service program. No changes were deemed necessary in the overall college objectives (institutional goals), but the faculty did find that not all courses contributed to the objectives in ways that could be substantiated.

The official letter from ABHE was received in March 2007. The commission re-affirmed accreditation for an additional ten years and accepted the financial exigency plan. They deferred action on the substantive change request for starting a degree completion program in Independence, Kansas, until the college could supply additional information to them—financial impact of opening the site, full list of instructors, plans to provide library service and monitor Christian service, and a review of the curriculum.

The college met twice with Sterling College to discuss a possible joint program that would allow students to enroll in an elementary education program at Barclay then transfer to Sterling and finish with state teaching credentials. In the end this did not work out. Another venture which did work, however, was the creation of a program that would allow students to earn a certificate using only Home College (correspondence) courses and not having to do classes on campus. In addition, a set of Home College courses were "web-enhanced" with an on-line component to assist a cohort program as a study group that was formed among Hispanic pastors of Northwest Yearly Meeting—the Latin American Center for Theological Studies, or Centro de Estudios Teologicos Latinamericano "in cooperation with Barclay College Online." Classes were set up using a platform called Moodle and a computer lab was set up at Vancouver First Friends Church. Several Hispanic pastors completed a Bi-lingual Bible Ministry Certificate through this program. Efforts to restart the degree completion program in Colorado Springs were unfruitful. The advertising resulted in only two leads one of which was a former student who had not completed the program.

A short conference, "Re-discovering Your Teenager" was held in February with a good response. This was a joint project with the Youth Ministry and Pastoral Ministry majors from the college and the Youth department of Haviland Friends Church. A second conference, a Church Planting Summit was scheduled for April 20 to 22.

Emily Harkness did an outstanding job as Director of Library Services and progressed on her MLS. Dave Williams began working on a doctorate with George Fox University and continued to occasionally provide Sunday morning pulpit supply. Dr. Francis Payette served several local churches by filling pulpits or by completing church plant evaluations. Lois Kendall continued her ministry, "Something for Moms." Dr. Prosperly Lyngdoh had opportunity to fill pulpits and to work with a large Indian population in Wichita as an evangelist. Jared Ross judged several high school music events and was involved regularly with the worship team at Haviland Friends Church. Pam Fulbright made many good contacts and smoothed out some existing relationships with the Haviland and Mullinville school districts. She also spoke at a weekend conference in Meade. Dr. Leppert preached at two churches and taught a regular Sunday School class. He also had the privilege of serving on an ABHE evaluation team at Montana Bible College in Bozeman, Montana in April. The book, *Founded By Friends*, for which he wrote the chapter on Barclay College, went to press in June.[128]

---

[128] Glenn Leppert, "2006/2007 Report to the Board," April 2007.

But, what really made the 2006/2007 year memorable was the initiation of a new almost outlandish program to attract students and the May 2007 F5 tornado that ripped through the neighboring city of Greensburg.

Throughout the 2006/2007 academic year Herb Frazier was working on ways to attract additional students to campus. Reviving the distance education program increased the overall numbers but did not address the empty dorms and classrooms on campus. Herb reached out to the accrediting association and to presidents of other small Bible colleges inquiring what they had tried and discovered two colleges that had come up with a bold plan to offer free tuition. Instead of having a small number of students on campus paying full tuition why not have the dorms and classrooms full of students paying only for room and board? Would the income from room and board for a full campus be greater than the income from tuition for a partial campus? These two colleges (St. Louis Christian and Central Christian College of the Bible) had tried this and found that was the case. Herb arranged for a visit and a discussion with both colleges. He learned what had happened to them and then, in October 2006, he approached the Barclay Board with his proposal. After the initial shock, the Board determined to give the plan a try. They approved the plan in December after much discussion and in Spring 2007 the college announced: "Starting in the Fall 2007 semester Barclay College will be offering a FULL-TUITION SCHOLARSHIP to ALL on-campus students. This scholarship is worth $10,000 per year and is good each year the student attends Barclay. The total cost for room, board and fees for the entire year is only $8,300."[129] Because students did not normally respond to mailings, the Internet, church bulletins, and advertisements in magazines and on radio were used.

The second momentous event of the 2006/2007 year was what happened over the May 4-6 Alumni Weekend. Friday evening, May 4, an F5 tornado struck neighboring Greensburg and moved slowly to

---

[129] *Barclay College Progress*, Spring 2007, 6.

the north making a mile wide swath through the countryside. Victims of the storm were brought to Haviland and housed for the night in the basement of the Friends Church, in the high school gymnasium, and in Jackson Hall. Food and water were arranged in the college cafeteria. Hours of planning and arranging for the annual Alumni Banquet and for the Baccalaureate and Commencement Services for Sunday, May 6, had been completed, but should these activities be continued? All day Saturday the college phones were ringing with people attempting to find family members in Haviland and increased activity with various agencies showing up to help. After debate, the alumni determined to go on with the banquet and although the attendance was down from what was expected the meal began only to be interrupted by tornado sirens. Those gathered in Hockett Auditorium for the banquet quickly moved to the basement of the library where they sang songs of praise and prayed. When the "all clear" was given they returned to Hockett to continue the banquet. A tornado had approached Haviland, lifted up, crossed over and sat down north of the city.

The banquet did not last long and as soon as the banquet materials were cleared out numerous agencies began to move into the gym to be ready to assist the victims. By Sunday morning the gym was packed full. There would be no way to hold the commencement service there. What should be done for baccalaureate and commencement? Working most of the night the college Registrar prepared a prayer service for Sunday morning which would conclude with the presentation of diplomas. There would be no regalia or any of the traditional speeches or components of the two traditional services; instead, groups of graduates led the congregation in a prayer concert praying for the victims of the tornado, the city of Greensburg, and the county. The church was packed as there were no churches left in Greensburg and numerous camera crews for local and area news services crowded the back of the church. From May 7 to near the end of July the campus was crowded with representatives from governmental agencies, insurance companies, and others as relief was given to the victims and various cleanup crews were hosted by the college.

Dr. Glenn W. Leppert in an article in the Summer 2007 *Progress* wrote:

> There have been times in the past when the staff at the college has asked itself, "What would it be like to have the campus used all summer?" This summer we received, at least in part, an answer. Just before the end of the semester the campus filled with displaced Greensburg residents, agencies connected with relief efforts, and volunteers who came to lend a helping hand. For most of the summer the gymnasium was crowded. In addition to the Salvation Army and all the goods they had to disperse, the gym housed several FEMA groups plus some 30 or more agencies-insurance adjusters, loan companies, counselors, department of motor vehicles, veterans, and more. But the activity was not limited to the gym. The Iroquois Mental Health Center occupied a classroom in Jackson Hall. The Red Cross set up in the cafeteria. The Kiowa County Hospital and the Greensburg Clinic took rooms in the library and the student center. A Greensburg church office was set up in Phillips Hall and shared the second floor with the offices of South-central Kansas Youth For Christ. Most of these remained on campus until late in July.
>
> In the weeks just after the tornado besides having the dorm rooms full, a tent city sprang up beside the gym, next to the men's dorm, and behind the women's dorm. The largest tents were for the Air National Guard, but many were for volunteers coming to lend a helping hand. While the tents came down in June, the dorms remained full all summer. At first the rooms housed FEMA and Red Cross personnel. Then, at their departure, the dorms housed the many volunteers who used Haviland as

a base. Overall several volunteer groups, mostly youth groups from churches, have stayed at Barclay.

While all of this activity happened on campus a similar scenario played out all across town. Immediately after the tornado displaced families stayed at the Friends Church, in the High School gym, and at Jackson Hall. Then, after they found places to stay, the Friends Church began to house volunteers. A special shower facility was set up near the church, and a laundry was established in the city park. The Methodist Church became a distribution point for supplies. Several displaced Greensburg businesses- Greensburg State Bank, Fleener's Funeral Home, and the Greensburg School District shared space at the Haviland Telephone Company.

Haviland changed in several ways. Houses, long on the market, sold. Rentals filled. Traffic increased. At least one new business, a barber shop, has been established downtown.

When we asked what the campus would be like in full use during the summer, we were thinking about classes meeting, and perhaps several conferences or camps using the campus. We looked forward to hosting the EFC-MA Ministry Conference. These conferences did not happen but nonetheless we found out what the campus was like with lots of activity.[130]

The college students were also busy that summer. The Summer edition of the *Barclay Progress* contains articles detailing student summer mission trips. Jessica Windorski was a participant in the Saltshaker group which went to Nepal. Kathryn Lawski and Julie

---

[130] *Barclay College Progress*, Summer 2007, 2-3.

Penna also spent two and a half months ministering in Nepal. Amanda Carlson was part of the Saltshaker trip to Alaska. Martha Hodson completed a mission internship in Ireland. Andrea Holguin went to Colombia on a mission trip. Other students shared as counselors and in led worship in a number of camps.[131]

The Fall 2007 semester was anticipated with excitement. Would the campus be cleared out in time to be ready for classes? Would the offer of free tuition for campus residents be accepted? What could be expected for enrollment? The campus was vacated just in time to prepare for students coming and the offer of free tuition was accepted. The fall enrollment reversed the drop experienced in 2006. Although the overall college headcount was not quite what it was in Fall 2005 when there were still active degree completion cohorts (one hundred and thirty-one) it came close with one hundred and twenty-nine. Full-time headcount for the campus program went from only seventy-three in Fall 2006 to one hundred and three, a forty percent increase. The total college full-time equivalent (FTE) was one hundred and ten, which was thirty-two more than for Fall 2006. The retention rate, which had only been sixty-eight percent in 2004 and fifty-nine percent in 2005 jumped up to eighty-eight percent for 2007.[132] This trend continued. The fall FTE for the college in Fall 2006 was at only seventy-three, it rose to one hundred and ten in Fall 2007, one hundred and thirty-two for Fall 2008 and was at one hundred eighty-three in the Fall 2009.

While the offer of free tuition attracted students it also created some challenges. Not all students who applied because of the free tuition were born-again Christians. Should the college accept students who were seeking the Lord? Would they find the Lord on campus, or would they be a deterrent to the spiritual growth of other students? The college responded by prayerful consideration of these questions, strengthening the acceptance policy and procedures yet allowing

---

[131] *Barclay College Progress*, Summer 2007, 5, 6, 7 and *Barclay College Progress*, Fall 2007, 8.
[132] *Barclay College Progress*, 2007, 2.

students who were not Christians to apply if they were open to a faith in Christ.

Fall 2007 was the last semester for Everett Jantz to teach philosophy and Spring 2008 was the last semester that Mark Newland, who began teaching computer classes for the college in 2002. That fall was the year that Willard and Doris Ferguson, who had been on the mission field in Africa for over forty years, teamed up to teach the missions class. Willard also that semester taught Doctrine of Holiness.

In the Fall 2007 soccer season the soccer team had few wins but found much value in their approach to ministry. They adopted a theme for the season of "Glory to God" and they let that theme describe their actions on the field. They made certain that each team they played heard a testimony of who Jesus was and what it meant to follow him.[133]

One highlight of the Fall 2007 semester was the 76th annual Ladies Auxiliary Auction which drew alumni and friends back to Haviland from eleven different states (Arizona, Colorado, Illinois, Kansas, Minnesota, Missouri, Nebraska, Oklahoma, Oregon, Texas, Washington). The total raised was $76,556.00. The highest priced item was a jar of BJ's Salsa donated by John and Tacy Hamm which sold for $1,300.00.[134]

The Fall 2007 semester ended in a rather unusual way. First a new occasion on campus was initiated called "Campus of Light." On December 9th students and community members gathered on the lawn to hear the Haviland Grade School Choir, several individuals and small groups and the College Choir and Barclay Singers provide musical numbers between segments of a program. Each segment was concluded by a reminder of the spiritual lessons of light and then one by one each building was lit up with Christmas lights

---

[133] *Barclay College Progress*, Fall 2007, 6.
[134] *Barclay College Progress*, Fall 2007, 11.

accompanied by fireworks until the entire campus was ablaze in lights. The second event was a tremendous storm on Monday December 14th which left not only the college but the entire community without electricity until the end of the week. Monday was the last regular classes and final exams were scheduled for Wednesday, Thursday, and Friday.

Tiffany Van Dame wrote of the event:

> The ice storm created some issues as well as excitement for most of the students. Many students went outside throughout the day to take pictures and see how much debris and ice there really was . . . Tuesday night . . . groups of students studied for their exams with candles, flashlights, and even cell phones. Throughout the night [one could hear] the cracking and breaking of trees all around the campus.
>
> When Wednesday morning came, the power was still out, and many students were wondering what was going to happen with the finals they were supposed to take that morning. In order to address the issue, a meeting was held with the President's Cabinet followed by a meeting with the entire student body. The decision was made that final exams would be cancelled on an individual basis. It was the responsibility of each student to talk to his or her teachers about whether or not taking the exam would affect the final grade. After students cleared everything with their professors, they were free to go.
>
> Some students did not have to take any finals, some exams were taken as scheduled, and some students even made up their work at the beginning of this semester. The Barclay campus cleared out rather quickly once students were able to go. Food service was offered until Thursday evening with only close

to a dozen students left in the dorms. Power and heat were back on by the end of the week, after all the students had begun their Christmas break.[135]

The ABHE Commission in their February 2008 meeting gave the college a good report in response to the exigency plan, abstract, and progress report submitted in November 2007. No new exigency plan or updated progress report was asked for Fall 2008, but instead the commission requested a progress report due November 1, 2009 to address the college's ongoing efforts to address assessment and planning, library resources, ministry formation, and assessment of student learning and development. While thankful for the good response from ABHE and committed to keeping Association for Biblical Higher Education accreditation the college again began the process for achieving regional accreditation. A letter of intent was written early in 2008 and submitted to NCA to open a two-year window to complete once again a Preliminary Information Form (PIF) and then upon approval of the PIF to begin a self-study in the Fall 2008. That engaged the faculty in gathering and editing materials through the 2008 spring, summer, and fall semesters. In January 2009, the preparation of the initial document—the Preliminary Information Form—was completed and accepted by NCA. The next two years (2009 and 2010) the college completed a self-study. and was ready for a visit by NCA. Candidacy was granted in 2014 and full accreditation came in 2018.

Early in February, 2008, Dr. Royce Frazier was hired to create an online program for the college. While working on that project he was offered, and he accepted, the position of Vice President for Academics. Dr. Leppert who had filled this position became the Vice President for Registration and Records.

The first semester for the online program was Fall 2008. A selection of nine classes was offered which were part of four majors (Bible, Christian Leadership, Missions, and Psychology). Twenty-two

---

[135] *Barclay College Progress*, Winter 2007/2008, 3.

students from nine different states and one foreign country enrolled. Of those twenty-two students eleven completed the full course and graduated. From 2008 to the time of this writing there have been eighty-eight graduates from the online program, but numerous others have completed classes.[136]

Joining the adjunct faculty to teach Teachings of Friends Spring 2008 was Dr. David Kingrey. In the Fall 2009 he assumed the role of chair of the Bible/Theology major and in the Fall 2014 semester he began to pick up full-time teaching loads teaching both in the undergraduate and the graduate divisions and giving leadership to the master's program. He continued at the college until the conclusion of the Spring 2021 semester only leaving because of his health. In the Spring 2022 he and Dr. Glenn Leppert were named faculty emeritus.

As early as Fall 2007 the president's cabinet had begun to discuss the need for having a formal tutoring program in place for students.[137] A grant proposal was written to seek funding for such a center and a grant was received from the South-Central Kansas Community Foundation in March 2008. A senior student, Jon Harkness, was hired to initiate the center and he did so preparing help sheets and setting up available hours. He continued this after his graduation. This tutoring center eventually morphed into the Writing Center.

As the third year for Herb Frazier ended he had this to say:

> As I near the end of my third year as president, I look back with a thankful heart. I was quite ignorant of the potential risks I faced with few financial resources and little hope for a change in our donor income.

---

[136] At the time of this writing there were twenty-six with hours short of graduation still marked as pursuing in the data base.
[137] Cabinet Minutes 2007/2008 Academic Year, Minutes 52, 65, 71, 102.

However, a major cash gift that first fall and 80 acres of land given to the college set the stage for what has happened between then and now. There have always been major gifts along with all of the regular monthly gifts that have been faithfully given to help us pay our monthly bills. I owe credit to the Lord for His provisions and to you who have faithfully supported the college. These have been three wonderful years in my life, and I will always be thankful that the Lord let me experience them.

As I look to my final two years as president, it is with anticipation for what lies ahead. It seems as though the miracles keep coming. That is one of the rewards for us who have the opportunity to work at Barclay College. It seems like there is a new miracle nearly every day. One of the miracles I hope we experience this fall is overflowing dormitories, which we have not experienced since the new Women's Dormitory was built. The influx of new students is exhilarating as I get to know more students who are preparing to serve.

The Matching Gift given by a couple who cares deeply for the college has given us a new chance to change the financial picture. As the Matching Fund continues to build there comes new hope for the needs we face. The only way Barclay College is able to continue to grow is to provide more student housing. If all beds on campus are filled during the fall semester of 2008 (which is very likely) there will be no chance for future growth. It is not wise to provide additional housing when we have a large debt on our present dormitory. Your help in matching the gift that has been offered will make it reasonable to get additional housing on campus.

Barclay continues to hold to the tenets its founding fathers set when they opened the doors, ninety-one years ago this fall. Students at Barclay continue to hold high standards in their personal lives and strive to be Godly examples as they prepare to serve Him. The book entitled *Founded by Friends*, which has given the history of the 15 colleges started by Friends, states in its conclusion; "Barclay is the only institution in the volume that continues as a school where the focus . . . is the Bible."[138]

Those miracles continued on through the last two years that Herb was president. For the Fall 2008 semester Herb was able to report the full-time student body had increased twenty-three percent over the full-time number for Spring 2007 and that the college was contemplating the need for additional dorm space. The college presidential home was pressed into service to house the overflow from the men's dorm. The Vice President for Registration and Records reported that Fall that the campus headcount was the highest since 1985. He noted that that fall there were fifty new students on campus. Trent Jacks reported that the Lord had definitely blessed the ministry of the college by nearly doubling the student body in an eighteen-month period. Athletic teams were fielding full squads and having successful seasons and the choir was full and active.[139] In fact the choir had a problem as the Spring 2008 semester began. The fall choir had thirty-three students and fit snug but comfortably in the choir room. The choir for spring grew to be fifty-four students and could not in any way fit. The solution, since there was no other larger room, was to move the admissions office from what had been the public affairs office (and before that the library) to the former business office and establish the vacated room as the choir room.[140]

---

[138] *Barclay College Progress*, Spring 2008, 2.
[139] *Barclay College Progress*, Summer 2008, 2 and Fall 2008, 1.
[140] *Barclay College Progress*, Winter 2007/2008, 3.

Several new campus faculty members were added in the Fall 2008. One was Dr. Jerry Simmons, a 1975 graduate of the college who came to chair the Elementary Education major as well as to teach science and mathematics. Dr. Simmons had a Ph.D. from the University of New Mexico in Multicultural Teacher and Childhood Education in addition to degrees from the New Mexico Institute of Mining and Technology. Another was Tim Hawkins who accepted the position of chair of the English department. Mr. Hawkins had experience teaching at Kansas State University and completed a graduate degree in Fine Arts with an emphasis on creative writing at the University of Alaska in the spring of 2008.[141]

Missions was given special emphasis that fall. Evangelical Friends Church—Mid America Yearly Meeting began sponsoring a scholarship for missions students in 2005. These scholarships were given to students intending to serve in the context of the Friends Church. In order to raise additional funds for this, the EFM-MAYM Mission Mobilizers sponsored a "run for missions" in November 2008. Two men, Adam Monaghan, and Allen Smelser ran the one hundred miles from Wichita to Haviland and solicited sponsors to pay for the run and raised $11,000.00. This engendered a run for missions event which began in Haviland in 2010. A set of shorter distance races were set up in and around Haviland and involved many runners for several years. Also in the Fall 2008 the college provided a successful missional conference in September (what previously was known as "mission emphasis week"). With the theme "The World is my Parish" the conference featured Bob Adhikari, a Friends Missionary from Nepal, as main speaker and Mr. and Mrs. Brad Carpenter from Rwanda. Students who had been in Bangladesh in the summer also spoke and the Matsiko Children's Choir from Uganda was present. Before the conference, Barclay students organized a weeklong prayer meeting to pray for the meetings.

Their prayers were effective, and the Missional Leadership Conference sparked a revival on campus. Mark Healton wrote in the Fall

---

[141] *Barclay College Progress*, Summer 2008, 7.

2008 Progress that when Bob Adhikari agreed to share in the conference he likely counted on speaking during each chapel service but that the Holy Spirit had different plans. "On a number of occasions, Bob either changed the contents of his message completely, or did not speak at all!" Under the Spirit's leadership, students sang, lifted up prayers for each other, and surrendered themselves more fully to the Lord.[142]

Before the close of the Spring 2009 semester new faculty and staff to join the college for the Fall semester were named. Dr. Tony Wheeler from Phoenix began part time in June in the area of Advancement and continued to be employed by Strong Families under the direction of Gary Smalley. Mr. Steve Teter from Ohio began as Vice President for Institutional Advancement on the first day of June. Mr. Kevin Lee from California assumed his position of Associate Dean for Distance Learning in August. Mr. Josh Bunce from Oregon joined the faculty as Chair of Youth Ministry in the fall of 2009. In Spring 2015 he would hand the Youth Ministry major to Jesse Penna and take on the chair of Bible and Theology. Dr. David Kingrey, who had been teaching as an adjunct in November became the Chair of Bible/Theology. Mike Temaat joined the staff as Director of Technology. Each of these men added depth to the Barclay team. Depth came also with the degrees received in 2008 and 2009 by current faculty members. David Williams, professor of pastoral ministry and Bible, graduated from George Fox Evangelical Seminary with a Doctor of Ministry (DMin) degree in Leadership and Spiritual Formation. Ryan Kendall, Vice President for Student Affairs, received a Master of Arts degree in Christian Leadership from Liberty University. And, Emily Harkness, Director of Library Services, earned a Master of Library Science from Emporia State University.[143]

Several new staff and faculty were added to the college in Fall 2009. The Indiana *Advantage!* program was re-started in Fall 2009 with

---

[142] *Barclay College Progress*, Fall 2008, 3.
[143] *Barclay College Progress*, Spring 2009, 2, 5.

two sites, one at Plainfield in the west suburbs of Indianapolis and the other was at the Brandywine Friends Church in Greenfield, Indiana east of Indianapolis. Dr. Marlene Pedigo and her husband Steve, who were co-superintendents of Western Yearly Meeting, gave leadership at Plainfield. At Brandywine Mark and Kathy Wright, and Gary and Carol Wright were leaders. Dr. Tony Wheeler joined the faculty to teach psychology and to direct the Institute of the Blessing. Kendy Johnson joined the adjunct faculty in Education. Kevin Lee joined the staff as Associate Dean for Distance Education, Randi Shetley joined the staff for drama. Dorothy Simon joined the *Advantage* staff as an adjunct in business while Kayleen Stevens became an adjunct in business. She later became full-time. Jack Holliday returned to college (was here 73-92) as adjunct in Bible. Stacy Wheeler was added to the campus faculty splitting her time between teaching music and English. Morris Jones became an adjunct for Ministry and Arden Kinser for Bible and Ministry. Ryan Haase was added to the adjunct staff on campus. Laurie Reinhart joined the adjunct staff for business, and Shelby Williams began teaching as an adjunct both online and campus.

The miracle of the revival of the college from the despair in 2005 to the continued excitement still in 2009 was evident. The spiritual revival that had begun at the Missional Leadership Conference in September 2008 continued to spread and Barclay maintained its role as a Spiritual Center. Students from various backgrounds across the country were blessed by the spirit-filled chapels and classes on campus. Enrollment made records. The campus FTE for Fall 2009 was one hundred sixty-two. The overall college FTE came to one hundred eighty-three on the official reporting date, but several new students were then added to online programs which began after that date. The Registrar reported about midterm an overall FTE of two hundred eight. The third floor of Phillips Hall received significant updates as new office space was needed to accommodate the growing programs. Operation John 13 the short-term mission ministry through which students had gone to Lafitte Louisiana to help victims of Hurricane Katrina and had helped in Greensburg after the

2007 tornado, and had helped build houses in the 9th ward of New Orleans planned a trip in conjunction with Christian Service International to Haiti and also to Kentucky. A "service day" in which Barclay students gave a full day of service (September 30, 2009) to the community was initiated. That first service day focused primarily on clean-up efforts for the community of Haviland. Haviland mayor, John Unruh bragged later that the day was "the talk of the town." Overall Fall 2009 was a great last fall semester for President Herb Frazier.

The fall semester was also a great one for the Barclay College Lady Bears Volleyball team who were crowned the Association of Christian College Athletics (ACCA) National Champions. The *Progress* Winter 2009/2010 issue stated:

> The Lady Bears were the number one seed going into the tournament and successfully overcame five strong opponents. Junior Renee Gonzales from Andale, Kansas was named the ACA National libero of the Year as well as the tournament MVP. Senior LeAnn Carlson from Haviland was named ACCA Academic All-American as well as Honorable Mention All-American. Freshman Adele Wheeler also from Haviland was named to the All-Tournament team and Second All-American. The Lady Bears finished the season with an overall record of 15-7.[144]

As Dr. Frazier prepared his last President's Perspective column for the *Progress* in Spring 2010 before handing the role of president to his son, Dr. Royce Frazier, he reflected on the many changes at the college and thanked the supporters and friends of the college for making them all possible. He listed several major items:

---

[144] *Barclay College Progress*, Winter 2009/2010, 4.

- Initiation of an online degree completion program.
- The *Advantage!* Program successfully restarted.
- Indebtedness decreased by $1,500,000.
- Net worth increased by $2,500,000.
- Full time enrollment increased 150% from what it was five years before.
- Student income 117% higher than it was before the Full Tuition Scholarship.
- Food service significantly improved.
- A 62 bed men's residence hall under construction on campus.[145]

There were many other items he could have listed. The Spring 2010 semester added several items worthy of his list. One item was that the Kiowa County Chamber of Commerce presented the Business of the Year Award to Barclay College for its significant contributions to the Kiowa County region. Another item was the creation of the Barclay College Park that leveled the space between Phillips Hall and the Library and added sidewalks and planter boxes to the landscape. A third item was the construction of the new parking lot to serve both Phillips Hall and the new men's dorm. A fourth item was the house just east of Lemmons Hall which was purchased to relieve overcrowding in the women's dorm. The house, a two-story structure built in the early 1900's had five bedrooms.

The house was named the Binford House in honor of Allen and May Binford long-time supporters of the college who gave the majority of the funds to purchase the house.[146]
On campus the Spring 2010 semester went well. Jeremie Frazier joined the adjunct online faculty to teach biology online and Ryan Haase took on his first faculty role as instructor for Yearbook. However, the Spring 2010 semester was the last semester for Emily Harkness who went with her husband Jon who graduated to take the pastorate of a Friends Church. As the semester ended a number

---

[145] *Barclay College Progress*, Spring 2010, 2.
[146] *Barclay College Progress*, Fall 2010, 14.

of students headed out on mission trips and prepared to serve churches through the summer. The college Physical Science 108 class headed out on a trip to the Grand Canyon and the Petrified Forest in Arizona. And as a final item, Lois Kendall, professor of psychology and encourager of all students was awarded the Faculty of the Year award at the annual Alumni Banquet just before commencement.

CHAPTER EIGHT
MOVING ONLINE
2008-2023

The 2010 Summer edition of the *Progress* contained a number of exciting articles that indicated great enthusiasm and excitement on campus. First in the message from the president, Dr. Royce Frazier, who had only been in his presidential position for two months, was able to speak of the opening of a new men's residence hall, of a record number of new students on campus, of a new record high for enrollment (total enrollment for the college was two hundred forty-five), of an FTE that was triple what it had been just three years previous. Then, Dr. Adrian Halverstadt, the new Vice President for Academic Services in describing the college's locale reported how God was using the area, 67059, "to script a sequence of events that [would] have global impact and lasting influence through the ministry of Barclay College." Part of that script was from articles in the issue concerning summer mission endeavors that Barclay students participated in, and from the accounts of the new well qualified faculty and staff joining the college.

New faculty becoming part of the team in Fall 2010 included Dr. Adrian Halverstadt who had been an integral part of putting the online Christian Ministry Leadership degree program together as he was still serving as pastor at Willoughby Hills Friends in

Northeast Ohio. Adrian moved to Haviland to be the Vice President for Academics. Dr. Halverstadt was intent "on keeping the quality of academics and Spiritual direction" at a high level in the college. Assisting Dr. Halverstadt was Linda Snyder, who took on the role as Administrative Assistant to the V.P. of Academics. Linda was a student at Barclay in the 1970's who joined the online program to complete her degree and was thus a current student as she accepted this role. Pat Hall, a 2006 graduate of the college, earned a Master of Library Science degree after his graduation from Barclay and came in the Fall 2010 as Director of Library Services. Royce Bryan accepted a position as coach and as the Athletic Director. He also became an adjunct to teach in education and the social sciences. Coach Bryan stated that his goal was to recruit athletes that, 'love Jesus, care about their education, and are gifted athletically and want to develop their gifts." [147] Traci Ballard began as an adjunct to teach physical education, Adam Monaghan joined the campus faculty as adjunct for Bible, and Matthew Chesnes joined the online staff for Bible and Ministry. Gary Jones began to teach online as an adjunct for ministry as well.

A presidential Inauguration happened October 8 and 9. A concert with Marilyn Ham began the activities Friday evening. Marilyn was an instructor at the college in the early 1980's. On Saturday, delegates were received and registered, and an educational symposium was held in which various members of the college administration spoke on how the college mission and purpose had been merged into all aspects of the college and how that "merger had a significant impact on the ministry life of evangelical denominations, especially of the Friends." Then at 2:30 the inauguration took place in the Hockett Auditorium which began with a procession of faculty, administration, and delegates. Several from the college, the community, and other colleges participated in bringing messages and prayers for the incoming president and the years ahead for the college. President Royce Frazier shared his hopes and dreams for the future of the college.

---

[147] *Barclay College Progress*, Summer 2010.

One significant event related to the college and its continuation happened in June 2010. Actually what led up to this event began well before June. As has been mentioned earlier, in 2007 Dr. Glenn Leppert contributed the chapter about Barclay College to the book, *Founded by Friends; the Quaker Heritage of Fifteen American Colleges and Universities*. In the introduction to that book, Thomas D. Hamm made several references to Barclay highlighting that among the Quaker colleges Barclay did not sense her Quaker identity as a hindrance but rather as a critical element to be embraced. Hamm noted that for Barclay its Quaker identity meant "upholding older moral standards and seeing truth as best ultimately understood through Christian Revelation." He also noted that student life at Barclay was still anchored strongly in holiness Christianity.[148]

John W. Oliver Jr. in the conclusion to *Founded by Friends* singled out Barclay as "the only institution in this volume that continues as a school where "the focus . . . is the Bible." Basically the suggestion was made that Barclay College was the one Friends college that had not changed its purpose in the course of its history.[149] That realization gave the editors of the book, John Oliver and Charles and Caroline Cherry, an idea for the June 2010 session of the annual Quaker Historian and Archivist's Conference. They asked five Quaker colleges—Azusa, Barclay, George Fox, Malone, and Wilmington—to submit a paper on the topic, "The founding purpose then and now."

Dr. Leppert wrote the paper for Barclay.[150] Dr. David Kingrey presented it. The *Progress* reported:

---

[148] Thomas Hamm, "Introduction," *the Quaker Heritage of Fifteen American Colleges and Universities*, edited by John L. Oliver, Charles L. Cherry, and Caroline L. Cherry, The Scarecrow Press, 2007, xi, xvii-xviii.

[149] John W. Oliver, "Conclusion," *the Quaker Heritage of Fifteen American Colleges and Universities*, edited by John L. Oliver, Charles L. Cherry, and Caroline L. Cherry, The Scarecrow Press, 2007, 267.

[150] Glenn W. Leppert, "The Purpose of Barclay College at its founding in 1917 and now in 2010," March-April 2010.

> Barclay College was founded in 1917 as a center that would give practical training focused on the doctrine of baptism with the Holy Ghost that would draw young people to Haviland rather than removing them from it. The stated purpose was to answer the necessity and demand for sound orthodox teaching of the Word of God. Is that still the purpose of the college? Has the mission of the college changed since its founding? This short paper suggests that it has not. Comparing statements from the literature of the college as it began with current literature and survey responses of students, faculty, and board members the author concludes that Barclay has remained true to the founding purpose. The reasons for establishing this small college on the prairies remain the reasons for continuing it today.[151]

Two important announcements were made in the Fall 2010 semester. First was the tremendous announcement that the Barclay College School of Graduate Studies was accredited. Preparations creating a graduate studies program began before Royce Frazier became president. Everything necessary—faculty, curriculum, resources, had all been hammered out and descriptions and documents had been submitted to ABHE during the Spring 2010 semester. This first graduate program was a Master of Arts in Transformational Leadership (MATL). The program officially began Fall 2011. (See Chapter 9.)

The second great announcement was that the Self-study for seeking candidacy status with the Higher Learning Commission of the North Central Association was complete. The materials were ready to submit and a NCA visiting team was scheduled for April 25-27, 2011. Since the process for gaining regional accreditation actually

---

[151] *Barclay College Progress*, Summer 2010, 4.

had begun back in the mid 1990's this was a wonderful announcement of progress.[152]

The NCA visit that spring came off extremely well. President Royce Frazier reported, "We had a very positive response from the visitation team from the Higher Learning Commission (HLC) during the last week of April. The team was impressed with the united reply of Board members, faculty, staff, and students who all articulated the mission and purpose of Barclay College. At the closing session of the visit the team chairman offered a prayer of blessing over the college and our work. He noted that he had never done that before on an HLC visit." Dr. Glenn Leppert, V.P. for Registration & Records described the visit in the *Progress* for Spring 2011:

> Four members of a North Central Association peer evaluation team representing the Higher Learning Commission visited the Barclay College campus the last week of April. They came to check files, to interview faculty and students, and to verify the data found in the college's Self Study. The four-day visit (Sunday evening through Wednesday noon) went well. The team was pleased with the supporting documentation they were given. They were impressed with the caliber of the faculty, staff, and students that they found—team members commented more than once on "the people" they encountered because of the commitment exhibited for the college. The team was surprised that so many of the college community knew the college's mission statement; the faculty actually recited it for them in unison. This was something team members had not encountered before. Each one they asked, whether staff or student, not only knew what the purpose of the college was but explained how it was being accomplished. The team shared a brief preliminary report as they left

---

[152] *Barclay College Progress*, Winter 2010/2011, 3.

which had only a few items that the college will need to address. Official word from the Commission, whether the college will be given candidacy status with North Central, is expected in the late summer.[153]

Word from NCA did come late that summer but rather than announcing candidacy the college was given a two-year window to address certain issues and then host another visit. The names of that visiting team were given to the college during the Fall 2013 semester and a date for the visit was set in April 2014.

With the launch of the master's degree in transformational leadership the focus of the college seemed to be on transformation. Transformation became a theme that was repeated in publications and messages during these years. During the spring of 2011, the college celebrated the transforming power of Christ and how God used individuals in making those transformations. To celebrate alumni and friends of the college were asked to send financial gifts and cards honoring those God used to help them in their transformational journey. Well before the conclusion of the project, the college had received $30,000.00 and many cards with detailed stories of transformations which had taken place while at the college. The Spring *Progress* listed names of ninety-two individuals and groups who were honored this way.[154]

Dr. Tony Wheeler, a graduate of Barclay, returned to the college in 2009 to work part time in the area of Advancement and as an adjunct professor. His first class, Fall 2009, was the Research Methods in Psychology class. His passion at the time concerned the *Blessing*, a program based on the book, *The Blessing*, by Gary Smalley and John Trent. While Tony was working for the college he also continued to be employed by Strong Families an organization under the direction

---

[153] *Barclay College Progress*, Spring 2011, 1, 2.
[154] *Barclay College Progress*, Spring 2011, 4

of Gary Smalley. An institute, The John Trent Institute for the Blessing at Barclay College, was set up to be the academic arm for Strong Families and for the Blessing Challenge launched in May 2011 by Focus on the Family.

Tony's dream was to create a set of classes about the Blessing that could be added to the college offerings, and as a set, would lead to a certificate. His excitement for the Blessing was contagious and the college added courses and a certificate. Nine classes were added to the college catalog with four of them having sufficient enrollment to open at the undergraduate level and two at the graduate level. These classes ran in the Fall 2010 and Spring 2011 semesters in both campus and online offerings. Sadly, there was never sufficient interest to keep the Blessing certificate viable. Dr. Wheeler taught in the graduate program until the conclusion of the Spring 2018 semester.[155]

The Summer 2011 issue of the *Progress* came out late enough that it was able to report some early fall items. Three reports proved again that the hand of God was upon the college. An estate that the college had counted on to cover the needed cash flow through the summer was delayed by the IRS and thus was unavailable. Alumni and friends of the college stepped up their giving, and their generous gifts allowed the college "to move carefully but confidently through the summer months."[156] A second report was just as positive. Lee Anders, V.P. for Business Services, wrote that it was certain the annual audit would show Barclay finished in the black for the 6th year in a row. Lee credited this to "increased student enrollment and outstanding financial support" from the college donors. Lee added several other encouraging facts. He said:

> Over the past six years the college's net worth has tripled with an increase in net property and equipment of over $1.8 million and at the same time reduced liabilities by over $1 million! It is clearly evident that

---

[155] *Barclay College Progress*, Spring 2011, 10.
[156] *Barclay College Progress*, Summer 2011, 2.

the Lord has blessed Barclay College with a growing student population, donors that have continued to give generously, and new donors that are seeing the need for Barclay College in today's world. Praise the Lord for His abundant goodness![157]

The third report concerned anticipated enrollment figures. Enrollment day was exciting with a record number of undergraduate students, but also for the first time in the college's history a cohort of graduate students began the semester as well. The first MATL courses went online with "Transformational Leadership in Biblical Perspective" taught by Dr. Dave Kingrey, "Spirituality and the Transformational Journey" taught by Dr. David Williams, and "Calling and Community" taught by Dr. Royce Frazier.[158] While the anticipated headcount for Fall 2011 when the Summer *Progress* was sent out was one hundred ninety-eight the number on the official reporting date was higher at two hundred and two. Thus, the campus headcount broke the two hundred barrier. The headcount for the online program on the official reporting date was forty-four, and there were twelve students in the new graduate program giving a total headcount of two hundred and fifty-eight. The overall FTE came out at two hundred thirty-one.

In the Spring 2011 semester, several new faculty members were added to the college. On campus, Derek Brown, a 2010 Barclay graduate, taught as an adjunct; in the Fall 2012 he accepted the full-time position as head of the Pastoral Ministry major and also as College Chaplain. Kevin Mortimer, also a 1986 Barclay graduate, moved from Iowa to Haviland in the spring of 2011 and taught that semester part-time. In the Fall 2011 semester he took on the full-time role as the head of the Missions major. Jesse Penna joined as an adjunct for ministry courses and then later became full-time and took on the role as Youth Ministry Professor. Online, Ned Arthur and

---

[157] *Barclay College Progress*, Summer 2011, 5.
[158] *Barclay College Progress*, Summer 2011, 5.

Derek Wilder became adjuncts for ministry, Roger Powell picked up the online math class, and Carol and Gary Wright assumed roles as professors of Bible and ministry. Gayle Mortimer, wife of Professor Kevin Mortimer, began as Accounts Payable clerk in January 2012.

On September 28, 2011, students, faculty, and some community members worked together on a serve day that resulted in twenty houses in Haviland being painted and twenty-two locations with trash removed. One group of students went to Greensburg to help clean up the Kiowa County Lake. Mid-morning each group enjoyed refreshments at either Haviland Hardware, Origins Coffee shop, or the Green Bean Coffee Shop. In Fall 2012 the serve day had similar results and brought praise for the jobs well done from Haviland's mayor, John Unruh. [159] In October, the annual Ladies' Auxiliary Auction went well beyond all expectations. This being the 80th anniversary of the college, the hope was to raise $80,000.00. Instead, the total at the end of the sale was just shy of $102,000.00. Throughout the fall the soccer team, and the volleyball team both had good although not spectacular seasons. The same was true for both the men's and women's basketball teams. There were thirty-eight students in the choir. The choir made the Christmas Pageant that December a huge success. In the spring the choir toured Kansas and Oklahoma.

A new program was added to the online offerings beginning Spring 2012. Business Administration a major which had been available on campus since 1983 was formed as an online major, Business Management, for the online venue.

Sadly, in February 2012, Steve Teter, Vice President for Institutional Advancement, lost his battle with lymphoma cancer and went home to be with Jesus. Steve, a 1993 graduate of Barclay College, became the Advancement officer in 2009.

---

[159] *Barclay College Progress*, Fall 2011, 4; Fall 2012, 3.

Fall 2012 also saw several new faculty and staff. Dr. Jim Le Shana assumed the role as Vice President for Academics and instructor in Bible and ministry allowing Dr. Halverstadt to take on the role of Chancellor. Dr. Keith White, a 1973 Barclay (FBC) graduate, began teaching part-time in the graduate school. In 2015 he moved to Haviland and became a full-time professor on campus. Not long after that, he became, in addition, coordinator of assessment. Cheryl Couch was named Associate Vice President of Distance Learning and then in 2012 as the head of the Elementary Education major. Also on campus Jeanine Le Shana joined the music department teaching both voice, and piano and Kay Unruh began teaching classes for Elementary Education. In the online division Brian Easley and his brother, Ray Easley, began to teach ministry courses, while Jon Kershner began to cover classes for Bible. Maria Smith started to teach business classes, and Linda Snyder-Patterson joined the online adjunct staff in psychology; later she taught part-time on campus.

Fall 2012 experienced several changes to the Christian School Elementary Education major. Dr. Jerry Simmons handed over the chair of the major to Cheryl Couch, and Cheryl began the process of gaining accreditation for the program. The name of the major was changed to Elementary Education (K-6) and accreditation was sought from both the Kansas State Department of Education (KSDE), and from the Association of Christian Schools International (ACSI). ACSI sent a visiting team to campus in February 2013 and gave full accreditation then. The KSDE process took longer but was as successful with candidacy status received in Fall 2013 and approval for full accreditation gained in 2018.

Like many previous fall semesters, Fall 2013 welcomed a number of new faculty and staff. Staci Derstein, a local teacher/administrator with years of experience with ACSI joined the professors in the Elementary Education major. Angie Wetmore agreed to teach media for the education major as an online class, and she accepted the position of administrator of the online program. Larry Lewis and

Michael Couch also joined the Education faculty. Chelle Leininger accepted a position to teach Spanish, while Steven Mann became an online adjunct for Bible, Paul Romoser for psychology, and Mark Triplett for business.

Although the admissions team was diligent in seeking new students and putting together large lists of accepted potential students, not all were actually enrolling. For the Fall 2012 there were sixty-five students on the accepted list but only fifty came. This was a problem for the college. A large enrollment was desired but at the same time the admissions process needed to be selective since not every student could be deemed a fit for the college and its mission. The college wanted only those students that God wanted on the campus—students who would see the world as their mission field with a passion for Christ and the church. Thus, the thirty days before the beginning of the fall semester were bathed in prayer with the anticipation that God would provide the necessary students. New undergraduate students that fall, campus and online, totaled sixty-six. (An interesting note—there were sixty-six new students on campus for the Fall 2013, and the graduating class of 2014 had sixty-six members. Also, in May 2013 the college graduated the largest graduating class in its history with sixty-five graduates.)[160]

The Writing Center, which had its beginning in the Tutoring Center established in 2008, was strengthened in the Fall 2012 through a grant from the South-Central Kansas Community Foundation. The grant enabled the center to add resources that bolstered the center's philosophy of emphasizing tutoring over editing, and improved students' writing skills. The Writing Center student staff was able to focus on being better peer tutors and thus empowered students to edit their own writing, a skill they could take with them well beyond their undergraduate coursework. Anissa Riggs (Potter), the director stated:

---

[160] *Barclay College Progress*, Summer 2013, 4.

As the Writing Center has grown in scope and influence, it has become a powerful resource for Barclay College students and professors. The stigma surrounding the Writing Center as a place only for students who struggle with writing has begun to fall away. As more instructors are encouraging students to use the Writing Center, it has become a part of the Barclay culture, which has led to a greater number of students utilizing this resource.[161]

In 1982 the college was blessed when a group of investors created the Haviland Housing Corporation which built a complex of sixteen apartments. This housing—College Hill Apartments—although not owned or managed by the college provided housing for many married and non-traditional students through the years. The loan that the corporation had taken out from the United States Department of Agriculture (USDA) was paid off in 2012, and in January 2013, the Haviland Housing Corporation asked to meet with officials from Barclay College. At the meeting, the college was given the opportunity to purchase the complex. A "For Sale" sign was placed on the property. Bids were submitted and a date set for the opening of the bids. Barclay College and one other bidder offered the same amount of money. Since the offers were identical, the Haviland Housing Corporation was given the opportunity to select the bidder that it preferred. The "nod" went to Barclay College, and on April 29, 2013, the college became the owners of the College Hill Apartments.[162] This gave the college overflow space for when the dorms might be full and space for married students.

During the fall once again the students participated in an annual serve day giving themselves to serve the communities of Haviland and Greensburg as a service to the Lord. Four groups used trucks to carry trash that had been collected by homeowners. Four gardening

---

[161] *Barclay College Progress*, Summer 2013, 7.
[162] *Barclay College Progress*, Summer 2013, 7.

teams cleaned yards, two window washing crews washed windows, one group stained the Gazebo in the park, six crews painted houses, six other crews painted garages and small buildings. One group formed a Greensburg clean up team, another dismantled a house while still another helped build a museum building. One group cleaned trash from the city's drainage ditch. A crew cleaned Antique Junction, the local antique shop, while another worked in the community garden, and several worked at Home Again, the local retirement home. Still another crew scraped a house.[163]

Three steps forward occurred in Spring 2014 regarding accreditation. Notice was received from the visiting accreditation team which had been on campus in April that they were recommending the college to the Higher Learning Commission (HCL) of the North Central Association for candidacy. And, second, the college also received notice from the Institutional Action Committee of the HCL that it was recommending candidacy status. Third, notification came from the Kansas Department of Education that the Elementary Education program had been recommended for full accreditation. Each of these notifications was great news and held tremendous potential for the college. In response to all three, President Royce Frazier reminded alumni and friends that these accreditations would open many opportunities for change for Barclay but that they would not move the college away from its mission "to prepare students in a Bible-centered environment for effective Christian life, service, and leadership."[164]

Some changes happened in the Summer 2014. One was that Dr. David Williams who had been the head of the Pastoral Ministries major since 2002 and Chaplain from 2004 accepted the position as superintendent of Evangelical Friends Church—Mid America Yearly Meeting and withdrew from his teaching and leadership positions at Barclay. On June 15th Jared Ross, music chair, graduated

---

[163] *Barclay College Progress*, Fall 2013, 3.
[164] *Barclay College Progress*, Spring 2014, 2.

with a Doctorate in Worship from the Robert E. Webber Institute for Worship Studies in Florida.[165] After obtaining his degree Jared brought a sharper focus on worship to the Music major changing the program from a performance Music major to a Worship Arts major with classes such as History of Christian Worship and Theology of Worship. Another change was that the college was able to drill a well that would supply water to keep the landscape improvements at the college thriving. As the college was a major user of water in Haviland the water allotment for the city was being exceeded.[166]

Summer 2014 like many summers before had many students serving in ministry. Nineteen ministries—camps, short term missions, youth groups, internships—involved thirty-seven students. Six of these students were part of a new program initiated by the college which gave students opportunity to serve in a different culture for three or four weeks. The program, called Juniors Global, was made available to students having completed six semesters at Barclay. During the spring semester the students would attend a class to explore facts about the country and the ministries that they would visit. The first two Juniors Global trips were available in the Spring 2014 semester. One was a trip to Brazil led by faculty member Ryan Kendall. The other was a trip to Greece, led by Dr. Jim Le Shana.

Both Summer 2014 trips went well. Dr. Jim Le Shana reported to the President's cabinet in June that the Juniors Global trip that he led exceeded his hopes and expectations. He saw leadership and spiritual growth in the students and knew that they expanded their understanding of ministry.[167] Ryan Kendall returned with a similar report. From 2014 through the Spring 2019 semester seventy students completed Juniors Global trips to ten countries (Asia (2), Belize, Brazil, Cambodia, Greece (7), India, Ireland (2), Kenya (4), Rwanda, and South Africa.) Each trip was led by a member of the Barclay College faculty.

---

[165] *Barclay College Progress*, Spring 2014, 3.
[166] *Barclay College Progress*, Summer 2014, 3.
[167] President's Cabinet Minutes for June 25, 2014, minute 13/14-272.

Herb Frazier had a wonderful idea to connect all ages of people to the college and to promote the annual Ladies Auxiliary sale in the Fall 2014. He sent out invitations for a "Senior Camp on the Prairies" inviting seniors to come spend a week leading up to the sale on campus. He arranged an extensive list of activities that would connect the participants not only with the campus and students but with the local area. Herb described the results of the three-day camp in the Fall 2014 *Barclay College Progress* as "an exciting three days," and he recapped each of the activities that was shared. The camp was successful enough that a 2015 camp and a 2016 camp followed.

One highlight of the Fall 2014 semester was the first National Friends Church Multiplication Conference sponsored by Barclay and held on the Barclay campus, August 8-9, 2014. This was the first of four such conferences until the venue moved online in 2020. The main speaker was Dr. Tim Roehl, the Director of Training and Development for One Mission Society (OMS). His doctorate was in Transformational Leadership for Church Multiplication Movements.

There were other high points for the Fall 2014. On November 14, the college heard from the Kansas Department of Education that Barclay had been given "Limited Accreditation" which was the highest level of accreditation given to an institution at the entry level. This meant that graduates of the Elementary Education major could have state credentials and that the teacher certification endorsement came from the college itself, not through another college as had been the case previously (St. Mary of the Plains, 1978-1992; Tabor College 1992-1993; none, 1993-2014). A third, particularly important highpoint was the notice received on November 17. On that day, formal notification was received that the recommendations of the visiting evaluation team, and the report of the Institutional Actions Council (IAAC) which had met with college representatives earlier in Chicago, had been favorable and Barclay was granted candidacy status. It would take another four years to gain full accreditation, yet candidacy status brought with it a number of benefits.

Yet another high point for the fall semester came from the successful season for the Barclay soccer team. President Frazier while listing the November highpoints in the fall issue of the *Barclay College Progress* was happy to report:

> The Barclay College soccer team won the Conference Championship, the MCCC Tournament Championship, the NCCAA DII Southwest Region Championship, and, on November 8, placed fifth at the NCCAA DII National Championship in Florida by winning the consolation bracket. Both wins at the National Championship went into overtime periods. The soccer team finished with a 17-2 record. Kingsley Assibey was the MCCC MVP and two players, David Hernandez, and Josh Moore, were placed on the NCCAA All-American DII first team.[168]

Spring 2015 was the last semester for the *Barclay Advantage!* program in Indiana; the *Advantage!* sites were each folded into the online program. Kenn Dirrim in Greece was added to the adjunct faculty as an instructor for Juniors Global Greece. Ben Staley joined the online adjunct faculty in ministry and Bible. Then in the Fall 2015 Anissa Riggs (Potter) became part of the faculty for the Elementary Education K-6 major, and later accepted the role as Director of the Writing Center as well as of the coordinator of Juniors Global. David Mabry was added to adjunct staff to teach Bible online. Ryan Haase began teaching more than Yearbook; by teaching the class on Transformational Leadership. Lora Meredith joined the adjunct staff online teaching English. Joshua Bunce, who had chaired the Youth Ministry major, was named chair of the Bible and Theology Department replacing Dr. Dave Kingrey who moved on to be the director of the Master of Arts in Spiritual Formation and the Master of Arts in Quaker Studies.

---

[168] *Barclay College Progress*, Fall 2014, 2.

This was the same semester that an LED sign was erected alongside Highway 54/400 near the entrance to Haviland. A generous donation made this possible. The sign makes it possible to post announcements about college events, and the college's programs visible to travelers on the highway. Barclay hosted the MCCC tournament in February and won the championship. It was a good season with the Bears ending the 2014/2015 season with a 7-1 home record against MCCC opponents and a 12-16 overall for the year. Ryan Kendall, chair of the Sports and Recreation major in April presented a synopsis of a book he was writing to the 41st Conference on Value Inquiry at Neumann University in Ashton, Pennsylvania. What he presented concerning discipleship and transformational leadership through coaching was well received, and he was affirmed in his philosophy of discipleship through coaching. The Barclay College Choir wrapped up the 2014/2015 year with a successful tour through Iowa, Indiana, and Kansas.[169]

Several exciting things were announced in the 2015 summer issue of the *Progress*. First, President Royce Frazier reported that the campaign to build a Fine Arts Center had received a welcome boost with the donation of a $750,000.00 challenge gift from the Mabee Foundation. The need for better space for the music department had spurred on a campaign for a Fine Arts building and up to this point the campaign had been in its silent phase. But over 200 donors had already given more than $3.5 million including a gift of $1.5 million from the descendants of Robert and Minnie Belle Ross. With the Mabee gift the campaign was moving into its public phase. Second, after being unable for a while to field a volleyball team the college now had a team that were good contenders for the Midwest Christian College Conference. The fall possibilities were looking up. Third, the 84th annual Barclay College Auxiliary Auction brought out some five hundred people and raised $93, 923.00. Fourth, Barclay College was represented on three continents in the Summer of

---

[169] *Barclay College Progress*, Spring 2015, 3, 9, 8.

2015 with Juniors Global teams experiencing wonderful trips to Greece, Cambodia, and Kenya.[170]

Four Juniors Global teams began preparing in Spring 2016 for their summer opportunities. "Partnering with Friends in other countries fifteen students and four professors [would] be serving alongside missionaries and national leaders."[171] One team to be led by Professor Derek Brown and hosted by Sam and Rebecca Barber was preparing to go to Belize to share in youth ministry and after school tutoring. Sam and Rebecca were missionaries in Belize who had several of their children attend Barclay. A second team would be led by Missions Professor Kevin Mortimer and hosted by Karen Bauer. They were to be a second team to go to Kenya to work in a project building huts for widows. The third team was headed to Ireland led by Professor Josh Bunce and hosted by Evangelical Friends Mission's missionary Kathi Perry. The fourth team was headed to Greece to work with Kenn and Lisa Dirrim in work with refugees.

In December 1985, a simple Christmas Pageant was created in the basement of the Haviland Friends Church. This simple pageant augmented by live animals—camels, donkeys, sheep—moved to larger building on Highway 54 for the next two or three years before moving to the Barclay College campus. President Robin Johnston arranged for the side door to the Hockett Auditorium to be heightened to allow access for the camels. The pageant ran each Christmas for many years until it began to run every other year. Each year it brought hundreds of people to Haviland and served a good ministry for the community. The cast each year was composed of Barclay College choir members, Barclay personnel, and community members. The 2015 pageant was a bittersweet one as it would be the last to be held in the Hockett Auditorium. The Winter 2015 *Progress* contained a two-page collage of scenes from the pageant.

---

[170] *Barclay College Progress*, Summer 2015, 2, 3, 4, 6-7.
[171] Hannah Kendall, *Barclay College Progress*, Winter 2015, 3.

God blessed the college two special ways in 2016. While the campaign for the Ross Center was gearing up and would typically take donations for day-to-day expenses away a timely legacy was received from Carl and Janie Bieshaar. The Bieshaars had been generous supporters of the college and had a great interest in the college's business department. The trust they left to the college endowment was vital for the college.[172]

The second blessing came from a rather unexpected source—the Lilly Endowment Inc. The Lilly Endowment Inc. was an Indianapolis based private foundation established in 1937 by three members of the Lilly family who had a pharmaceutical business. This foundation made available grants to Christian colleges to be used for programs "to deepen and enrich the religious lives of American Christians." Barclay College wrote a grant proposal for a program to introduce high school youth to theological study and to enable them to explore ways to serve Christ in ministry. The grant proposal was accepted. Brockie Follette (Harvey) was hired by the college to establish the program. She put together a theology camp and mentoring program called Kaleo (from the Greek word for "call.") The program was at first referred to as the Kaleo Academy for Friends Youth Theological Training. In 2016 it was called the Kaleo Academy National Friends Youth Training.

The program worked in partnership with Evangelical Friends Mission and the local Friends leadership with means to offer online interactions with teachers, global Friends leaders, and other students, mentorships in local churches, residency camps on the campus of Barclay College to explore Scripture and Theology, and service training. The first residency camp took place in the summer of 2017.[173]

---

[172] *Barclay College Progress*, Winter 2015, 2.
[173] *Barclay College Progress*, Winter 2015, 7.

Two additional mileposts in the accreditation process were passed in the Spring 2016. In April, the College hosted visiting teams from both the Higher Learning Commission (HLC) and from the Accrediting Association for Biblical Higher Education (ABHE). The HLC team was on campus for a biennial evaluation or "progress check" since the college was halfway through the four-year candidacy process. The team gave Barclay a positive review, recommending that the college could maintain its candidacy status. The peer-review team from ABHE was to reaffirm the College's relationship with ABHE. The team made a few recommendations for improvement, but ultimately determined that Barclay continued to meet ABHE's criteria for accreditation, saying, "The Team was unanimously enthusiastic about its interaction with all Barclay College personnel and is deeply appreciative of the School's ethos, overall quality, and devotion to its mission."[174] President Royce Frazier reported of the visits that both teams noted the evident community exhibited by the college—"Barclay College does community. At Barclay College there is a rich community. It's more than just a buzz word."[175]

Still another significant milestone was reached during the alumni weekend when the college broke ground for the new $7.5 million Ross-Ellis Center for the Fine Arts. Robert and Anita Ellis, longtime residents of Haviland who supported the college joined their donations with that of the Ross family. At the time of the groundbreaking $6.5 million had been raised and the hope was to complete the last million by October 13, 2016, in order to receive the promised Mabee grant. This happened as hoped. Because major campaigns nearly always draw funds away from the day-to-day needs the college issued a call for $400,000.00 to see the college through the summer. This also came in.

---

[174] *Barclay College Progress*, Summer 2016, 3.
[175] *Barclay College Progress*, Summer 2016, 2.

The Ross-Ellis Center had an auditorium with five hundred and eighty seats and a large stage. The auditorium allowed the entire population of the college to attend chapels and programs together and was used for a number of community events. The local elementary school held their spelling bees, awards ceremonies, and graduations there. The Yearly Meeting met in ministry conference there, and other conferences such as the Mission Multiplication Conference were hosted. The drama department made use of the space for some excellent productions. In addition four large rooms could be used as classrooms, for recitals, and rehearsals and configured for symposiums, for receptions, and even a "tea party" before the showing of the play "Cinderella." The hallways had offices, practice rooms, and smaller rooms that were effective for smaller classrooms.

In the early summer of 2016, the college received a number of recognitions. The president reported three, *"Best Educational Programs* listed our Elementary education program #1 in the state of Kansas. *Best Value Schools* ranked Barclay College the #1 best value college in the state of Kansas, and *Value Colleges* ranked Barclay College #7 in the nation in best value."[176]

For the college, the value was found in the spiritual life of the students and staff and the opportunities to grow in that life. One opportunity was an annual event arranged in connection with the college's preview days for prospective students. It was a student-led night of worship which emphasized the event's title: "With Everything." The three student leaders of the Spring 2016 event, Nathan Vanderploeg, Katie Newton, and Aaron Kick shared the belief that worship was not limited to music, but that worship was much, much more immersive, pervasive, and transcendent than that. They created an environment and experience for students that offered different mediums to connect with God beyond just music, with five different stations/worship activities that all required a response of

---

[176] *Barclay College Progress*, Summer 2016, 3.

the heart, including one done all together. Following the 'with everything' theme, they had cards that read, "I give you my. . ." Students finished the sentence with whatever they believed was keeping them from worshiping Him with everything. It was such a rich experience! Their goal was that anyone who walked into the sanctuary that night would be able to give everything up to the Lord in order to be able to worship Him fully.[177]

For the Fall 2016 there were numerous changes and additions to the faculty and the staff. Ryan Haase, who had been titled Director of Financial Aid was given a new title of Executive Assistant to the President. His new role included also being the Director of Marketing. Tiffany Van Dame, who had served as an Assistant Director for Admissions and as Women's Resident Director, became the Vice President for Student Services. Aaron Stokes, who had returned to the college to work in the kitchen and to pursue a Master of Arts degree assumed the role of Director of Distance Learning replacing Angie Wetmore who had accepted a position at Point Loma Nazarene University. With the pending retirement of Dr. Glenn Leppert, as Registrar for thirty-two years, Mark Miller became an Assistant Registrar, as a "Registrar in Training." Jesse Penna, an adjunct since 2010 in various Bible and ministry classes while serving as Associate Superintendent of Student Ministries for Evangelical Friends Church Mid-America continued on as part-time for both positions but assumed the role as chair of the Youth Ministry major. Heather Thornburg, who had been assisting in graduate admissions, took on the role of Assistant Director of Admissions while Shandy Brodhead became the Assistant Director for Financial aid and an Admissions Counselor. Shelly Barber became the Director of Graduate and Distance Learning Admissions. Jeannie Ross gained a second role in housekeeping. She became the Director of Food Service and the Director of Housekeeping. Martha Hodson became the Women's Resident Director. Pilo Miranda-Troup, a former Barclay College soccer player, took on the role of Soccer Coach along with Austin Ogle. Whitney Kreger assumed the role as Head Cross

---

[177] *Barclay College Progress*, Summer 2016, 11.

Country Coach. Brockie Follette was named Director of Kaleo Academy.[178]

During the summer before the Fall 2017 semester several additional changes happened. Larry Lewis, who had been working in the Institutional Advancement department, accepted a major role for the Sports and Recreation major to fill that position Ryan Kendall's leaving had vacated. In addition, Lauren Sill joined the major as a part-time professor. Steven King came to cover all of the math and science classes. Steve came to Barclay from both teaching at Cowley County Community College and being the curator at the Museum of World Treasures in Wichita. Dylan Palmer was promoted to Associate Director of Food Services while Jeannie Ross was released from being Director of Food Services to serve as the Director of Library Services. Charles Brodhead was named as Athletic Director and Men's Basketball Coach. Recent graduate, Justin Dahmer, was hired as Admissions Counselor and Financial Aid Assistant.[179]

There were two departures at the conclusion of the Spring 2017 semester. Dr. Jerry Simmons, a 1975 graduate of the college who had come to Barclay in 2008 to teach science and math, retired to give his full attention to the Heart of America Science Resource Center. Dr. Glenn W. Leppert partially retired. For thirty-two years Dr. Leppert had served the college as Registrar or as Vice President for Registration and Records. In those years he filled the role of Dean/Vice President for Academics for three periods of time, was interim president for a year, worked as the IT coordinator, in fact taught the early computer classes, served as faculty secretary and as secretary for the President's cabinet, functioned as the accreditation liaison, and taught full-time. He left his V.P. position but remained as a full-time professor teaching Greek, Bible, and history. He retired, almost, at the end of Spring 2022 (he returned to the classroom in the Spring 2023 to cover the Greek class left vacant at the death of Dr. Gene Pickard.)

---

[178] *Barclay College Progress*, Fall 2016, 4-6.
[179] *Barclay College Progress*, Summer 2017, 10-11.\

As the college moved into 2017, the year of its centennial, President Frazier mused on the prayer (the request for wisdom) of Solomon in 2 Chronicles 1 and the blessings the college had received:

> It occurred to me that, possibly, the intentional and deliberate decision of the Board of Trustees of Barclay College in 2006 to remain a ministry focused institution serving the Friends Church and the larger church universal was the request God used to determine if Barclay College could be gifted with other blessings. Is it possible that Lewis Hall, the College Hill Apartments, and now the Ross-Ellis Center are a result of God's blessings on the faithfulness of the leadership of this institution to stay its course, through its historic mission, in the most trying of times?

He then set some goals for the year:

1. to finish the accreditation process.
2. to broaden the degrees through which the college prepares students for "effective Christian life, service, and leadership."
3. to improve the campus "quality of life."
4. to increase the endowment.
5. to expand the college's impact on the Evangelical Friends movement by additional graduate programs.
6. to continue to speak effectively to the Friends movement.

Regional accreditation was received in 2018. The degrees were expanded, most notably, by the addition of criminal justice and nursing. Increasing the endowment was a steady ongoing process. The doctorate program envisioned in this goal is yet to be. The Robert Barclay Institute was created to keep the college in conversation with the Friends movement.

It was in the Fall 1917 that the first classes at Barclay College opened (as the Kansas Central Bible Training School), thus Fall 2017 marked the completion of one hundred years and the opening of a new era for the college. A centennial committee had met throughout 2016 to plan events to celebrate the centennial. The first event was on May 6, 2017, when a presentation was made to the alumni at the annual Alumni Banquet where a 6-foot-tall centennial birthday cake, lit with 100 electric candles, was on display. During the dinner, a 100-year historical presentation of the college was made, recounting the 16 presidents' years of service at the college. Representatives from the families of the presidents were present to represent their parent or grandparent who had been president. There were about 450 guests at the banquet. A centennial birthday party was held in the school's cafeteria after the banquet in honor of Barclay's birthday.[180]

In August at the very first chapel of the new academic year a special presentation to the students was made that included a history of the college. Placed around campus were special displays some of which were interactive. Then at the Ladies Auxiliary Sale in October patrons were encouraged to check out the displays and some special displays were set up in the sale area. In December at the Christmas Pageant a brief video informed the audience of the centennial before the pageant began. The final celebration was the presentation to and of the 100th graduating class at commencement, May 5, 2018.

A visiting team from the Higher Learning Commission of the North Central Association was on campus April 23-25, 2018, and in November the process that had begun back in the 1990's ended with the announcement that regional accreditation was fully achieved. President Royce Frazier was able to announce:

---

[180] Barclay College Progress, Summer 2017, 4.

Barclay College is pleased to announce that it is now accredited by the Higher Learning Commission, a regional accreditation agency recognized by the U.S. Department of Education. When our students pursue post-graduate education, other colleges, universities, seminaries, and schools of theology will recognize even more the quality of a Barclay education . . . This is a great achievement for Barclay College and an endorsement of the quality of education it offers. There are many more wonderful surprises ahead.

In May, 2018, the college kicked off a new campaign to increase the endowment for the college. The challenge was to have $20 million by 2020. Coming right at the heels of the fund raiser for the Ross Ellis Center for Ministry this was, perhaps, the most ambitious venture in the college's 100-year history. But if successful the endeavor would ensure that Barclay College could always stay committed to Kingdom work. Endowing the ministry departments and majors with Great Commission professors who appreciate the rich evangelical Friends tradition would ensure the vision of the college would always exist. By the time of the *Winter Progress* the college had $7.3 million of the $20 million goal. The goal was not reached by 2020 and in 2020 COVID made visiting possible donors impossible and giving was greatly curtailed. However, at the end of 2022, the endowment stood at $18.5 million and was growing.

In the Fall 2018 additional changes took place among the faculty and staff. Several of these changes reflected the growth of the college's programs. Dr. Jim Le Shana accepted the position as superintendent of Northwest Yearly Meeting and thus left the Vice President for Academics position open. It was filled by moving Tim Hawkins from Associate Vice President for Academic Services to be the Vice President for Academic Services. Dr. Derek Brown was named Vice President for Graduate Studies. He retained his role as Chair of Pastoral Ministry. Ryan Haase was named as Vice President of Student Services. Brockie Follette added a new role. In addition to directing Kaleo Academy she assumed the title and role of Chaplain and Assistant to the President. Two staff members were added in the Fall of 2019. Shane Shetley took the position of Athletic Director and Scott Post as Recruiting Coordinator.

A happy event happened in the Fall 2019 semester. Crossland Construction, the company that built the Ross-Ellis Center, donated a completely refurbished Ebony 9-foot Baldwin grand piano. A special humidity-controlled room was built on the stage where the piano could be housed.[181]

In the Fall 2019 the Barclay College Board of Trustees initiated an aggressive vision to pursue accreditation for an Associate of Nursing degree (ADN) and a Bachelor of Nursing degree (BSN). The college hired a director/administrator to initiate the accreditation process when the fundraising goal was met. At the time the Board announced this decision they had nearly $485,000 in gifts and pledges toward their $800,000 goal over three years. In this venture the college had the support of Pratt Regional Medical Center, regional rural medical facilities, and pursued affiliations with western Kansas community colleges.[182]

Early in 2020 Barclay College kept the new Ross Ellis Center busy. On February 9, the center hosted a marriage seminar, "Momentous," with couples and singles coming to hear "Roger Gibson, marriage pastor at a thriving five-campus church in Dallas, Texas, son-in-law of Gary Smalley, and well-known marriage and relationship counselor." The seminar was fun and taught attendees "to communicate better, deepen intimacy, 'fight' well, have fun together, and raise healthy families." On February 22, there was a concert with Prince Ivan, an American songwriting, production, and performing duo from Branson, Missouri, with a mission "to change lives, to tell a story [to] connect, captivate, and transform the lives

---

[181] "What's UP at Barclay" e-mail newsletter, 12/2/2019.
[182] "What's UP at Barclay" e-mail newsletter, 9/1/2019, 11/1/2019.

of individuals, families, and cultures."[183] But, then COVID shut most everything down. The spring production, "Mary Poppins," was postponed, and the college faced the question of whether to close the semester early or find an alternative way to complete the semester.

First, near the beginning of the semester, the college began to inform the campus concerning hygiene, masks, and the proper protocols to prevent the spread of the virus. Kim Hansen, the chair of the in-process nursing program, sent e-mails and did chapel presentations. Then, Barclay extended Spring Break by one week (Mar. 16-29) hoping the situation would change,[184] but since conditions were unchanged, they moved all classes online and adjusted the grading options for all classes.

All spring events including commencement were cancelled. In place of commencement a video introducing each of the graduates was made and distributed to alumni and friends of the college, and tentative plans were made to hold commencement exercises in October after the annual sale—if that were to happen.[185] In Haviland during the graduation weekend there was a parade to drive by the homes of the graduates who were in the community. Students stepped out of their homes to wave at the long line of cars snaking through town. The procession was led by the flashing lights of a highway patrol escort. The parade included homes of students who lived in Greensburg.[186]

Introductions to the online system were made available to all campus students and some classes moved on to the college's Learning Management System (LMS) while others were set up rather like independent studies utilizing Zoom and e-mails. A chapel time was

---

[183] "What's UP at Barclay" e-mail newsletter, 3/3/2020.
[184] "What's UP at Barclay" e-mail newsletter, 3/16/2020.
[185] "What's UP at Barclay" e-mail newsletter, 5/12/2020.
[186] "Barclay Update," 5/12/2020.

put together, and all students were invited to join together via Zoom. To keep up morale Shane Shetley sent out a weekly video of encouragement.

The college began building a *Mitigation Plan* for the potential return of students in the fall, anticipating classes in the fall would happen as scheduled. The concern was to be ready and able to safeguard the health of the Barclay College family and the surrounding community. Means for doing health checks and space for quarantine were prepared.

From the time the classes moved online the Barclay College family was invited to an *11:00 Moment in Prayer*. Students, alumni, friends of the college, and people who believed in prayer joined this effort.[187]

Kaleo Academy, the Friends Youth Leadership Training program, made the difficult decision to lay down the 2020-2021 Kaleo Academy Cohort, trusting God had a plan. (Kaleo was back and strong in 2022.

Classes on campus for Fall 2020 did return to face-to-face. Numerous things were put into place to keep students and the community safe. These included temperatures taken on arrival on campus, extra time for registration so that students could be distanced from each other, regular temperature reports, restricted travel off campus, resident assistants performing regular monitoring, required masks, space in classrooms adjusted, no public use of the cafeteria, Sunday services were limited to gatherings on campus, sports games were delayed, and cafeteria access was scheduled to assure proper distancing. As new students came to campus travel restrictions did make for some interesting happenings. It caused one incoming student from Florida to have to come early for quarantine, however before she got to campus Florida was taken off of the list!

---

[187] "What's UP at Barclay" e-mail newsletter, 3/30/2020.

The Ladies Auxiliary Sale did not happen; the ladies made the hard decision to postpone the sale doing so "to provide safety for vulnerable BC students, faculty, and alumni."[188] In place of the auction donations were requested and the "What's UP at Barclay" e-mail newsletter added a "track the donations" feature. The commencement did happen, but attendance was limited to graduates and their guests.

During the summer before the Fall 2020 semester, Randi Shetley, Director of Fine Arts, received the M.A. of Theater Arts from Regent University. Of her degree she said,

> The studies gave me a deeper understanding of acting methods and theater management. Studying theater at a Christian university with Christian values was wonderful. I look forward to taking what I learned into our program at Barclay.[189]

During the fall, together, Barclay College, Evangelical Friends Church-Mid-American Yearly Meeting, and Youth Core Ministries presented a third annual Youth Ministry Workshop in November of 2020. Steve Argue was the speaker. The topic was *Faith, Doubt, and Creating Spiritual Depth in Young People*. A second such workshop with Andrew Root as speaker was held June 29, 2022; this one was titled, "Have We Lost Them?" Also in the fall Kaleo Academy offered free mini versions of several Kaleo classes designed for high schoolers and ideal for youth groups, small groups, or personal reflection. The classes were posted on social media and were available for download. [190] In November Brockie Follette, as Chaplain, invited the Barclay College community to participate in a period of fasting. Training on fasting was done in chapel, participants signed up for a meal that would be replaced with a fast, a special prayer room was prepared, and daily emails were sent out

---

[188] "What's UP at Barclay" e-mail newsletter, 9/8/2020.
[189] "What's UP at Barclay" e-mail newsletter, 8/7/2020.
[190] "What's UP at Barclay" e-mail newsletter, 10/7/2020.

with a centering thought, reading, or scripture for the day. Some Barclay Board members and adjunct professors even participated in locations outside of Haviland.[191]

One bright spot in the Fall 2020 was the publication of Barclay College Publishers' first book. Barclay College determined to create a publishing arm that could publish the work of faculty and students and thus encourage research and sharing of truth. Over the years former students and faculty have authored books. Jim Towne, *My Senior Year;* David Crisp, *The View from Here;* Dr. Fred Johnson, *Toward Conformity to the Image of Christ,* and *When Beliefs Collide with Culture . . . What Then?* and active faculty such as Dr. Derek Brown, On *Quakers and Pastors.* The first Barclay College Publishers' book, *The Heart of Friends; Quaker History and Beliefs,* was published in August 2020. It was written by Dr. Glenn Leppert with contributions by Dave Kingrey. The next book was by Dr. Keith White, *Kings and Queens in the Kingdom of God,* April 2022. The third was *Quaker Leaders Who Transformed the World* by Dr. Dave Kingrey, 2022.

In the December 2020 issue of "What's UP at Barclay" President Frazier was able to announce that the goal of raising $800,000.00 for the nursing program was exceeded. By the end of November, $1,003,000.00 had been received. Once again the hand of God's blessing was seen. Support came from individuals as well as from Pratt Regional Hospital and Kiowa County Hospital. After the first goal in fundraising had been met, in July 2019, the college hired Kim Hansen, B.S.N., M.S.N., as the Director of Nursing Education. She began the arduous task of lining out all that would be required to gain accreditation.[192]

In the Spring 2021 the Lady Bears clinched the MCCC conference title with a record of 10-1, they clinched the #7 seed for the DII NCCAA National Basketball Tournament. After a good showing

---

[191] "What's UP at Barclay" e-mail newsletter, 11/6/2020.
[192] "What's UP at Barclay" e-mail newsletter, 12/10/2020.

at the tournament, they finished in 6th place! Lady Bears' head coach Scott Post said,

> I'm super proud of the entire season. Our girls accomplished a lot. To finish 6th in the country with the youth we have and my first year as coach is really nice. I'm happy with our results. Both Men's and Women's teams secured the regular season MCCC Conference Titles! The potential for doing so in 2021 was heightened as Tanner Huck joined the athletic department in Fall 2011 as Men's Basketball coach. Mallorie Scott accepted the position of Volleyball coach for Fall 2021. Ashley Hatton became an assistant coach.[193]

In February, 2021, Angie Wetmore returned to Barclay as the Associate Vice President of Distance Learning[194] and in the fall, Aaron Stokes, who had been the Associate Vice President for Distance Learning, replaced Mark Miller as Registrar.[195] Mark Miller took on the role of Vice President for Institutional Advancement when Larry Lewis retired from that position to be full-time as chair of the Sports and Recreation major.[196] Also, that fall Chelle Leininger took over the chair of the Elementary Education K-6 major from Cheryl Couch.[197] Jeannie Ross added the title Vice President for Student Success and Kim Stewart assumed the role as music director for the college choir and singers. In the spring Dr. Derek Brown had been named Vice President for Academic Services beginning July 1, 2021. That position put academic programs under his office—Campus, Online, and the School of Graduate Studies. Tim Hawkins, who had been the Vice President for Academic Services, began work on a Doctorate in Education (Ed.D.) at Johns Hopkins University,

---

[193] "What's UP at Barclay" e-mail newsletter, 4/1/2021.
[194] "What's UP at Barclay" e-mail newsletter, 1/8/2021.
[195] "What's UP at Barclay" e-mail newsletter, 7/8/2021.
[196] "What's UP at Barclay" e-mail newsletter, 5/13/2021.
[197] "What's UP at Barclay" e-mail newsletter, 7/8/2021.

focusing on pedagogy and professional development at small, rural, and private institutions.[198]

Another highpoint for the summer of 2021 was the first annual Boys & Girls Basketball Youth Camp on the Barclay campus. The camp was coached by Barclay College Men's Basketball players and staff. Over thirty boys and girls participated in that first camp led by Barclay coach Tanner Huck and the Barclay Bears.[199] In connection with the Barclay Bears coaching a basketball camp later in the fall, in September, Barclay students submitted names for the Barclay Bear's mascot. The name chosen was "Benny Bear." The name comes from the Latin meaning, "blessed." The prayer was for the Bear community to be a blessing to the world around them.[200] Speaking of blessings; the 90th annual Ladies Auxiliary Auction, October 2, 2021, brought in a record amount of $129,306.00.

A new major was crafted in 2021 and had classes begin online in the Spring 2022. The major, Criminal Justice, chaired by Dr. Adrian Halverstadt focuses on "restorative justice and how people are reconciled, and communities are transformed." Dr. Halverstadt said of the program:

> Evangelically minded Friends advocate that justice be administered in a restorative manner, so it is fitting that Barclay College offer Criminal Justice as an area of study. It serves as a means for bringing healing into the wounded areas of humanity and allows Barclay College to contribute its influence to the criminal justice system of our country.[201]

The tireless work put in by Kim Hansen resulted in the great announcement in February 2023 that Barclay College was approved to

---

[198] "What's UP at Barclay" e-mail newsletter, 5/13/2021.
[199] "What's UP at Barclay" e-mail newsletter, August 2021.
[200] "What's UP at Barclay" e-mail newsletter, September, 2021.
[201] "What's UP at Barclay" e-mail newsletter, October 2021.

offer the traditional Bachelor of Science in Nursing (BSN) degree program by the Higher Learning Commission (HLC). The Kansas State Board of Nursing approved the program in July 2022.

President Frazier stated:

> The challenge of adding a nursing program fits well within the mission of Barclay College . . . Both supporters and people in the medical profession affirmed that an institution that is committed to both faith and healing has a relevant place in our culture and our world today . . . Holding to our deeply grounded roots in partnering any degree with an additional degree in biblical studies sets our students apart.[202]

Several staff and faculty changes happened in 2022. Sherry Ward joined the faculty for the nursing program, Kim Hansen was named Dean of the Nursing program, Kevin Lee returned to the college to be the Director of Online Recruiting. Elyse Birdsong became Director of Recruiting and Scott Post accepted the role as Athletic Director. Richard Thompson was named Men's Head Basketball Coach and Recruiter.[203] Dave Kingrey, faculty emeritus who had left because of health, was able to return to be the chair of the online Biblical Studies program. His role was to advise and recruit Biblical studies students. Shane Shetley was named chair of the Friends Ministry Training program, a certificate program offered online. Michale Johnson became the Graduate Admissions Counselor.[204]

Athletics had a good season and several individuals received honors. The December newsletter declared, "Maddie Yost went off to the National NCCAA Women's DII Cross Country National Championship and came back a winner for Barclay." Davion Knight and

---

[202] "What's UP at Barclay" e-mail newsletter, February 2023.
[203] "What's UP at Barclay" e-mail newsletter, October 2021, December 2021, Summer 2022, 2021.
[204] "What's UP at Barclay" e-mail newsletter, September 2022.

Jamia Jackson both scored one thousand points in their basketball season. The March newsletter reported that DJ Hudspeth was named to 2nd team, NCCAA DII All-Conference, and 1st team MCCC All-Conference. Davion Knight was named to the 3rd team, NCCAA DII All-Conference, and 2nd team MCCC All-Conference. Sarah Robinson and Cambrey Ballard were named 2nd team All-Conference at the 2022 MCCC Volleyball Tournament.[205] Cambrey was named the MCCC student Athlete of the week in December.

The goal for Christmas Wreath for the 2021 fall was $100,000.00. Mark Miller was able to express in January 2022:

> On behalf of President Frazier and myself it is with joy that we report to our alumni and friends that through our Christmas Wreath appeal we received $130,934.51 from 201 households. There were multiple examples of people giving their largest donation, people donating out of their retirement accounts, new donors, people who gave more than one gift, and amazing generosity from so many. Thank you for your continued support of Barclay College. Our partnership with our alumni and friends is a vital component that allows the college to remain true to its mission.

At the conclusion of the Spring 2022 semester two faculty members and one Board member were granted emeritus status recognizing their long-time contributions to the college. The first was Dr. Dave Kingrey, a professor at the college from 2008 to 2022 gave tirelessly in the classroom and in leadership in the Theology department on campus and as a Director of several concentrations in the Graduate Division. Dave was the motivation behind the Institute for Pastoral Leadership Development from 2005 to 2021. The second to be

---

[205] "What's UP at Barclay" e-mail newsletter, December 2021, March 2022.

given faculty emeritus status was Dr. Glenn Leppert who served the college in various capacities from Fall 1985 to Spring 2022. Trustee emeritus status was awarded to Dr. David Robinson who served many years on the Barclay College Board.

In May, the college also celebrated three retirements—Dr. Dave Kingrey, Dr. Keith White, and Dr. Glenn Leppert. During the summer and then early in the spring of 2023 the college experienced the homegoing of two professors—Dr. Keith White and Dr. Gene Pickard.

Granting emeritus status speaks well to the concept of longevity, of continuation for those given the honor have persisted in their commitment. Retirement and Homegoing are illustrative of change. Change is constant as we have seen with the coming and going of personnel at the college, with innovative programs, new goals, new ways to address the day-to-day needs. Yet there is also stability, and some things remain, some things we hold sacred, and hold tightly to. Dr. Frazier expressed this when he spoke of the college and in essence summarized his first thirteen years at the helm:

> Today the work of Barclay College continues. We provide Full Tuition Scholarships through your gifts to educate students who might otherwise not receive a college education. We [have prepared]a Nursing Program... We are creating effective Bible translators who will proclaim the Good News to the unreached. We will continue to be the global community for higher education for evangelical Friends ministry. Barclay College will always stand firm.[206]

---

[206] *Annual Report*, 2020.

CHAPTER NINE
GRADUATE STUDIES
2011-2023

The college began to explore the possibility of a graduate division as early as August 2009 and through the fall of 2009 inquiries were sent to the State Board of Regents to ascertain if there were state regulations or standards that would need to be met. Inquiries also went to the Association for Biblical Higher Education and to the North Central Association. There were no state regulations, and ABHE replied that no special administration would be needed for a graduate division.[207]

The college began preparing in 2010. Everything necessary—faculty, curriculum, resources, had all been lined out and descriptions and documents had been submitted to ABHE during the Spring 2010 semester. ABHE gave approval that fall.

---

[207] President's Cabinet Minutes for 2009/2010, minutes 09/10-36, 09/10-104e, 09/10-235 c d, 09/10-243a, b, 10/11-41.

This first graduate program was a Master of Arts in Transformational Leadership (MATL) with a concentration in Spiritual Formation (SF). The concentration under the leadership of Dr. David Williams officially began Fall 2011. In 2014 when Dr. Williams accepted the superintendency of EFC-MAYM Dr. David Kingrey assumed the leadership of the MATL-Spiritual Formation concentration.

The MATL was created in response to many alumni and other college constituents who had contacted the college desiring additional education at the graduate level. Surveys of Barclay graduates indicated there was strong interest in two different areas—in studies of leadership and in studies of spiritual formation. Transformational leadership focused on both of these areas. Scriptural leadership is transformational and spiritual formation is integral to any transformation. The program was online but included a week-long "face-to-face" component each semester. Students could complete the thirty-six required hours in four semesters.[208]

The first public announcement for the MATL program stated that in keeping with Barclay's commitment to a "high-touch, high-quality education" the enrollment would be limited. This was to assure small, close-knit cohorts with low faculty to student ratios.

The first cohort began with twelve students from five different states (California, Colorado, Iowa, Idaho, and Kansas). The first semester was the first of four modules, and contained three classes, an apprenticeship, and a project for a total of 9 hours. Dr. Dave Kingrey taught the three-hour class, "Transformational

---

[208] *Barclay College Progress*, Fall 2010, 3.

Leadership in Biblical Perspective." Dr. David Williams covered a two-hour class, "Spirituality and the Transformational Journey," as well as was responsible for the one-hour apprenticeship which offered opportunity each week for students to meet with a mentor.[209] Dr. Royce Frazier taught another two-hour class, "Caring and Community." Dr. Adrian Halverstadt was responsible for the one-hour project. October 10-19, 2011, the students, and faculty met in Woodland Park, Colorado, for a face-to-face session at the Quaker Ridge Conference Camp.[210]

In the Summer 2012 issue of the *Barclay College Progress* the graduate division announced a second concentration and also a $1,275.00 scholarship then available. This second concentration was Professional Studies (PS) under the leadership of Dr. Jim Le Shana. The MATL in Professional Studies promoted the same overall aim as the Spiritual Formation track—to equip men and women for effective Christian life, service, and leadership. The PS emphasis was designed especially for the Christian professional who would benefit from a degree in leadership for their business, career, or educational objectives, but for whom time and money remained a pressing issue. Ten students formed the first PS cohort in Fall 2012.

In 2014 the Graduate School changed the names of the two concentrations. What was known as the MATL-PS (Master of Arts in Transformational Leadership—Professional Studies) became the MA in Transformational Leadership (MATL). What had been the MATL-SF (Master of Arts in Transformational Leadership—Spiritual Formation) took the new name, MA in Spiritual Formation (MASF). The Graduate school at that time

---

[209] *Barclay College Progress*, Winter 2011/2012, 4.
[210] *Barclay College Progress*, Summer 2011, 5; Fall 2011, 3.

was exploring other concentrations or emphases that could be added. By Spring 2015 three additional concentrations were available—Quaker Studies (MAQS), Family Ministries (MAFM), and Pastoral Ministries (MAPM).

Two new graduate faculty were added in 2014. Dr. Kent Walkemeyer joined the faculty for Spiritual Formation, and Dr. Stan Leach began teaching the "Spiritual Direction and Soul Care" class.[211] Lisa Christiansen, who had been the admissions coordinator for the Graduate School, also received a new title—Director of Graduate Student Services.[212]

In Fall 2015 enrollment was up to thirty-four students. The Fall 2015 face-to-face was held in Haviland. Through the Spring 2016, details for yet another concentration were worked out and the new program, a Master of Arts in Missional Multiplication (MAMM) was added to the schedule. The MM concentration was designed to prepare men and women to serve in a variety of ministry settings, both globally and locally. The emphasis was on preparing leaders to "shed the maintenance-mentality" and instead to contribute to a church multiplication movement, being aware of global concerns, and desiring to connect with people from every cultural group.[213] Fall 2017 a seventh concentration, Master of Arts in Sports Outreach (MASO) was added.

The August issue of "What's UP at Barclay" announced an eighth concentration for the Barclay College School of Graduate

---

[211] *Barclay College Progress*, Summer 2014, 6,7.
[212] President's Cabinet Minutes, Spring 2014, minute 13/14-272.
[213] *Barclay College Progress*, Summer 2016, 7.

Studies—a Master of Arts in Biblical Translation (MABT). The program was created in partnership with Wycliffe Associates and was designed to train people in the Mobile Assistance Supporting Translation (MAST) methodology of biblical translation. MAST, a methodology enabling the church to quickly learn, implement, and own the translation process, allowed native language speakers to participate in both written and oral translations. Dr. Dan Kramer, Vice President of Strategic Initiatives at Our Daily Bread, was named to direct the program, and brought with him decades of missions and administrative leadership experience to Barclay College. Derek Brown, Ph.D., Vice President for Graduate Studies at Barclay College reported, "The MA in Biblical Translation prepares our students to be on the cutting edge of translation methods, allowing them to contribute in making the Word of God available to every tongue and nation."[214] The first cohort of students in this major graduated in December 2021.

In January 2012 David Mabry took on the position of the Director of the Master of Arts in Transformational Leadership. He served as the Director of the M.A. in Family Ministry. Mabry had served as a professor in Theology and Biblical Studies and in Organizational Leadership. David's full title as listed in the July newsletter was, "Dean, School of Graduate Studies Director, Master's in Family Ministries, Transformational Leadership, and Practical Theology."[215]

Three new faculty were added to the graduate division in the fall. Dr. Paul Hoffman and Dr. Clifford T. Winters were added to the Master of Arts for Family Ministry, teaching the "Ministry of Community" class, and Dr. Marva Hoops joined the faculty for Master of Arts for Family Ministry teaching the "Ministry of

---

[214] "What's UP at Barclay College" e-mail newsletter, 8/7/2020.
[215] "What's UP at Barclay College" e-mail newsletter, 1/21/2021.

Family" class.[216]

---

[216] "What's UP at Barclay College" e-mail newsletter, 8/7/2020.

CHAPTER TEN
THE BEST KIND OF DRAMA
1990-2023

Since 1976 a drama class has been on the schedule for students desiring or needing credit for participation in a drama team. The class was defined as, "A performance group that employs plays, skits, readings, and other dramatic forms to share God's love. Audition required." Mostly, drama at Barclay consisted of small teams which sometimes travelled with music groups to present the Gospel in music and drama. While this was usually a ministry to churches near the college, in the summer of 1990 the Barclay College Drama Troupe, working with Del Covington, visited a number of camps and churches in Indiana, Michigan, Ohio, Virginia, North Carolina, and Tennessee. And in the Summer 2000, the Barclay College Singers and the Drama Team visited six nations in Europe.[217] To fund the trip the Singers and the Drama Team presented a dinner theatre on May 5, 2000. The production was titled "Salt and Light."

Sometimes the teams did more than skits and short dramas. In 1997, first semester drama students worked on a variety of skits for chapel and local church services, but they also presented a major production, "Jonah and the German Whale" a tale of Jonah and his

---

[217] *Barclay Progress*, Volume 70, No. 2 Summer 2000, 3.

disobedience. In the spring semester of 1998, another major production, "Book Mark", was given. The play was about how the Gospel of Mark was written.[218] In the Spring 1999 two members of the drama team, Sean McGilberry, and Angelique Kavalski, wrote a full-length drama for the team. Titled "The Way He Leads Me", it was a drama that portrayed a young man who chose to go the way the Lord led him instead of the direction his father had gone. Margaret Pent was the instructor that semester.[219] There were two teams in the 2002/2003 academic year—a fall team and a spring team. Two of the favorite skits that they did were "Oh Lord!" and "How to Fold a Shirt." The 2003/2004 teams performed short dramas regularly in chapel. Spring 2005 the drama team presented a set of one-act plays. In 2006 Barclay College student, Tara Healy, wrote and directed an adaptation of "Princess Bride" that the team performed. Amber Smitherman was the princess, Andy Adair was the "farm boy," and Justin Schamberger the king.[220]

Del Covington (90-94), Janet Johnston (94-96), Margaret Pent (99-00), Steve Elmore (02-03), Jared Ross (03-08 and 18), Andrea Grace (08-09), and Randi Shetley (09-13 and 19-23) were assigned over the years as instructors. Randi commuted from Fowler to the college beginning in 2009 to instruct the Drama Ensemble. That fall she had a group of seventeen students to work with and they presented a play, "Harvey." Spring 2010 each member of the drama class wrote and directed a play with their classmates as the actors.[221] Spring 2011 a wonderful presentation of "Beauty and the Beast" with Katelyn Butler as Belle, and Tim Coleman as the beast was given. For the Fall 2011 semester, the drama team did an "exquisite" performance of "Monday Night Live" showing off their talents in many different skits, through poetry, stories, and monologues, along with one big play. There was no drama class for the Spring 2012, but a large class for Fall 2012 which began work on a

---

[218] *Crimsayvista*, 1998, 7.
[219] *Crimsayvista*, 1999, 51.
[220] *Crimsayvista*, 2003, 38; 2004, 32; 2005, 46-47; 2006, 58-59.
[221] *Crimsayvista*, 2010, 64-65.

production for the Spring 2013. That play was Rodger's and Hammerstein's "Cinderella." The production involved some twenty-one or so students and was a remarkable success. It ran three nights (April 5, 6, and 7) to pleased audiences. Christianne Agbuya played Cinderella and Joel Pedigo was Prince Charming.

Professor Shetley was away from the college, living and working in Branson, Missouri, from the end of the Spring 2013 semester until Spring 2018 when she returned to the college to direct drama and to be the Director of Fine Arts. There were no drama classes nor drama teams from Fall 2013 to Fall 2017. Spring 2018, however, saw a major production that wowed audiences—"Joseph and the Amazing Technicolor Dreamcoat." Isaac Cox played the part of Joseph. Each year since there has been an over-the-top major production.

Spring 2019. "Beauty and the Beast" with Natalie Forest (Stewart) and Jarod Daniel.

Fall 2019 saw William Shakespeare's "Much Ado About Nothing" with a little bit of Swing. This was the original script, but had a 1945 setting, just after WWII. The production had great costumes, live swing music, and a little swing dancing as well.[222]

Spring 2020/Fall 2020. "Mary Poppins" was postponed because of the Coronavirus. It was to have played in April 2020 and was moved to the Fall 2020 and opened in September.[223] Chase Groth stared a tradition in which every night before the cast of Mary Poppins took the stage, they sang "I Love You Lord," and after the "Amen" Chase reminded the cast, "to go out and tell a story!" This tradition has continued till now. Tickets were re-issued with "social distancing" in mind. A request was sent out to friends and family to raise

---

[222] "What's UP at Barclay" e-mail Monday 9/16/2019.
[223] "What's UP at Barclay" e-mail newsletter, 3/16/2020, 6/8/2020, 9/8/2020.

$7,000.00 to rent the fly rig from a fly specialist company (ZFX). The needed funds were raised in less than three weeks making it possible for Mary Poppins to "fly" onto the stage.

Spring 2021. "Newsies" a true David and Goliath story straight from the streets of New York. It was a rousing tale of Jack Kelly, a charismatic newsboy and leader of a band of teenaged "newsies." When titans of publishing raise distribution prices at the newsboys' expense, Jack rallied newsies from across the city to stand for what was right.

Fall 2021. In November Barclay College joined thousands of theatrical organizations around the globe by producing their own local production of Music Theatre International's *All Together Now!: A Global Event Celebrating Local Theatre*. At Barclay, this musical revue featured songs from *Annie, Mary Poppins, High School Musical, Frozen, Matilda, Rent, Newsies*, and more!

Spring 2022. "The Play that Goes Wrong" which was a whacky crazy comedy that kept everyone in the audience laughing and then some.

Fall 2022 saw the production of "*The Lion, the Witch, and the Wardrobe.*" This was an outstanding performance with many great lessons tucked in. More than 1,600 people attended the production.

Spring 2023. "Cinderella" was another major production. It was not the same play as in Spring 2013. Instead, it had a few twists and turns that caught the audience by surprise. Elizabeth Johnson was the lead player as Cinderella and Logan Rosales was the prince.

An amazing creative team of Deb Folkerts, Traci Ballard, Jared Ross (Joseph, Beauty and the Beast and Much Ado) Kim Stewart (all the later shows), Casey Roberts, and Shane Shetley have worked alongside Randi in these productions. Randi stated, "I couldn't do this without them!"

CHAPTER ELEVEN
SYMPOSIUMS AND COLLOQUIUMS
2016-2023

The administration, faculty, and board members of Barclay College, and sometimes community members, met each summer as a visioning community to dream and plan for the future of the college. At the visioning community in June 2016, as the strategic plan for the college was considered, a concept that earlier had been discussed by the Bible and Ministry Division and approved by the division (March 4) and by the faculty (March 11) was presented. The idea was that it would be well for the college to create a way that research and exploration, by faculty and students, of Quaker writings and thought could be encouraged and dialogue with Friends be facilitated.

The idea was to create an institute, which would be named for the Quaker theologian, Robert Barclay, with the purpose to "give Robert Barclay's thought a vibrant place in campus life and to allow Robert Barclay and other early Quaker voices to speak effectively in today's world." The goals and aims of the Robert Barclay Institute were to be under the identity, mission, and strategic plan objectives of Barclay College. This institute would be made up of faculty, students, alumni, and affiliated interested scholars. The Institute was added to the college's Long-Term Plan on June 10, 2016.

An original statement describing the institute declared, "The Robert Barclay Institute is an organization created to encourage and broaden Quaker scholarship among Evangelical Friends. The Symposium is the Institute's vehicle for giving such research a voice with the intent of inspiring informed and passionate discussion."

Objectives for the institute were to:

- Research the early voice (writings) of our Quaker leaders.
- Articulate how the early Quaker movement speaks into today's culture.
- Reinvigorate evangelical expressions of historic Quaker faith and practice.
- Align contemporary social issues with evangelical Quaker faith and practice.
- Nurture vocational callings amongst evangelical Quaker Christians.

The faculty discussed the institute and made clarifications between the institute and other such entities in a faculty meeting on August 9, 2016—the college had recently adopted a colloquium to encourage academic research and sharing. The faculty did not want to have the two confused with each other. The colloquiums would entertain research and presentation of any worthy academic topic; the Robert Barclay Institute would share their research in symposiums. While topics for colloquiums could be from any discipline, topics for the symposiums were to be limited to topics germane to Friends history or beliefs. The first colloquium was held in November, 2016. The first symposium was in the Spring 2017. Dr. Derek Brown coincidently was the presenter for both. In a colloquium the presenter gave a presentation of their research and then generally had a time for questions and answers. Symposiums followed a pattern of a presentation followed by a formal response by another scholar, and then questions and answers.

A Robert Barclay Institute Board of Advisors was gathered and approved by the faculty on August 9, 2016. The members were: Royce Frazier, Derek Brown, Dave Kingrey, Jared Ross, Aaron Stokes, Jesse Penna, Glenn Leppert, and Director—Kevin Mortimer. The Board had their first official meeting on January 27, 2017. The inaugural Robert Barclay Institute Symposium was on Saturday, March 4, 2017 with Derek Brown as presenter, and Aaron Stokes as the responder. The lengthy title of the presentation was, "All Are One in Christ Jesus: the Social Justice Actions of Early Quakers as an Example to Contemporary American Evangelicalism."

The second symposium was held on Tuesday, September 12, 2017, with Brockie Follette presenting and Jesse Penna, responding. Brockie shared "An Exploration of "Calling" Among Friends Students." The next symposium was in the spring and was a presentation by a recent Barclay graduate, Nate Perrin. Nate spoke on, "The Gospel of Kashkawa: A Call to Peace" in which he shared about being part of a peace envoy in the Middle East. Jesse Waller, also a recent graduate who was serving as a prison chaplain, was the respondent. Dr. Dave Williams did the Fall 2018 symposium speaking about "Rhythms of Grace" with Manuel Garcia responding. The Spring 2018 presentation was by Barclay Board member, and teacher, Chelle Leininger, considering the topic "From Trauma to Resilience Through Relationships." The next symposium was again by Nate Perrin this time with the title, "The Peace of Christ: Peacemaking in Syriac Orthodoxy & Friends Theology." The one to respond was Aaron Kick, like Nate a recent graduate of the college. On October 24, 2019, Dr. Glenn Leppert presented "Virtue and a More Perfect Union." He explored the concept of virtue as a characteristic of Friends. Dr. Gene Pickard responded. For Fall 2020 Dr. Glenn Leppert gave a synopsis of his recent book, *The Heart of Friends; Quaker History and Beliefs*, and in very summary fashion outlined Quaker history.

Rather than responding to Glenn's presentation, Dr. Dave Kingrey, who contributed to the book, outlined the significant beliefs of Friends. For Fall 2021, Kevin Mortimer spoke about, "The

Christian Heart of Quakerism" which was a synopsis of his graduate thesis. Dr. Jim Le Shana responded. The most recent symposium to the writing of this book was in March 2022 by three presenters, Aaron Stokes, Dr. Debby Thomas, Dean of the College of Business at George Fox University, and Barclay student, Jakob O'Brien, titled "Countering the Secular When it Invades the Sacred."

During this time six colloquiums were presented. The first was presented in the Fall 2016 by Dr. Derek Brown who shared concerning the pastoral system among Friends, "A Friendly Ecclesiology: an Exploration of Pastoral Theology in American Quakerism." The next was a presentation in March 2017, by Dr. Jared Ross on "Renewing Corporate Worship: a Framework for Friends." Dr. Jim Le Shana presented the history of early Friends in North Carolina, "A New View of History of Quakerism: Friends in Colonial North Carolina." For Spring 2018, Dr. Glenn Leppert shared a study of the infamous Order #11 issued by General Thomas Ewing in the border conflict between Kansas and Missouri during the American Civil War. The paper was titled, "Something Desperate: the Infamous Order #11." The Fall 2018 colloquium featured was Kevin Mortimer sharing a paper "Soteriology and Theosis as Prognosis: What Will Become of the Church in the Midst of Missional Challenges?" As can be seen by the titles the distinction between symposium and colloquium was not always followed.

CHAPTER TWELVE
THE FUTURE
2023-

The observant reader has surely picked up a repeated theme in the pages just read. They have noticed the many times the words same, change, and remain have been used to describe Barclay College.

- While the college has changed its name twice, it has never changed its focus.
- The purpose for the college stated in the 1930 catalog at the time of the first name change remained the same as the statement of purpose in each of the earlier catalogs.
- This name change did not change the purpose of the college.
- The current statement of mission for Barclay College is the same: "The mission of Barclay College is to prepare students in a Bible-centered environment for effective Christian life, service, and leadership."
- Second, changing the name would in no way change the purpose and mission of the college.
- The MATL in Professional Studies promoted the same overall aim as the Spiritual Formation track—to equip men and women for effective Christian life, service, and leadership.

- Has the mission of the college changed since its founding? This short paper suggests that it has not.
- There was a strong commitment to remain as a member of AABC. Second, changing the name would in no way change the purpose and mission of the college.
- The author concludes that Barclay has remained true to the founding purpose. The reasons for establishing this small college on the prairies remain the reasons for continuing it today.
- Our partnership with our alumni and friends is a vital component that allows the college to remain true to its mission.

The commitment to remain the same, with the same focus, and the same mission foretells the future of the college. As long as Barclay keeps to the mission of preparing students in a Bible centered environment for effective life, service, and leadership the many blessings related in this volume will surely continue. Throughout Scripture there are many "if . . . then" statements. They nearly all have the same message—if one abides, remains, stays true, then God does likewise and pours out blessings just as he has done throughout the life of this college. May Barclay College abide in him!

APPENDIX 1
CAMPUS FACULTY FALL 1990 THROUGH SPRING 2023[224]

Lee Anders	F90 ...	FT, Business manager, business
Chris Anderson	F97-S01	FT, coach, ministry
Jeremie Anderson	S00-F00	athletics
Ray Anderson	F05-S16	history
Bernard Ashlock	F03-S10	psychology
Irwin Bales	S02	ministry
Traci Ballard	F16 ...	physical education
Jim Beeler	S01-F01	FT Dean of Students, athletics, ministry
Bruce Bell	S12	Bible
Jeff Blackburn	S92 ...	Bible, ministry
Karen Blasi	F16-S17	education (art)
Gail Boisseau	S21	education (art)
Charles Brodhead	F17-S19	basketball
Derek Brown	S11 ...	FT, Academic Dean, Bible, ministry
Kasey Brown	F03-S04	yearbook
DeWayne Bryan	F93-F93	soccer
Joyce Bryan	F19 ...	education
Royce Bryan	F09 ...	FT, Athletic director, athletics, history
Stanley Bryant	F07-F07	Bible science
Joshua Bunce	F09-S23	FT, Bible, ministry
Michael Burns	F02-F04	Bible
Jeff Carpenter	F99-F04	soccer
Jerry Clarkson	S03-F03	ministry
Mark Clodfelter	S10-F19	education
Curt Cloud	S97-S98	athletics
Marc Compton	S12-S13	ministry
Cheryl Couch	F12-S21	FT, education
Del Covington	F87-S95	FT, ministry
Sherry Covington	F93-F94	language
Isaac Cox	F20-F21	TA, Bible, ministry
Gary Damron	S06	history

---

[224] Faculty marked FT are full-time teaching administrators or full-time faculty. Those not marked are adjuncts. TA signifies teaching assistant. Semesters represent first semester of very first class and last; the range does not imply constant employment. Teaching areas are generalized categories.

Elmer Davis	S12-S14	math
Staci Derstein	F13-F15	education
Kenn Dirrim	S15	ministry
Clance Doelling	S06-S08	business
Alyssa Donelly	F03	education
Robert Ellis	F78-S07	aviation
Steven Elmore	F00-S03	FT, music
Lucy Entz	F22-S23	TA, Tch Friends
Doris Ferguson	S07-F10	science, holiness, missions
Willard Ferguson	S07-F10	science, holiness, missions
Jeanie Fitch	S94-F99	FT, math, science, ceramics
Amy Fleener	F96-S01	volleyball
Herb Flinkman	S98-S05	FT, Bible, apologetics
John Fly	S05	Bible
Brockie Follette	S18 ...	FT, Chaplain, Kaleo, ministry
Elkie Frans Burnside	S02-S03	yearbook
Herb Frazier	F11	FT, President, math
Jeremie Frazier	F02	science
Royce Frazier	F90 ...	FT, President, psychology
Dennis Fulbright	F06-S08	literature
Pamela Fulbright	F06-S08	FT, education
Tim Garrett	F01-S06	FT, Dean of Students, ministry
Tayler Gentry	F21	TA, math
Jeff Gillingham	S96-F96	athletics
Ron Ginther	F90-S91	FT, language
Steven Given	F98	soccer
Andrea Grace	F07-S09	drama
Karen Grossman	S90-S92	education
Ryan Haase	S10 ...	FT, various roles, leadership
Pat Hall	F09-S17	FT, Librarian
Adrian Halverstadt	F10 ...	FT, holiness, philosophy, justice
Elaina Halverstadt	F20 ...	language
Adrian Halverstadt III	S12	business
Duane Hanks	F22	piano
Kimberly Hansen	S21 ...	FT, nursing
Emily Harkness	F07-F11	FT, Librarian
Jonathan Harkness	F09-F11	Bible
John Harrell	F97	science
Charity Harvey	F19 ...	FT, Assessment, psychology
Ariel Haskin	S19-S21	education
Tim Hawkins	F08 ...	FT, Dean, language
Mark Hayes	F99-S00	psychology
Bruce Hicks	F84-S95	Academic Dean, Bible
Dorothy Hicks	F92-S95	FT, education

Bobby Hinderliter	S04	education
Tom Hinderliter	F88-S04	FT, Dean of Students, Bible, education
Jerry Hodges	S06-S11	Bible
Travis Hodges	F01-F02	soccer
Jack Holliday	F73-F91	FT, Bible
Will Hoving	S21	TA, critical thinking
Del Huff	F89-S92	FT, music
Sheldon Jackson	F93-S95	history
Nathan James	F05-F07	yearbook
Everett Jantz	F98-F07	philosophy
Kathy Jay	F90-F91	missions
Elizabeth Johnson	F22-S23	TA, Bible
Fred Johnson	F65-S09	holiness
Kendy Johnson	F09-S13	education
Michale Johnson	S21	TA, adjunct, admissions, Bible
Janet Johnston	F71-S96	missions
Mark Kelley	F90 ...	FT, Academic Dean, ministry
Kathleen Kellum	F95	general psychology
Dick Kelsey	S04	camping
Hannah Kendall	F06-S15	art
Lois Kendall	F99-F22	FT, psychology
Ryan Kendall	S03-F16	FT, Dean of Students, sports ministry
Roger Kerr	S08	language
Keith King	F95-S97	ministry
Steven King	F17 ...	FT, math, science
David Kingrey	S08-S21	FT, Institute, Bible, ministry
Sheila Knepper	F97-F00	math
Doug Kunsman	F92-F94	business
Judy Kunsman	S92-F93	physical education
Diane Lambrecht	S94	education (art)
Michael Landon	S98-S01	FT, missions
Lori Larsh	S19 ...	business
Jeanine Le Shana	F12-F18	music
Jim Le Shana	F12-F18	FT, Dean of Students, Bible, ministry
Kevin Lee	F09-S16	FT, Dean of Students, Bible, ministry
Chelle Leininger	S94 ...	FT, holiness, education
Jim Leininger	F72-S04	FT, math, science
Roberta Leininger	F72-F96	FT, Librarian, ceramics
Glenn Leppert	F85-S23	FT, Registrar, Bible, Greek, history
Jo Lewis	F85-S90	FT, language

Name	Term	Role
Larry Lewis	F13 …	FT, Public Relations, athletics, sports ministry
Brad Lingafelter	S05	basketball
Gregory Linville	F16-S17	ministry
Heidi Longstroth	F96-F01	FT, Librarian
Prosperly Lyngdoh	F04-S10	FT, missions
Manny Magana-Garcia	F16	ministry
Marvin Mardock	S01	youth ministry
Maggie Marsh	S22	TA, Bible
Megan Metcalf	F19-S20	TA, Bible, ministry
Mark Miller	S17-S20	FT, Registrar, Public Relations, music
Brian Mills	F01	general psychology
Walter Moody	F97	psychology
Ed Moreland	F97	education
Sylvia Morley	F96-S06	FT, language
Jason Morones	S04	youth ministry
Kevin Mortimer	S11 …	FT, missions, cross-cultural ministry
Michelle Murray	S15	Juniors Global
Chuck Mylander	S12	missions
Patrick Neifert	S95-F12	yearbook, ministry
Mark Newland	F02-S08	math
Wesley Norman	F97	business
Dave Ohlde	S98	science
Tricia Oren	F02-F08	language
Charles Orwiler	S01	Bible
Brandon Palmer	F22-S23	athletics
Jeanette Parker	F04-S06	FT, Librarian
Sarah Patterson	F94-S95	FT, Librarian
Skip Payette	F04-S09	FT, youth ministry
Abby Penna	F19	education (art)
Jesse Penna	S11 …	FT, youth ministry
Kim Pennington	S05	FT, Dean of Students, yearbook
Margaret Pent	F98-S00	FT, music
Nathan Perrin	S19	Juniors Global
Gene Pickard	F82-S23	Bible, ministry
James Pinkerton	F05	Bible
Anissa Potter	F15-F20	FT, Juniors Global, lang., educ.
Gail Pritchard	S91-F93	education
Jim Rahenkamp	F91-S93	FT, psychology, education
Savannah Read	F21-S22	TA, orientation, Bible
Delbert Regier	F04-F06	Bible
Viola Regier	S05-F05	education

Pamela Rhodes	S08	language
Erik Ritschard	F99-S03	FT, Academic Dean, orientation
Casey Roberts	F17 ...	media
Dave Robinson	F90-F96	Bible, ministry
Geoff Robinson	S94	basketball
Pam Roe	S94	music
Ron Roe	F97	general psychology
Paul Romosser	S91-S92	youth ministry
Jared Ross	F00 ...	FT, music
Jeannie Ross	F17 ...	FT, Librarian
Randall Rucker	F96-F97	Bible
Arden Sanders	F95	linguistics
John Sanders	S01	psychology
Michael Sanders	S16-S18	education
John Sarver	F91-S97	FT, youth ministry
Christine Savery	S21	Bible
Heather Sazama	F04-F05	education
Joyce Schmidt	F11-S12	piano
Mallorie Scott	S23-F23	education
Kate Semeniuk	S23	TA, Bible
Randi Shetley	F09 ...	FT, drama
Shane Shetley	S20-S21	athletics
Lauren Sill	S17-F21	sports ministry
Jerry Simmons	F08-F17	FT, math, science
Dorothy Simon	F09	business
Jeannie Sneed	F91-S92	language
Linda Snyder-Patterson	S15 ...	psychology
Christa Songer	F06-F08	Bible
Mary Spaulding	S01-F03	Bible
Jeff Starkey	S04-S06	ministry
John Steiner	F95-F96	FT, language
Pam Steiner	S96	yearbook
Nicholas Sterner	F18	Bible
Kayleen Stevens	S09 ...	FT, business
Kim Stewart	F07 ...	FT, music
Donald Stimpson	F99-F00	science
Aaron Stokes	F16 ...	FT, Registrar, Tch Friends
Steve Svoboda	F97-S98	FT, music
Mike Temaat	S10	FT, IT, computer
Susan Teske	S14-F16	language
Steve Teter	S11	business
Denise Unruh	S98	business
Kay Unruh	F13 ...	education
Karen Utt	S98	Bible

Tiffany Van Dame	S15	youth ministry
Joyce Veenstra	S05	education
Brian Wachtel	F02	volleyball
Robert Wambold	F03	piano
Ruth Ann Wedel	F00-F02	FT, Computer manager, education
Janet West	F06	language
Cathy Westerhaus	F97-F98	general psychology
Stacey Wheeler	F09-S16	FT, language
Tony Wheeler	F09-F15	FT, Blessing, speech
Ethan White	F19	TA, ministry
Keith White	F15-S22	FT, Assessment, psychology
Sheryl White	F95-21	FT, ministry
Nancy. Whiteman	F01-S02	volleyball
David Williams	F00-F21	FT, ministry
Jeremiah Williams	F14-S15	Bible, ministry
K. Williams	F96	psychology
Shelby Williams	F09-F22	FT, psychology
Elaine Worden	F92-F94	music

APPENDIX 2
ADVANTAGE! FACULTY
1996-2023

Jimmie Allen	S00	psychology
Lee Anders	S98-S04	business
Michelle Arbeleaz	F98-S00	psychology
Mitch Arbeleaz	F98-F02	church history
Ned Arthur	S11-S15	business
Joel Bardwell	F01-F05	Bible
Bruce Bell	S11	Bible, ministry
Donna Botinelly	F00-S01	psychology
David Breeden	S99	Bible
David Brookman	F03	business
Michael Burns	F02-F03	Bible
Ryan Carpenter	F99-F05	Bible
R. Justin Carswell	S05	Bible
William Clendineng	S11	Bible
Melba Cook	F99-F03	business
Herman Diaz	F07-S08	ministry
Doug Diel	F00-F04	psychology
Bryan Easley	F12-S14	Bible, church history
Ray Easley	S12-S14	Bible, missions
Leonard Eniss	F01-S04	Bible
Gregory Enos	F02-F04	Bible
Andy Flink	S10	Bible, church history
Herb Flinkman	F01-S02	Bible
John Fly	F04-S05	Bible, ministry
Tim Garrett	S03-FO3	life assessment
Elizabeth Griffin	S99-F03	business
Jonea Hartshorn	F02-F03	business
Mark Hayes	S00	life assessment
Jack Holiday	S10-S15	ministry
John Hunt	S00-F05	Bible
Gary Jones	F10-F12	ministry
Mark Kelley	S98-S99	ministry
Lois Kendall	S00	psychology
Stan Kenny	F98-S99	business
Sheila Knepper	S99	science
Michael Landon	F98-F00	Bible, ministry
Jason Le Shana	S15	Bible
Glenn Leppert	F96-F04	Bible
Jim Lund	F98-S03	psychology
Billy Manning	S98	psychology

Janyne McConaughy	S15	math
Dan Miller	S10	missions
Brian Mills	F01-F05	psychology
Howard Moffatt	S99-F00	Bible, ministry
Walter Moody	F98-F99	psychology
Kraig Moore	F98-F99	psychology
Sylvia Morley	S01	language
Don Mueller	S03-F03	church history
Sharon Norman	F01	ministry
Charles Orwiler	F01-S03	Bible
Marlene Pedigo	F10	Bible
Steve Pedigo	S10	Bible
Margaret Pent	F99	music
Steve Prieb	S99-F01	Bible
Erik Ritschard	F98-F02	life assessment
Paul Romoser	S13-S15	ministry
John Sanders	F99-S04	psychology
Anita Scarbrough	S99-F05	Bible, ministry
Jack Schultz	F99	business
Daniel Scott	S98-F03	business
Dianne Seibert	F04	psychology
Greg Smith	S10-F10	Bible, ministry
Mary Spaulding	S01-S05	Bible
Della Stanley-Green	S11	ministry
Jerry Storz	F99-F04	Bible, ministry
Stephen Talley	F98-S02	psychology
Hunter Taylor	S98-F05	psychology
Mike Thornburg	F10-S11	Bible, theology
Paul Till	F00-F01	business, life assessment
Becky Towne	S99-F05	Bible, ministry
Richard Troup	S01-F03	Bible
Kevin Ulmet	F98-S99	Bible, psychology
David Upp	S01-S02	Bible
Joyce Webb	F02-S04	psychology
Justin Weber	S10	Bible
CG White	S10-F11	Bible
Charles White	F00-S03	Bible
Sheryl White	F02-S05	Bible, ministry
Derek Wilder	S12	ministry
David Williams	F03-F05	ministry
Gene Williams	F03-S05	ministry
Carol Wright	S12-S15	ministry
Gary Wright	S11-S15	ministry
David Yocum	F00-F05	Bible

APPENDIX 3
ONLINE FACULTY
2008-2023

Name	Term	Subject
Ray Anderson	S11-S16	social science
Ned Arthur	S12	business
Bruce Bell	F12 …	Bible, ministry
Derek Brown	S14 …	Bible, ministry
Matt Chesnes	F10-S20	ministry
Lisa Christensen	S22 …	ministry
Paul Cochrane	S17 …	Bible, ministry
Cheryl Couch	F12-S19	education
Rick Darden	S10	ministry
Lucy Entz	F22	TA, Tch Friends
Brockie Follette	S18 …	ministry
Jeremie Frazier	S10	biology
Royce Frazier	S08 …	psychology
Brandie Freitas	F19	psychology
Laura Gallagher	F20 …	Bible
Ryan Haase	F15 …	leadership
Adrian Halverstadt	F09 …	Bible, ministry, justice
Elaina Halverstadt	F20 …	language
Adrian Halverstadt III	S13	business
Kimberly Hansen	S23 …	nursing
Tim Hawkins	F09-F20	language
Cameron Hays	F22 …	nursing
Gregory Hinshaw	F17 …	Tch Friends
Chay Howard	S20 …	justice
Morris Jones	F09-S12	psychology
Mark Kelley	S11 …	ministry
Lois Kendall	F15	psychology
Ryan Kendall	S16	ministry
Jon Kershner	F12 …	theology
Steven King	S18 …	science
Arden Kinser	F09 …	Bible, ministry
Lori Larsh	S19 …	business
Marius Lazau	S19 …	business
Jason Le Shana	S14-S18	Bible
Jim Le Shana	S18-S20	Bible, ministry
Kevin Lee	F09-F22	Bible, ministry
Glenn Leppert	S09-S22	Bible, ministry, history
Larry Lewis	F16	sports ministry
John Luton	F21	Bible
Prosperly Lyngdoh	F09	missions

David Mabry	F15 ...	ministry
Trent Maggard	F21 ...	justice
Steven Mann	F13 ...	Bible
Janyne McConaughy	S15 ...	education
Lora Meredith	F05-S20	language
Chris Phillips	F14-F14	language
David Phillips	S17 ...	ministry
Gene Pickard	F17	Bible
Patricia Pope	S11-S13	Bible, speech
Roger Powell	S11-S13	math
Laurie Reinhart	S16 ...	business
Paul Romoser	F15 ...	ministry
Jared Ross	F10-F22	music
Michael Sanders	F16	education
Paul Shelton	S14-S15	business
Shane Shetley	S21 ...	ministry
Jerry Simmons	S14-S17	science
Marie Smith	F12-S15	business, history
Mason Smith	F22 ...	orientation
Linda Snyder-Patterson	F13 ...	psychology
Benjamin Staley	S15 ...	Bible, ministry
Kayleen Stevens	S14 ...	business
Aaron Stokes	S17 ...	orientation, Tch Friends
Mark Triplett	S13-S17	business
Sherry Ward	S23 ...	nursing
Angie Wetmore	F13 ...	orientation
Tony Wheeler	F15	speech
Keith White	F15-S22	psychology
Shelby Williams	F09 ...	psychology
Clifford Winters	F21	Bible
Elisha Wisener	S23 ...	research
Carol Wright	F18 ...	ministry
Gary Wright	F17 ...	ministry
David Yocum	S09-S10	Bible

APPENDIX 4
GRADUATE FACULTY
2011-2023

Alan Amavisca	S20	MAMM
Paul Anderson	S16 ...	Bible
Bruce Bell	F22 ...	MAPM
Curtis Blasiman	F22 ...	English Competency
Derek Brown	S16 ...	MAPM/MATL
David Byrne	S18 ...	MAMM
Matt Chesnes	F12-S20	TLSF/MAPM
Lisa Christensen	F21 ...	MATL/Applied Research
Diego Chuyma	F20	MAMM
Steve Cunningham	S21-S22	MABT
Wayne Evans	S18	MAMM
Mark Foster	S21	MABT
Carolyn Frazier	S21	Orientation
Royce Frazier	F11-F20	TLSF
Bill Galipault	S21 ...	MASO
Adrian Halverstadt	F11 ...	Theology
Elaina Halverstadt	F20 ...	Orientation
Thomas Hancock	F19-F21	Applied Research
Paul Hoffman	S21	MAFM/MAPM
Marva Hoops	F20 ...	MAFM/MAPM
Michale Johnson	F22 ...	Orientation
Jon Kershner	S16	MAQS
David Kingrey	F11-F21	TLSF/MASF/MAQS
John Knox	S23 ...	Theology
Daniel Kramer	F20 ...	MABT
Jim Le Shana	F12 ...	TLPS/MAMM/MAQS/Theology
Stanley Leach	S17-S21	MASF
Glenn Leppert	S20	Theology
Gregory Linville	F17-S20	MASO
John Luton	S20 ...	MABT
David Mabry	F18 ...	MAFM/MAQS
Manny Magana-Garcia	F22 ...	MASF
Steven Mann	F15 ...	Bible
Gloria Maquez	S21 ...	MABT
David Mercadante	F22 ...	MAQS/MAPM/MAFM
Kevin Mortimer	S12	TLSF
Folashade Oloyede	S22 ...	MABT
Deanna Oxner	S21 ...	MABT
Emmanuel Oyemomi	S21 ...	MABT
Gene Pickard	S13-F22	TLSF/MAMM/MAQS

Tim Roehl	F17	MAMM
Jared Ross	S18-S20	MAPM
Jeannie Ross	F20	Orientation
Rusty Savage	S23	MAMM/MAQS
Stacy Shawiak	S21	MABT
Paul Shelton	F13	TLPS/Applied Research
Ron Stansell	S17	MAMM/MAQS
Aaron Stokes	F16	Orientation
Kent Walkemeyer	S15	TLSF/MASF
Angie Wetmore	F14	Orientation
Tony Wheeler	S12	TLSF/MAFM
David Williams	S11	TLSF/MASF/MAPM
Clifford Winters	S21	MAFM/MASF
Keith White	F12	TLPS/Applied Research

Regular font = teaching field
All Caps = core classes for concentration

MABT	Master of Arts Biblical Translation
MAFM	Master of Arts Family Ministries
MAMM	Master of Arts Missional Multiplication
MAPM	Master of Arts Pastoral Ministries
MAQS	Master of Arts Quaker Studies
MASF	Master of Arts Spiritual Formation
MASO	Master of Arts Sports Outreach
MATL	Master of Arts Transformational Leadership
TLPS	Transformational Leadership Professional Studies
TLSF	Transformational Leadership Spiritual Formation

APPENDIX 5
GRADUATES OF THE COLLEGE
1990-2023

These graduate lists were built from the commencement programs for each year and thus reflect maiden names rather than married names. Also the lists will contain names of some students who were approved for graduation with outstanding requirements who may not have completed those requirements and thus are not technically graduates.

Graduates 1990

Bachelor of Arts

Brott, Ellen Marie	Eastlake, OH	Elementary Education
Brown, Anthony Daniel	Haviland, KS	Christian Missions
Ferguson, Pamela Nichols	Melba, ID	Bible
Puga, Socorro Horta	Mexico City, Mexico	Christian Missions
Stephens, Melvin Wayne	Argonia, KS	Pastoral Ministry

Bachelor of Science

Hernandez, Frank	Wagoner, OK	Elementary Ed.
Harvey, Brockie Renee	Wichita, KS	Christian Ministries
Lowry, Ronald Jay	Melba, ID	Christian Ministries
Martin, Karl N.	League City, TX	Christian Ministries & Business Administration
Ogstad, Brian Jerry	Caldwell, ID	Business Administration

Graduates 1991

Bachelor of Arts

Butler, Bruce Alan		Pastoral Ministry
Harrison, Kirk H.		Pastoral Ministry & Christian Ministry
Yater, Timothy Dwain		Pastoral Ministry

Bachelor of Science

Robinson, Geoffrey David		Youth Ministry
Roher, Tina Rae		Elementary Education
Roher, Thad Joseph Roher		Elementary Education
Tomp, Carmen Marcela		Christian Education

Graduates 1992

Bachelor of Arts

Chuyma, Diego T.	La Paz, Bolivia	Pastoral Ministry
Hearon III, David Miles	Hugoton, KS	Pastoral Ministry
McClaren, Thomas Edward	Damascus, OH	Pastoral Ministry
Nunnally, Evan R.	Mentor, OH	Pastoral Ministry

Bachelor of Science

Carlson, Amy Marie	Rock Springs, WY	Church Music
Fitch, Brian G.	Argonia, KS	Bible
Hinderliter, Heather Anne	Haviland, KS	Elementary Education
Kennison, Kimberly Ann	Edwall, WA	Elementary Education
Kyger, Anthony Wayne	Ridge Farm, IL	Bible Theology
Roe, Pamela (Neifert)	Haviland, KS	Church Music
VandenHoek, Logan (Kendall)	Haviland, KS	Christian Ministries

Graduates 1993

Bachelor of Arts

Crisp, David Asher	Haviland, KS	Pastoral Ministry
Hernandez, Carlos Huerta	Haviland, KS	Pastoral Ministry & Business Administration
Kunsman, Judith Marie	Haviland, KS	Business Administration
Schroeder, Bryan Scott	Paonia, CO	Bible Theology
Whitaker, Robert Dean	Newberg, OR	Bible Theology
Worden, Mark Standley	Houston, TX	Pastoral Ministry

Bachelor of Science

Bell, Kathryn Joan	Hutchinson, KS	Christian Education
Belt, Kathryn Lyn	Greenleaf, ID	Business Administration
Bolton, Melissa	Friendswood, TX	Elementary Education
Bontrager, Colleen	Kendall, KS	Business Administration
Brokar, Amanda	Greensburg, KS	Elementary Education
Chitwood, Lynnetta	Haviland, KS	Business Administration
Gillingham, Jeffrey	Rock Springs, WY	Christian Ministries
Hada, Jamie	Bartlesville, OK	Elementary Education
Hartig, Tena	Emporia, KS	Christian Ministries
Neifert, Patrick	Citrus Heights, CA	Christian Missions
Parker, Jodi	Wichita, KS	Elementary Education
Schroeder, Teri	Paonia, CO	Business Administration
Temaat, Michael	Pratt, KS	Youth Ministry
Teter. Steven	Greenleaf, ID	Business Administration
Trainer, Jackie	Friendswood, TX	Youth Ministry

Graduates 1994

Bachelor of Arts

Colfax, Gary	Talent, OR	Christian Missions
Howell, David	Talent, OR	Youth Ministry & Pastoral Ministry
Friedrich, Jeremy	Haviland, KS	Pastoral Ministry
Thomas, Danny	Coyle, OK	Pastoral Ministry

Bachelor of Science

Colfax, Christine	Talent, OR	Business Administration
Crowder, Laura	Mentor, OH	Elementary Education

Hickman, Darby	Goddard, KS	Elementary Education
Howell, Patricia	Grants Pass, OR	Elementary Education
Lee, Kevin	Wichita, KS	Business Administration
Libby, Deborah	Macksville, KS	Business Administration
Szamosi, Geda	Budapest, Hungary	Church Music
Temaat, Shannon	Bettendorf, IA	Christian Missions
Thomas, Carrie	Rock Springs, WY	Church Music
Winters, Gregory	Harper, KS	Youth Ministry

Graduates 1995

Bachelor of Arts

Boyd, Dana	Akron, OH	Business Administration
Carlson, Heather	Rock Springs, WY	Bible Theology
Cuevas, Brandon	Westminster, CA	Business Administration
Kneeland, Kevin	Carpinteria, CA	Business Administration
Moissant, David	Cleveland, OH	Pastoral Ministry

Bachelor of Science

Friedrich, Carrie	Silverton, OR	Elementary Education
Fugate, Regina	Ramona, OK	Business Administration
Fulbright, Mae	Kim, CO	Elementary Education
Gates, Charles	Haviland, KS	Business Administration
Harris, Michael	Rose Hill, KS	Youth Ministry
Metcalf, Jeff	Greenleaf, ID	Elementary Education
Neifert, Christy	Booker, TX	Christian Missions
Riggs, Rachelle	Pratt, KS	Elementary Education
Self, Chris	Lawrence, KS	Elementary Education
VandenHoek, Randy	Haviland, KS	Elementary Education

Graduates 1996

Bachelor of Arts

Gilpin, Nicholas	Hamilton, IL	Pastoral Ministries
Kasparie, John	Amelia, NE	Christian Missions & Bible Theology
Sorensen, Kris	Manly, IA	Pastoral Ministries
Whittaker, Ronald	Haviland, KS	Pastoral Ministries

Bachelor of Science

Fitch, Christina	Milo, IA	Christian Education
Durham, Deborah	Garden City, KS	Christian Missions & Spec. Children's Services
Holmes, Silfane	Manado, Indonesia	Christian Missions
Kneeland, Danette	Prather, CA	Christian Ministries
Lowe, Steven	Wickliffe, OH	Christian Ministries
Moyer, Scott	Macksville, KS	Christian Ministries
Shuck, Richy	Hugoton, KS	Christian Missions
Schuck, Betty	Minatitlan, Mexico	Elementary Education

Graduates 1997

Associate of Arts

Clark, Gary	Phoenix, AZ	Arts and Sciences
Gundling, Heather	Colorado Springs, CO	Arts and Sciences

Bachelor of Arts

Norlund, Cory	Escondido, CA	Christian Ministry
Velazquez Gastelum, J. Daniel	Wichita, KS	Pastoral Ministry
Zink, Mary Ann	Larned, KS	Pastoral Ministry

Bachelor of Science

Blackmore, Cheri	Van Wert, OH	Christian Ministry
Ellis, Jessica	Meridian, ID	Christian Ministry
Haase, Ryan	Ridge Farm, IN	Christian Ministry
Lowe, Scott t	Wickliffe, OH	Christian Ministry
Morones, Jason	San Antonio, TX	Business Administration
Ostrowski, Dean	Muscatine, IA	Bible as 2nd degree
Ostrowski, Susan	Muscatine, IA	Business Administration
Pinkerton, Anne	Escondido, CA	Christian Ministry
Pinkerton, James	Escondido, CA	Bible/Theology
Scott, Barbara	Minneola, KS	Christian Ministry
Smuck, Jeremy	Talent, OR	Christian Missions
Sorensen, Tamara K.	Northwood, IA	Bible/Theology

Graduates 1998

Associate of Arts

Davis, Janelle Lyn	Battle Ground, WA	Arts and Sciences
Smuck, Jannea Aileen	Alton, KS	Arts and Sciences

Bachelor of Arts

Becker, Christina Denise	Sherwood, OR	Missions
Jay, Michael David	Hutchinson, KS	Bible Theology
Myers, Kenneth Len	Derby, KS	Missions
Oren, Ronnie Howard	Jonesboro, IN	Pastoral Ministry

Bachelor of Science

Gundling, Jeremy Scott	Friendswood, TX	Youth Ministry
Leppert, Tricia Ann	Haviland, KS	Business Administration
Muhr, Adam J.	Hillsboro, OR	Youth Ministry
Pierce, John Charles II	Haviland, KS	Bible Theology
Sandstrom, Richard Michael	Greenleaf, ID	Business Administration
Sirkel, Tricia Rene	Penrose, CO	Business Administration
Stanfield, Christopher Wayne	Colorado Springs, CO	Youth Ministry
Thompson, Amy Lynn	Riverton, KS	Youth Ministry
Tucker, Tonya Joy	Seiling, OK	Christian Ministry
Winters, Kelvin Daniel	Harper, KS	Youth Ministry

ADVANTAGE! Bachelor of Arts
Devine, Stefanie   Larned, KS   Business Administration

ADVANTAGE! Bachelor of Science

Baugh, Cindy E.	Pratt, KS	Business Administration
Griffin, Elizabeth Grace	Larned, KS	Business Administration
Howell, Martha	Coats, KS	Business Administration
Huddleston, Cynthia Ann	Larned, KS	Business Administration
O'Connor, Theresa Lynn	Copperas Cove, TX	Business Administration
Pritchett, Kathy	Pratt, KS	Business Administration
Unruh, John W.	Haviland, KS	Business Administration

Graduates 1999

Associate of Arts

Alvarez, Eunice	Velasquez, Mexico	Biblical Studies
Brawner, Lynne	Arvada, CO	General Studies
Parker, Jeanette	Wichita, KS	General Studies
Phillips, Jennifer	Wichita, KS	General Studies
Pickard, Jason	Chiquimula, Guatemala	General Studies

Bachelor of Arts

Ballard, Traci	Haviland, KS	Business Administration
Demuth, Lawrence	Dodge City, KS	Business Administration
Haner, Carey	Riverton, KS	Pastoral Ministries
Haskett, Jason	Greenleaf, ID	Bible Theology & Youth Ministry
Hinderliter, Chris	Wichita, KS	Pastoral Ministry
Whiteman, Nancy	Haviland, KS	Missions

Bachelor of Science

Becker, Bruce	Newton, KS	Youth Ministry
Carpenter, Jeffrey	Wichita, KS	Youth Ministry
Snyder, Beverly	Woodward, OK	Psychology and Fam Studies

ADVANTAGE! Bachelor of Science

Bailey, Michael	Liberal, KS	Business Administration
Bensch, LaDonna	Seiling, OK	Christian Leadership
Bunker, Joni	Larned, KS	Business Administration
Burnside (Frans), Elkie	Dodge City, KS	Christian Leadership
Church, Elesia	Pratt, KS	Business Administration
Elliott, Sandra	Dodge City, KS	Business Administration
Herrmann, Mary Beth	Larned, KS	Business Administration
Kough, Sheila	Pratt, KS	Psychology and Fam Studies
Medina, Linda	Dodge City, KS	Business Administration
Miller, Kelly	Larned, KS	Business Administration
Moore, Calvin	Pratt, KS	Psychology and Fam Studies
Moore, Sharlet	Hot Springs, AR	Business Administration

Rader, Stephen	Oregon City, OR	Business Administration
Spurgin, Sabrina	Coyle, OK	Business Administration
Swafford, Shannon	Pratt, KS	Business Administration

Graduates 2000

Associate of Arts

Hughes, Anthony	Payette, ID	Arts & Sciences
Sugden, Liz	Auburn, WA	Arts & Sciences

Bachelor of Science

Factor, Arthur	Mulvane, KS	Youth Ministry
Livingston, Leah	Pratt, KS	Youth Ministry
Livingston, Daniel	Tacoma, WA	Business Administration
Phillips, Jennifer M.	Wichita, KS	Youth Ministry
Wood, Mica	Dickinson, TX	Youth Ministry

***ADVANTAGE!* Bachelor of Science**

Anderson, Jeremy	Shippensburg, PA	Psychology and Fam Studies
Croney, Judy	Dodge City, KS	Psychology and Fam Studies
Feril, Janet	St. John, KS	Business Administration
Gieswein, Ruby	Sharon, KS	Business Administration
Hamilton, Tamara	Ellsworth, KS	Psychology and Fam Studies
Haney, Rebecca	Larned, KS	Business Administration
Harris, Jerald	Mullinville, KS	Business Administration
Morgan, Wilma	Lakin, KS	Psychology and Fam Studies
Salyers, William	Ellsworth, KS	Business Administration
Salyers, Debra	Ellsworth, KS	Business Administration
Self, Archie	Gaffney, SC	Psychology and Fam Studies
Shaw, Thomas	Ellsworth, KS	Psychology and Fam Studies
Stevens, Marilyn	Pratt, KS	Business Administration
Stude, Marilyn	Larned, KS	Psychology and Fam Studies
Whitney, Keith	Fowler, KS	Psychology and Fam Studies

Graduates May 2001

Associate of Arts

Belland, Briana	El Dorado Hills, CA	General Studies
Browns, Joel	Kansas City, KS	General Studies
Fox, Elizabeth	Pratt, KS	General Studies
Lee, Tyrone	Dickinson, TX	General Studies
McGilberry, Sean	St. Louis, MO	General Studies
Penrose, Bryan	Arkansas City, KS	General Studies
Rusco, Stephanie	Caldwell, ID	General Studies
Smith, Rebekah	Wichita, KS	General Studies

Bachelor of Arts

Kelley, Nancy	Vancouver, WA	Bible Theology
Prather, Nicholas	Medicine Lodge, KS	Pastoral Ministry
Spurgin, Matthew	Pratt, KS	Pastoral Ministry

STILL SHINING

Bachelor of Science

Ballard, Marshall	Haviland, KS	Youth Ministry
Bashford, Kurt	Powell, WY	Business Administration
Bernardo, Deborah	Colorado Springs, CO	Christian Leadership
Briel, Theresa	Pratt, KS	Business Administration
Burke, Shannon	Valley Center, KS	Christian Sch Elem Educ
Burnett, Miriam	La Mar, CO	Christian Sch Elem Educ
Crain, Eric	Springfield, MO	Christian Sch Elem Educ
Embry, Richard	Fort Wayne, IN	Youth Ministry
Fitch, Mark	Argonia, KS	Business Administration
Foulk, Larry	Macksville, KS	Business Administration & Psychology and Fam Studies
Harris, Dori	Colorado Springs, CO	Business Administration
Haskett, Jason	Greenleaf, ID	Youth Ministry
Kellie, James	Larned, KS	Psychology and Fam Studies
Kelling, Michael	Dodge City, KS	Business Administration
Lantz, Heather	Dodge City, KS	Business Administration
Montes Eliza	Dodge City, KS	Psychology and Fam Studies
Morton, James	Dodge City, KS	Business Administration
Nath, Patrick	Garden City, KS	Psychology and Fam Studies
Odom, Mary	Colorado Springs, CO	Christian Leadership
Parker-Brown, Lois	Dodge City, KS	Psychology and Fam Studies
Reeves, Sandy	Wichita, KS	Psychology and Fam Studies
Rivera, Dennis	Brooklyn, NY	Christian Leadership
Sassaman, Acacia	Garden City, KS	Psychology and Fam Studies
Southammavong, Tony	Oklahoma City, OK	Business Administration
Tharp, Darren	Dodge City, KS	Business Administration
White, Laurie	Lyons, KS	Psychology and Fam Studies
Wise, Robert	Colorado Springs, CO	Christian Leadership
Yohn, Marilyn	Greensburg, KS	Psychology and Fam Studies

Graduates December 2001

Bachelor of Arts

Meehan, Jana	Colorado Springs, CO	Christian Leadership

Bachelor of Science

Belton, Bennie	Columbia, SC	Christian Leadership
Meyer, Erika	Colorado Springs, CO	Christian Leadership
Micheli, Karen	Pueblo, CO	Christian Leadership
Miller, Diana	Colorado Springs, CO	Christian Leadership
Moore, Cheryl	Pueblo, CO	Christian Leadership
Saunders, Joseph	Eliot, ME	Christian Leadership
Voelker, Clifford	Pawnee Rock, KS	Psychology and Fam Studies

Graduates May 2002

Associate of Arts

Gordon, Jolene	Colorado Springs, CO	General Studies
Yohn, Rebecca	Greensburg, KS	Associate of Arts

Bachelor of Arts

Bayouth, Sandra	Wichita, KS	Psychology and Fam Studies
Ewing, Melissa	Great Bend, KS	Psychology and Fam Studies
Martinez, Efrain	Dodge City, KS	Business Administration
Morford, Sheryl	Haviland, KS	Business Management
Rexroad, Amy	Rose Hill, KS	Psychology and Fam Studies

Bachelor of Science

Brown, Annette	Derby, KS	Psychology and Fam Studies
Brown, Toni	Citrus Heights, CA	Youth Ministry
Bunce, Joshua	Riverton, KS	Youth Ministry
Clark, Edward	St. John, KS	Psychology and Fam Studies
Coulson, Thomas	Larned, KS	Psychology and Fam Studies
Cox, Richard	Los Angeles, CA	Psychology and Fam Studies
Ekis, Ronald	Colorado Springs, CO	Business Administration
Fairchild, Sara	Garfield, KS	Psychology and Fam Studies
Fisher, Paola	Fayetteville, NC	Psychology and Fam Studies
Frazier, Stacy	Haviland, KS	Business Administration
Gean, Connie	Augusta, KS	Psychology and Fam Studies
Gobin, Kelley	Dodge City, KS	Business Administration
Gustafson Jim	Rock Springs, WY	Psychology and Fam Studies
Holopirek, Brenda	Dodge City, KS	Psychology and Fam Studies
Huang, Jack	Xiamen, China	Business Administration
Hughes, James	Hoisington, KS	Business Management
Jantz, Karen	Haviland, KS	Psychology and Fam Studies
Jensen, Eileen	Dodge City, KS	Business Management
King, Roger	Hays, KS	Psychology and Fam Studies
Kuykendall, Charles	Greenville, SC	Psychology and Fam Studies
McManus, La Una	Englewood, KS	Psychology and Fam Studies
Medved, Paul	Pueblo, CO	Bible Theology
Miles, Mary	Ellenwood, KS	Business Management
Morford, Michelle	Haviland, KS	Business Management
Morse, Christina	Maryville, TN	Psychology and Fam Studies
Mull, Pamela	Pawnee Rock, KS	Psychology and Fam Studies
Olson, Ronald	Miltonvale, KS	Psychology and Fam Studies
Pelzel, Susan	Larned, KS	Business Management
Penrose, Stacy	Silverton, OR	Psychology and Fam Studies
Penrose, Shawn	Bucklin, KS	Youth Ministry
Perez, Marilyn	Larned, KS	Psychology and Fam Studies
Redger, Kevin	Montezuma, KS	Psychology and Fam Studies
Ritschard, Greta	Haviland, KS	Psychology and Fam Studies
Smith, Sharlene	Kechi, KS	Psychology and Fam Studies
Steele, Vince	Pueblo, CO	Bible Theology

Tucker, Marc	Haviland, KS	Christian Sch Elem Educ
Turner, Brenda	Greer, SC	Psychology and Fam Studies
Uram, Carrie	Greenville, SC	Psychology and Fam Studies
Urbanec, Laura	Grand Island, NE	Business Administration
Van Nahmen, Kim	Offerle, KS	Business Management
Whiteman, Mark	Haviland, KS	Business Administration
Zeck, Julie	Greensburg, KS	Psychology and Fam Studies

Graduates December 2002

Bachelor of Arts

Nygren, Aaron	Sacramento, CA	Bible Theology

Bachelor of Science

Battles, Don	Cheyenne, WY	Bible Theology
Bowman, Scott	Houston, TX	Christian Leadership
Brannon, John	Bronx, NY	Christian Leadership
Dinh, Nichole	Dodge City, KS	Business Management
Doze, Marcina	Hoisington, KS	Psychology and Fam Studies
Ehrlich, Randall	Wichita, KS	Psychology and Fam Studies
Galaszewski, Janet	Colorado Springs, CO	Christian Leadership
Hall-Kleweno, Toni	Cimarron, KS	Business Management
Hoyt, Victoria	Salina, KS	Psychology and Fam Studies
Jones, Diana	Odesa, TX	Christian Leadership
La Rue, Heather	El Dorado, KS	Psychology and Fam Studies
McBride, Roy	Cheyenne, WY	Bible Theology
McKinney, Dianne	Lewis, KS	Psychology and Fam Studies
McWilliams, Sherri	Viola, KS	Psychology and Fam Studies
Orth, Jennifer	Larned, KS	Business Management
Seibel, Dianne	Kinsley, KS	Psychology
Shelton, Shirley	Hudson, KS	Psychology and Fam Studies

Graduates May 2003

Associate of Arts

Langden, Sandee	Sharon Springs, KS	Biblical Studies

Bachelor of Arts

Kuffel, Matthew	Sacramento, CA	Pastoral Ministry
Rodriguez, Sarah	Bixby, OK	Christian Leadership
Romano, James	Manitou Springs, CO	Bible Theology
Sack, Lisa	Hutchinson, KS	Psychology and Fam Studies
Sandstrom, Charity	Haviland, KS	Music & Pastoral Ministry
Taylor, Erletha	Colorado Springs, CO	Christian Leadership

Bachelor of Science

Atteberry, Larry	Larned, KS	Psychology and Fam Studies
Beemer, Angela	Dodge City, KS	Psychology and Fam Studies
Beus Cheri	Salina, KS	Psychology and Fam Studies

Boyer, Patsy	Greensburg, KS	Psychology and Fam Studies
Bunce, Marcy	Haviland, KS	Business Administration
Burns, Anita	Andover, KS	Psychology and Fam Studies
Calvin, Audrey	Dodge City, KS	Psychology and Fam Studies
Carpenter, Jennifer	Hutchinson, KS	Psychology and Fam Studies
Cousins, Jonya	Ellinwood, KS	Psychology and Fam Studies
Foster, Mike	Wichita, KS	Youth Ministry
Gadson, Larry	Ridgeland, SC	Christian Leadership
Gardener, Nicole	Great Bend, KS	Business Management
Hammeke, Kimberly	Great Bend KS	Business Management
Huggins, Benjamin	CO Springs, CO	Christian Leadership
Jamison, Lynda	Great Bend, KS	Business Management
Jones, Jeffrey	Pratt, KS	Business Management
Kempton, Marilyn	Pratt, KS	Business Management
Kennedy, Allen	Larned, KS	Psychology and Fam Studies
Kolterman, Brian	Kinsley, KS	Business Management
Landreth, Corey	Leon, KS	Psychology and Fam Studies
Lindal, Marlyn	Dodge City, KS	Psychology ad Fam Studies
Martin Gwen	Great Bend, KS	Business Management
Moore, Clifton	Kenansville, NC	Christian Leadership
Nusbaum, Beverly	Pratt, KS	Business Management
Ogollah, Celine	Nairobi, Kenya	Business Administration
Pierce, Olga	San Antonio, TX	Business Management
Prather, Jenelle	Medicine Lodge, KS	Christian Sch Elem Educ
Ray, Nicole	Lake City, KS	Christian School Elem Educ
Scarbrough, Joan	Pratt, KS	Business Management
Schwerdtfege, Patricia	Derby, KS	Psychology and Fam Studies
Shaw, Warren	Ellsworth, KS	Psychology and Fam Studies
Slaight, Jerry	Ellsworth, KS	Psychology and Fan Studies
Thompson, Marjorie	Haviland, KS	Psychology and Fam Studies
Wharton, Beth	Aurora, CO	Christian Leadership
Yohn, David	Pratt, KS	Business Management

Graduates December 2003

Bachelor of Science

Harrison, Eleanor	Colorado Springs, CO	Christian Leadership
Cephus, F. Cee	Larned, KS	Psychology and Fam Studies
Emeana, "Chi-Chi"	Wichita, KS	Psychology and Fam Studies
Foster, Christina	Minneapolis, MN	Psychology and Fam Studies
Simmons, Elizabeth	Wichita, KS	Psychology and Fam Studies
Staats, Shaleah	Greensburg, KS	Psychology and Fam Studies
Thompson-Williams, Loretta	Wichita, KS	Psychology and Fam Studies
Turner, Jennifer	Great Bend, KS	Business Management

Graduates May 2004

Associate of Arts

Bauer, Emily	Sedro-Woolley, WA	General Studies
Caldwell, Zakary	Walsh, CO	General Studies
Routon Farrah	Greensburg, KS	General Studies

Bachelor of Arts

Belasco, Michael	Arvada, CO	Christian Sch Elem Educ
George, Marvin	Greensburg, KS	Psychology and Fam Studies
Howard, Abigail	Saint Francis, KS	Youth Ministry
Kwiatkowski, Peter	Laurel, MD	Pastoral Ministry
Leppert, Emily	Haviland, KS	Christian Sch Elem Educ
Lugalia, Alfred	Nairobi, Kenya	Pastoral Ministry
Lugalia, Mabel	Nairobi, Kenya	Pastoral Ministry
Olson, Aaron	Brooklyn Park, MN	Bible Theology

Bachelor of Science

Aytes, Renelle	Great Bend, KS	Psychology and Fam Studies
Bauer, Dustin	Homedale, ID	Christian Sch Elem Educ
Bennett, Andrew	Wichita, KS	Psychology and Fam Studies
Byers, Linda	Dodge City, KS	Psychology and Fam Studies
Cobb, Gregory	Vancouver, WA	Bible Theology
Collom, Amber	Mazatlan, Mexico	Christian Sch Elem Educ
Cummings, Danny	Woodland Park, CO	Christian Leadership
Duggin, Thomas	Elizabeth, CO	Bible Theology
Freelain, Jamika	Wichita, KS	Psychology and Fam Studies
Fulbright, Lorraine	Pratt, KS	Psychology and Fam Studies
Gordanier, Byron	Wichita, KS	Psychology and Fam Studies
Hanson Serena	Wichita, KS	Psychology and Fam Studies
Haugaard, Joshua	Ellsworth, KS	Psychology and Fam Studies
Jones, Amy	Pratt, KS	Business Management
Jones, Kaylan	Glen Elder, KS	Psychology and Fam Studies
Lee, Tyrone	Alvin, TX	Business Administration
Musso, Jason	Bath, NY	Bible Theology
Nauertc Allison	LeRoy, KS	Psychology and Fam Studies
Ray, Jacqueline	Hutchinson, KS	Psychology and Fam Studies
Renner, Theresa	Haysville, KS	Business Administration
Routon, Ken	Greensburg, KS	Psychology and Fam Studies
Rust, Nichole	Sidney, MT	Psychology and Fam Studies
Skibbe, Connie	Newton, KS	Psychology and Fam Studies
Van Meter, Jessica	Brighton, CO	Christian Sch Elem Educ
Wiens, Marcia	Great Bend, KS	Psychology and Fam Studies
Wild, Roy	Fountain, CO	Bible Theology

Graduates December 2004

Bachelor of Arts
Kekoa, Curtis	Denver, CO	Bible Theology
White, Patsy	Stanwood, WA	Psychology and Fam Studies

Bachelor of Science
Kennedy, Lois	Larned, KS	Business Management
Stegman, Jerri	Offerle, KS	Business Management
Lundquist, Perry	Palos Verdes, CA	Bible Theology
Shields, Alton	Aurora, CO	Bible Theology
Farley, Anita	Cheyenne, WY	Christian Leadership
Milbattenler, Crystal	Littleton, CO	Christian Leadership
Miller, Peter	Littleton, CO	Christian Leadership
Nansel, Matthew	Westminster, CO	Christian Leadership
Goodwin, Velda	Greer, SC	Psychology and Fam Studies
Heath, Caleb	Wichita, KS	Psychology and Fam Studies
Webb, Ruthie	Greenville, SC	Psychology and Fam Studies

Graduates May 2005

Associate of Arts
Harding, Amy	Greenleaf, ID	General Studies
James, Nathan	Osawatomie, KS	Biblical Studies

Bachelor of Arts
Allred, Jeffry	Dayton, OH	Pastoral Ministry
Carpenter, Brad	Wichita, KS	Missions
Chambers, Amber	Great Bend, KS	Psychology and Fam Studies
Howard, Jason	Wray, CO	Pastoral Ministry
Huffstutter, William	Colorado Springs, CO	Biblical Studies
Kearns, Darin	Springfield, CO	Christian Leadership
Larsen, Brett	Colorado Springs, CO	Christian Leadership
Monaghan, Adam	Wichita, KS	Pastoral Ministry
Morin, Scott	Battle Ground, WA	Pastoral Ministry
Towne, Carly	Colorado Springs, CO	Bible Theology

Bachelor of Science
Adee, Stephanie	Caldwell, ID	Business Administration
Ankrum, Aaron	Colorado Springs, CO	Biblical Studies
Baker, Maria	Dodge City, KS	Psychology
Bradley, Leslie	Wichita, KS	Psychology
Bushman, Kevin	Littleton, CO	Biblical Studies
Carlson, Audrey	Rock Springs, WY	Youth Ministry
Chambers-Lesire, Carissa	Hutchinson, KS	Christian Sch Elem Educ
Delvo, Cindy	Pratt, KS	Psychology
Driskill, Amy	Wichita, KS	Psychology
Frazier, David	Haviland, KS	Music Ministry
Gresham, Laura	Valley Center, KS	Psychology and Fam Studies

STILL SHINING

Happle, Andrew	Towaco, NJ	Christian Sch Elem Educ
Herriges, Michael	Osawatomie, KS	Christian Leadership
Jamison, Jeffrey	Centennial, CO	Ministry Leadership
Jensen, Mary	Larned, KS	Psychology
Krier, Kerry	Holyrood, KS	Psychology and Fam Studies
May, Jason	Alva, OK	Business Administration
Patterson, Karen	Peck, KS	Psychology
Ross, Jadon	Haviland, KS	Youth Ministry
Studer, Sarah	Colorado Springs, CO	Biblical Studies
Thaut, Russ	Evergreen, CO	Bible Theology
Vanderploeg, Amber	Grinnell, IA	Music Ministry
Webb, Ruthie	Greenville, SC	Psychology and Fam Studies
Whitlock, Belinda	Oxford, KS	Psychology
Zeiger, Dava	Olympia, WA	Psychology and Fam Studies

Graduates December 2005

Bible Ministry Certificate
Collins, Bette "Jane"   Colorado Springs, CO   Bible Ministry Certificate

Bachelor of Theology
Gipson, Randall	Monument, CO	Biblical Studies
Knight, Wanda	Colorado Springs, CO	Biblical Studies
McClain, Donna	Colorado Springs, CO	Ministry Leadership
Melendez, Edgardo	Cayey, Puerto Rico	Biblical Studies
Pucci, Sara	Colorado Springs, CO	Biblical Studies & Ministry Leadership

Bachelor of Science
Preble, Relena   Greensburg, KS   Psychology and Fam Studies

Graduates May 2006

Associate of Arts
Bunce, Kara	Haviland, KS	General Studies
Gere, Jacob	Nampa, ID	General Studies

Bachelor of Theology
Cox, Theodore   Colorado Springs, CO   Biblical Studies

Bachelor of Arts
Goering, Karissa	Corn, OK	Business Administration
Hall, William "Pat"	Richland, WA	Bible Theology

Bachelor of Science
Allred, Michelle	Gap, PA	Psychology and Fam Studies
Batten, Andrew	Crestline, OH	Bible Theology
Caldwell, Zakary	Walsh, CO	Business Administration
Carlson, Aaron	Rock Springs, WY	Youth Ministry
Carlson, Nels Nathaniel	Huggins, MO	Church Music

Frazier, Megan	Miami, OK	Psychology and Fam Studies
Gilligan, Elizabeth	Savonburg, KS	Business Administration
Greene, Glenda	Great Bend, KS	Psychology and Fam Studies
Haley, Jared	Denver, CO	Music Ministry
Healy, Tara	Pittsburg, PA	Youth Ministry
Holton, Jennifer	Greenleaf, ID	Psychology and Fam Studies
Jensen, Sally	Great Bend, KS	Psychology and Fam Studies
Leake, Tavis	Wichita, KS	Psychology and Fam Studies
Melton, Thomas	Derby, KS	Psychology and Fam Studies
Peters, Rachel	Lincoln, NE	Youth Ministry
Preble, Relena	Greensburg, KS	Psychology and Fam Studies
Riggs, Anissa	Iuka, KS	Business Administration
Rogers, Cletis	Pearland, TX	Youth Ministry
Savage, Jennifer	Dodge City, KS	Business Administration
Van Meter, Jason	Brighton, CO	Youth Ministry
Williams, Josiah	Haviland, KS	Psychology and Fam Studies

Graduates May 2007

Associate of Arts

Fitch, Tessa	Kuna, ID	Biblical Studies
Custer, Shelby	Booker, TX	General Studies

Bachelor of Arts

Collins, Jewell	Upland, IN	Bible Theology
Korf, Sarah	Hanston, KS	Bible Theology
Leppert, Timothy	Haviland, KS	Business Administration
Roberts, Chelsea	Wichita, KS	Bible Theology
Williamson, Joel	Hastings, NE	Bible Theology

Bachelor of Science

Calderwood, Tamara	Whittier, CA	Christian Sch Elem Educ
Caldwell, Katrina	Corn, OK	Psychology and Fam Studies
Carlson, Annalisa	Huggins, MO	Christian Sch Elem Educ
Everhart, Heather	High Point, NC	Youth Ministry
Kind, Sarah Joan	Denver, CO	Christian Sch Elem Educ
Lesire, Sheldon	Silverton, OR	Christian Sch Elem Educ
Najjar, Samer	Aurora, CO	Biblical Studies
Ross, Travis	Haviland, KS	Business Administration
Smitherman, Kristopher	Haviland, KS	Youth Ministry
Therriault, Nicole	Pratt, KS	Business Administration
Williams, Shelby	Haviland, KS	Psychology and Fam Studies

Graduates May 2008

Associate of Arts

Mendenhall, LeAnn	Corona, CA	Biblical Studies
Reeser, Tahnee	Denver, CO	General Studies

Bachelor of Arts

Carlson, Nathaniel	Rock Springs, WY	Pastoral Ministry
Hodson, Martha	Lakin, KS	Missions
Linville, Eric	Douglass, KS	Pastoral Ministry
Pulido, Brandon	Citrus Heights, CA	Missions

Bachelor of Science

Bousman, Abigail	Arvada, CO	Psychology and Fam Studies & Youth Ministry
Bousman, Tyler	Arvada, CO	Youth Ministry
Bunce, Kara	Denver, CO	Christian Sch Elem Educ
Davis, Stacie	Ellsworth, KS	Psychology and Fam Studies
Harkness, Jonathan	Wichita, KS	Youth Ministry
Reeser, Keith	Springfield, IL	Youth Ministry
Schamberger, Justin	Alton, KS	Business Administration
Schlichting, Michael	Meade, KS	Christian Sch Elem Educ
Vance, Tyler	Caldwell, ID	Youth Ministry
Walworth, Joshua	Brighton, CO	Psychology and Fam Studies
Windorski, Jessica	Douglass, KS	Business Administration
Willems, Kate	Hutchinson, KS	Youth Ministry

Graduates May 2009

Associate of Arts

Binford, Seth	Wichita, KS	Biblical Studies
Coleman, Timothy	Central City, NE	General Studies
Rose, Nikkie	Lake Elsinore, CA	Biblical Studies
White, Andrew	Colorado Springs, CO	General Studies

Bachelor of Arts

Hancock, Sarah	Haviland, KS	Missions
Magana-Garcia, Manuel	Hutchinson, KS	Pastoral Ministry
Metzger, Timothy	Sacramento, CA	Bible Theology
Raber, Zane	Haviland, KS	Pastoral Ministry

Bachelor of Science

Gere, Jacob	Nampa, ID	Music Ministry
Hancock, Gabriel	Hugoton, KS	Music Ministry
Hollingshead, Stephanie	Douglass, KS	Bible Theology
Koerner, Joshua	Jacksonville, FL	Christian Leadership
Mareska, Michelle	Deadwood, SD	Psychology and Fam Studies
Oliver, Bryanna	Wichita, KS	Psychology and Fam Studies
Raber, Sarah	Haviland, KS	Psychology and Fam Studies
Rocha, Michele	Dodge City, KS	Business Management
Van Dame, Tiffany	Mentor, OH	Youth Ministry
Vance, Michael K.	Mt. Pleasant, IA	Youth Ministry

Graduates 2010

Certificate in Bible and Ministry
Mandujano-Contreras, Antonio   Newberg, OR   Bible Ministry Certificate

Associate of Arts
Brown, Jessica	Macksville, KS	Biblical Studies
Hinrichs, Adria	Temecula, CA	General Studies
Sullivan, Mindy	Wichita, KS	Biblical studies
Thiak, Georgina	Kathmandu, Nepal	Mission Nursing

Bachelor of Arts
Anders, Rebecca	Haviland, KS	Music Ministry
Brown, Derek	Macksville, KS	Bible Theology
Carlson, LeAnn	Haviland, KS	Business administration
Rose, Scott	Saginaw, MI	Pastoral Ministry

Bachelor of Science
Anthony, Dennis	Kirtland, OH	Psychology
Beck, Jason	The Woodlands, TX	Youth Ministry
Bousman, Cristine	Santa Ana, CA	Youth Ministry
Brunk, Kristy	Hesston, KS	Psychology
Goss, Cal	Henderson, TX	Business Administration
Hall, Julie	Richland, WA	Christian Sch Elem Educ
Hancock, Angela	Benson, AZ	Christian Leadership
Hayes, Barron	Hermitage, TN	Psychology
James, Alisha	Meade, KS	Music
Linville, Michael	Douglass, KS	Missions, and General Studies
Pfeifer, Dana	Russell, KS	Psychology
Roberts, Casey	Wichita, KS	Youth Ministry
Ross, Amanda	Rock Springs, WY	Psychology and Fam Studies
Routon, Farrah	Derby, KS	Christian Leadership
Schamberger, Jared	Natoma, KS	Business Administration
Wallace, Cynthia	Hastings, NE	Psychology
Woods, Timohy	Haviland, KS	Bible Theology
Yowell, Jaclyn	Hugoton, KS	Psychology and Fam Studies

Graduates May 2011

Certificate in Bible and Ministry
Velarde, Miguel   Woodburn, OR   Bible Ministry Certificate

Biblical Studies Certificate
King, Daniel	Georgetown, IL	Bible Studies Certificate
Trover, Paul	Dana, IN	Bible Studies Certificate
Trover, Ramona	Dana, IN	Bible Studies Certificate
Vincent, Kathy	Georgetown, IL	Bible Studies Certificate

Christian Leadership Certificate

Elliott, Dwight	Amboy, IN	Christian Leadership Cert.
Hensley, Martin	Greenfield, IN	Christian Leadership Cert.
Reeves, Joseph	Marion, IN	Christian Leadership Cert.
Smith, William	Greenfield, IN	Christian Leadership Cert.
Summers, Nathan	Greenfield, IN	Christian Leadership Cert.
Taylor, David	Franklin, IN	Christian Leadership Cert.
Vore, Jesse	Greentown, IN	Christian Leadership Cert.
Wright, Kathy	Greenfield, IN	Christian Leadership Cert.

Associate of Arts

Colliatie, Ashley	Wichita, KS	General Studies
Sanchez, Joshua	Magee, MS	General Studies
Williamson, Spring	Arkansas City, KS	General Studies
Zerger, Jacob	Derby, KS	Biblical Studies

Bachelor of Arts

Davis, Jesse	Winfield, KS	Pastoral Ministry
Healton, Julie	Wichita, KS	Missions
Healton, Mark	Sacramento, CA	Missions
Pence, Matthew	Harper, KS	Pastoral Ministry
Phillips, Cassandra	Wichita, KS	Missions
Tower, James	Silverton, OR	Pastoral Ministry

Bachelor of Science

Bailey, Brianna	Hutchinson, KS	Psychology and Fam Studies
Berry, Kathi	Mt. Pleasant, IA	Christian Leadership
Binford, Kimberly	Wichita, KS	Psychology and Fam Studies
Calson, Kyle	Arkansas City, KS	Christian Leadership
Coleman, Timothy	Central City, NE	Business Administration
Compton, Marc	Newton, KS	Youth Ministry
Copeland, Carla	Bucklin, KS	Psychology
Gallez, Hannah	Indianola, IN	Christian School Elem Educ
Haley, Cairistiona	Lochbuie, CO	Psychology
Henry, Andrew	Mt. Gilead, OH	Bible Theology
Jeki, Christina	Salem, OR	Christian School Elem Educ
Kelsey, Sarah	Hutchinson, KS	Psychology and Fam Studies
Lofgren, Ann	Haviland, KS	Christian School Elem Educ
Lopez, Carlos	Yorba Linda, CA	Business Administration
Mitchell, Marcus	Henderson, TX	Business Administration
Mullikin, Trent	LeGrand, IA	Music Ministry
O'Sullivan, Barry	Citrus Heights, CA	Youth Ministry
Richter, Samantha	Eastlake, OH	Youth Ministry
Rose, Nichole	Lake Elsinore, CA	Psychology and Fam Studies
Rose, Priscilla	Great Bend, KS	Psychology and Fam Studies
Sato, Makoto	Tokyo, Japan	Business Administration
Smith, William	Greenfield, IN	Christian Leadership
Snyder, Linda	Arkansas City, KS	Psychology
Switzer, Elisa	Coeur d'Alene, ID	Psychology and Fam Studies

Trunnell, Danae	Holland, MI	Psychology and Fam Studies
Trunnell, Eliot	Wilder, ID	Business Administration
Vanderploeg, Aaron	Grinnell, IA	Youth Ministry
Vanderploeg, Kayla	Arvada, CO	Business Administration
Wheeler, Isaac	Haviland, KS	Psychology and Fam Studies
Williams, Jeremiah	Haviland, KS	Bible Theology
Wright, Katherine	Greenfield, IN	Christian Leadership

Graduates May 2012

Associate of Arts

Breashears, Geoffrey	Tulare, CA	Biblical Studies
Brown, Hannah	Hayden, ID	General Studies
Konsky, Clara	St. Louis, MO	General Studies
Leininger, Andreia	Hugoton, KS	General Studies
Mull, Melissa	Coldwater, KS	General Studies
Palmer, Star	Burlington, IA	General Studies
Sullivan, Sarah	Universal City, TX	General Studies
Trunnell, Hannah	Greenleaf, ID	General Studies

Bachelor of Arts

Arnold, Darrell	Orange, CA	Pastoral Ministry
Merritt, Sue	Lone Wolf, OK	Pastoral Ministry
Spencer, Jesse	Lompoc, CA	Bible Theology
Stewart, Nash	Valley Center, KS	Bible Theology
Zerger, Erica	Strasburg, MO	Missions

Bachelor of Science

Anders, Barry	Pratt, KS	Business Administration
Blayney, Jill	Heyburn, ID	Psychology and Fam Studies
Collins, Sarah	Franklin, IN	Christian Leadership
Garrison, Patric	Eldora, IA	Youth Ministry
Hensley, Martin	Greenfield, IN	Christian Leadership
Hinshaw, Eliot	Haviland, KS	Worship Arts
Hunter, Caleb	Fairland, IN	Youth Ministry
Imsen, Claire	Denver, CO	Youth Ministry
James, Deborah	Osawatomie, KS	Christian Sch Elem Educ
Kachipapa, Vasco	Liongwe, Malawi	Christian Leadership
Macy, Emma	Union, IA	Psychology and Fam Studies
Newton, Jacob	Friendswood, TX	Youth Ministry
Osborn, Grady	Oxford KS	Christian Leadership
Reeves, Joseph	Greenfield, IN	Christian Leadership
Robinson, Crystal	Fountaintown, IN	Christian Leadership
Silva, Morgan	Rock Springs, WY	Psychology and Fam Studies
Summers, Nathaniel	Greenfield, IN	Christian Leadership
Taylor, David	Franklin, IN	Christian Leadership
Thomson, Linda	Larned, KS	Psychology and Fam Studies

STILL SHINING

Graduates May 2013

Associate of Arts
Becker, Stephanie	Denver, CO	General Studies
Butler, Katelyn	Glendora, CA	General Studies
Hays, Brianna	Fresno, CA	General Studies
Larsh, Jamie	Santa Cruz, CA	General Studies
Waller, Savannah Linville	Douglas, KS	General Studies
Mease, Titus	Union, WA	General Studies
Morin, Jennifer	Salem, IA	General Studies

Bachelor of Arts
Anders, Darin	Haviland, KS	Worship Arts
Austin, Sean	Wichita, KS	Pastoral Ministry
Helkenn, Amy	Lower Tonsina, AK	Psychology and Fam Studies
Johnson, Christopher	Benton, KS	Pastoral Ministry
Jones, Sharilee	Memphis, TN	Biblical Studies
Mardock, Timothy	Friendswood, TX	Bible Theology
Sanders, Ceress	Hutchinson, KS	Missions
Sanders, Samuel	Hutchinson, KS	Missions
Sterner, Michelle	Dewey, OK	Bible Theology
Sterner, Nicholas	Denver, CO	Pastoral Ministry

Bachelor of Science
Alexander, Geoffrey	Wichita KS	Youth Ministry
Becker, Matthew	Colorado Springs CO	Psychology and Fam Studies
Bowman, Zachary	Omaha, NE	Christian Sch Elem Educ
Brown, Adele	Haviland, KS	Christian Sch Elem Educ
Brown, Shane	Farmland, IN	Youth Ministry
Bush, James	Garfield, KS	Psychology
Climes, Artaya	Lawton, OK	Psychology and Fam Studies
Coleman, Caleb	Corona, CA	Psychology and Fam Studies
Cruse, Katie	San Dimas, CA	Psychology and Fam Studies
Day, Danielle	Oklahoma City, OK	Psychology and Fam Studies
Eadie, Russell	Manton, MI	Bible Theology
Eadie, Tacy	Wilson, KS	Sports Leadership & Psychology and Fam Studies
Gallez, Rebekah	Indianola, IN	Business Administration
George, Samantha	Haviland, KS	Psychology
Hatton, Toney	Irving, TX	Psychology and Fam Studies
Hays, Marsha	Cheyenne, WY	Psychology
Hinderliter, Casie	Wichita, KS	Sports Leadership & Psychology and Fam Studies
Imsen, Amanda	Cordell, OK	Psychology
Kendall, Shelby	Haviland, KS	Psychology
Linville, Kathryn	Wichita KS	Mission Nursing
Maselli, Deborah	Fairfield, IA	Psychology
McCarty, Janae	Pratt, KS	Christian Sch Elem Educ
Miller, Kaylee	Great Bend, KS	Business Administration

Mull, Melissa	Upland, CA	Psychology
Newton, Matthew	Friendswood, TX	Worship Arts
Patterson, Sarah	Los Angeles, CA	Youth Ministry
Rose, Brian	Haviland KS	Music Ministry
Shartzer, Kolbi	Yorktown, VA	Christian Leadership
Shepherd, Charity	Walsh, CO	Psychology and Fam Studies
Shetley, Shane	Fowler, KS	Biblical Studies
Simmons, Linda	Haviland, KS	Business Administration
Smidt-Helm, Paige	Woodland Park, Co	Christian Sch Elem Educ
Smith, Rachel	Great Bend, KS	Business Administration
Stokes, Aaron	Alliance, OH	Bible Theology
Wailes, Jonathan	Strasburg, CO	Youth Ministry
Wailes, Jonathan	Bennett CO	Youth Ministry
Willems, Jeffrey	Hutchinson, KS	Youth Ministry
Wilson, Ethan	Miami, OK	Youth Ministry
Wisener, Elisha	Limon, CO	Psychology and Fam Studies

Master of Arts

Berry, Kathi	Salem, IA	Spiritual Formation
Compton, Marc	Wichita, KS	Spiritual Formation.
Magana-Garcia, Manuel	Union, IA	Spiritual Formation
Robert Dwayne Hays	Fresno, CA	Spiritual Formation
West, Richard	Des Moines, IA	Spiritual Formation
Morin, Scott	Salem, IA	Spiritual Formation
Penna, Frank	Wichita, KS	Spiritual Formation
Ross, Jadon	Haviland, KS	Spiritual Formation
Smuck, Herschel	Mediapolis, IA	Spiritual Formation
Van Dame, Tiffany	Ashtabula, OH	Spiritual Formation

Graduates May 2014

Associate of Arts

Herbal, Elizabeth	Lakeside, AZ	General Studies
Howarth, Brandon	Dodge City, KS	General Studies
Lujan, Melynda	Caldwell, ID	General Studies
Maselli, Lucas	Fairfield, IA	General Studies
Wyss, Julianna	Colorado Springs, CO	General Studies

Bachelor of Arts

Fisher, Nathan	Haviland, KS	Pastoral Ministry
Fuentes, Isaac	Liberal, KS	Pastoral Ministry
Fuller, Nathaniel	Wichita, KS	Bible Theology
Platt, Caleb	Syracuse, KS	Bible Theology
Vance, Amanda	Coeur d'Alene, ID	Missions
Waller, Jessie	Caldwell, ID	Missions
Woodsmall, Morgan	Haviland, KS	Missions
Woodsmall, Sawyer	Haviland, KS	Pastoral Ministry
Zeiger, Kenneth	Haviland, KS	Bible Theology

Bachelor of Science

Auer, Joel	Alton, KS	Christian Sch Elem Educ
Augustenborg, Brittney	Reno, NV	Psychology
Brown, Amber	Riverside, CA	Biblical Studies & Psychology
Cochran, William	Fountaintown, IN	Youth Ministry
Duarte, Ben	Boise, ID	Biblical Studies
Fisher, Allissa	Haviland, KS	Psychology and Fam Studies
Garrison, Paige	Haviland, KS	Business Administration
Gray, Tracy	Fortville, IN	Christian Leadership
Gresham, Rochelle	Franktown, CO	Business Administration
Guthrie, Danyelle	Haviland, KS	Psychology and Fam Studies
Hinshaw, Jennifer	Miami, OK	Psychology and Fam Studies
Jaimes, David	Fullerton, CA	Bible Theology
Kendal, Nathan	Lompoc, CA	Business Administration
Maki, Mary	Fort Collins, CO	Psychology and Fam Studies
Maselli, Hannah	Fairfield, IA	Psychology
McKay, Richard	Hay Springs, NE	Christian Leadership
Mease, Hannah	Wilder, ID	Psychology
Miranda-Troup, Meghan	Portage, MI	Business Administration
Miranda-Troup, Porfirio	Arvada, CO	Business Administration
Moral, Brandi	Ulysses, KS	Business Administration
Newton, Leah	Meridian, ID	Psychology
Pachal, Hannah	Arvada, CO	Biblical Studies
Palmer, Brandon	Newton, KS	Business Administration
Reyes, Omar	Hugoton, KS	Psychology and Fam Studies
Ringwald, Mattie	Bucklin, KS	Business Administration
Roush, Theresa	Greenfield, IN	Christian Leadership
Sanchez, Joshua	Magee, MS	Sports Leadership
Shipley, David	Berthoud, OH	Psychology
Spencer, Jacob	Lompoc, CA	Business Administration
Starnes, John	Haviland, KS	Bible Theology
Sullivan, Sarah	Universal City, TX	Sports Leadership
Sulzbach, Marki	Branson, MO	Psychology
Tarver, Cullen	Haviland, KS	Business Administration
Thornburg, Heather	Potwin, KS	Psychology and Fam Studies
Varela, Kimberly	Houston, TX	Christian Sch Elem Educ
Vore, Jesse	Greentown, IN	Christian Leadership
Welter, Keaghan	Chandler, OK	Christian Sch Elem Educ
Williams, Hannah	Haviland, KS	Bible Theology

Master of Arts

Arnold Darrell	Haviland, KS	Spiritual Formation
Bryan, Ronald	Oskaloosa, IA	Professional Studies
Campbell, Neil	Calgary, AB, Canada	Professional Studies
Christensen, Lisa	Haviland, KS	Professional Studies
Haase, Ryan	Haviland, KS	Professional Studies
Haley, Jared	Salem, IA	Spiritual Formation
Hinshaw, Donald	Haviland, KS	Spiritual Formation
Kuffel, Matthew	Denair, CA	Spiritual Formation

Reich, Mark	Beloit, OH	Professional Studies
Ridley, Jeremy	Commerce City, CO	Spiritual Formation
Showalter, Thomas	Barberton, OH	Professional Studies
Summers, Nathaniel	Greenfield, IN	Professional Studies
Wharton, Jonas	Aurora, CO	Spiritual Formation
Williams, Jeremiah	Haviland, KS	Spiritual Formation

Graduates 2015

Associate of Arts

Cox, Abbey	Derby, KS	General Studies
Franco, Dallas	Lakin, KS	General Studies
Gray, Robbie	McCloud, OK	General Studies
Klein, Grace	Rock Springs, WY	General Studies
Leininger, Kaitlyn	Hugoton, KS	General Studies
Mardock, Shelby	Hutchinson, KS	General Studies
Palmer, Dylan	Newton, KS	General Studies

Bachelor of Arts

Arnold, Justin	Haviland, KS	Pastoral Ministry
Branson, Patricia	Haviland, KS	Education K-6
Clark, Bobby	Longmont, CO	Pastoral Ministry
Goodwin, Renee	Neodesha, KS	Biblical Studies
Harris, Tracy (Skip)	Red Banks, MS	Bible Theology
Kirkbride, Kathleen	El Dorado, KS	Missions
Read, Christopher	Newton, KS	Pastoral Ministry
Zeiger, Christi Anne	Haviland, KS	Bible Theology

Bachelor of Science

Barber, Nicolas	Salem, IA	Sports Leadership
Blanton, Derek	Colorado Springs, CO	Biblical Studies
Butler, Katelyn	Friendswood, TX	Psychology
DeRemer, Chandra	Freeman, MO	Business Administration
Dyson, Amanda	Kinsley, KS	Business Administration
Freitas, Brandie	Haviland, KS	Psychology and Fam Studies
Freitas, David	Haviland, KS	Youth Ministry
Graham, Antonio	Baltimore, MD	Business Administration
Gressel, Danielle	South Haven, KS	Business Administration
Herriges, Michael	Osawatomie, KS	Christian Leadership
Huiatt, Spencer	Weatherford, OK	Business Management
Hunter, Megan	Randleman, NC	Christian Leadership
Kershner, Kaylee	Great Bend, KS	Business Administration
Konsky, Clara	O'Fallon, MO	Psychology and Fam Studies
Maggard, Ginger	Haviland, KS	Business Administration
Mullikin, Tyler	LeGrand, IA	Worship Arts
Nolen, David	Indianapolis, IN	Christian Leadership
Ogle, Austin	Haviland, KS	Youth Ministry
Richmond, Angela	Aurora, CO	Business Administration
Schuck, Chelsea	Haviland, KS	Psychology and Fam Studies

Shuck, Kaelin	Liberal, KS	Education K-6
Spiegle, Joseph	Aurora, CO	Youth Ministry
Stander, Morgan	Omaha, NE	Sports Leadership
Vance, Michael	Haviland, KS	Youth Ministry
Workman, Stacie	Melba, ID	Psychology

Master of Arts

Albertini, Anthony	Van Alstyne, TX	Spiritual Formation
Bousman, Bonnie	Denver, CO	Spiritual Formation
Brown, Shane	Farmland, IN	Spiritual Formation
Herriges, Michael	Osawatomie, KS	Professional Studies
Kachipapa, Vasco	Liongwe, Malawi	Professional Studies
Nuako, Rose	Sandy Bay, NY	Spiritual Formation
Reeves, Joseph	Marion, IN	Professional Studies
Robinson, Crystal	Fountaintown, IN	Spiritual Formation
Shartzer, Kolbi	Yorktown, VA	Professional Studies
Stewart, Rodney	Dayton, OH	Professional Studies
Kathy Wiebe	Wichita, KS	Professional Studies

Graduates 2016

Associate of Arts

Bachert, Rachel	Two Buttes, CO	General Studies
Barber, Sean	Westminster, CO	General Studies
Entz, Nicholas	Valley Center, KS	General Studies
Lofgren, Bethany	Haviland, KS	General Studies
Maloney, Adrian	Wichita, KS	General Studies
Milton, Jaqualion	Paris, TX	General Studies
Morin, Brianna	Argonia, KS	General Studies
Rohde, Hannah	Denver, CO	General Studies
Stovall, Paul	Wichita, KS	General Studies

Bachelor of Arts

Kellum, Lauren	Halstead, KS	Missions
Lujan, Joy	Caldwell, ID	Business Management
Price, Ruth	Rozel, KS	Bible Theology
Wells-Lee, Amanda	Wichita, KS	Psychology

Bachelor of Science

Arnott, Jennifer	Greenfield, IN	Psychology
Dudley, Howard	Kennard, IN	Bible Theology
Edenborough, Shandy	Goodwell, OK	Business Administration
Entz, Emily	Valley Center, KS	Business Administration
Franklin, Donna	Greenfield, IN	Christian Leadership
Friesen, Susan	Hydro, OK	Business Administration
Gutshall, India	Yuma, CO	Youth Ministry
Hall, Preston	Corona, CA	Business Administration
Herbel, Elizabeth	Lakeside, AZ	Business Administration

Maggard, Trent	Woodward, OK	Business Administration
Mendenhall, Scott	Corona, CA	Business Management
Miller, David	Kotzebue, AK	Business Management
Miller, Sarah	Kotzebue, AK	Business Management
Morin, Jennifer	Vancouver, WA	Youth Ministry
Ogle, Katelyn	Wichita, KS	Worship Arts
Pribble, Jacob	Chandler, OK	Business Management
Racchini, Christopher	Rose Hill, KS	Education K-8
Smedley, Sharese	LeGrand, IA	Psychology and Fam Studies
Smith, Jeremy	Edmond, OK	Business Administration
Switzer, Kalyn	Weatherford, OK	Business Administration
Tarver, Rachel	Melba, ID	Psychology
Thompson, Samuel	Wichita, KS	Business Administration
Tracy, Kevin	Oakland, CA	Psychology and Fam Studies
Trad, Philip	St. Louis, MO	Youth Ministry
Young, Caitlin	Russell, KS	Youth Ministry

Master of Arts

Roy Dale Bogan	Hugoton, KS	Spiritual Formation
Daniel Duncan Cale	Hughesville, PA	Professional Studies
Martha Sue Hodson	Lakin, KS	Spiritual Formation
Dennis McDowell	Fowler, KS	Spiritual Formation
Richard Earl McKay	Hay Springs, NE	Spiritual Formation
James H. Moreland	Carthage, IN	Spiritual Formation
Michelle Susanne Murray	Orange, CA	Spiritual Formation
Janine Cross Saxton	Richmond, IN	Spiritual Formation
Sawyer Duane Woodsmall	Marshalltown, IA	Spiritual Formation
Kenneth Edward Zeiger	Grand Rapids, MI	Professional Studies

Graduates 2017

Associate of Arts

Arnold, Kenneth	Lawton, OK	General Studies
Brown, Hannah	Haviland, KS	General Studies
Fitch, Rebekah	Argonia, KS	General Studies
Herbers, Taylor	Wichita, KS	General Studies
Kearns, Christy	Colorado Springs, CO	General Studies
Kick, Karli	Haviland, KS	General Studies
Martin, Joshua	Wyandotte, OK	General Studies
Morales, Joseph	Wichita, KS	General Studies
Priebe, David	Rose Hill, KS	General Studies

Bachelor of Arts

Collick, Marcus	Salisbury, MD	Pastoral Ministry
Lujan, Joy	Caldwell, ID	Christian Leadership
Naillieux, Kimberlee	Derby, KS	Missions
Perrin, Nathan	Haviland, KS	Pastoral Ministry

Bachelor of Science

Andre, Jessica	Castle Rock, CO	Bible Theology
Bennett, Bethany	Sharon, KS	Youth Ministry
Bradley Jr., Jay	Wichita, KS	Sports Leadership
Brodhead, Charles	Riverside, CA	Sports Leadership
Colliatie, Aaron	Wichita, KS	Education K-6
Dahmer, Justin	Aurora, CO	Business Administration
Epp, Raelyn	Corn, OK	Business Administration
Fitzer, Shelby	Haven, KS	Business Management
Graham, Tiffany	Newberg, OR	Education K-6
Haack, Breanna	Branson, MO	Education K-6
Hernandez, Federico	Allentown, PA	Biblical Studies
Holliday, Tanner	Wilkinson, IN	Youth Ministry
Hooper, Karina	Haviland, KS	Psychology and Fam Studies
Huck, Tanner	Coldwater, KS	Sports Leadership
Humbert, Jonathan	Brighton, CO	Business Administration
Imada, Belinda	Prescott, AZ	Biblical Studies
Jarrell, Matthew	Brush, CO	Sports Leadership
Klotz, Sierra	Hamburg, NJ	Psychology and Fam Studies
Lee, Kristen	Blairsville, GA	Psychology and Fam Studies
Lujan, Melynda	Caldwell, ID	Education K-6
Malone-Fontenot, Vernell	Houston, TX	Biblical Studies
Miller, David	Palmer, AK	Business Management
Miranda-Troup, Porfirio	Haviland, KS	Business Administration
Moore, Angela	Augusta, KS	Psychology and Fam Studies
Munsell, Amber	Newton, KS	Psychology and Fam Studies
Newby, Brenton	Wichita, KS	Psychology and Fam Studies
Nicholson, Ezra	Valley Center, KS	Business Administration
Palmer, Samantha	Wichita, KS	Education K-6
Read, Abbey	Derby, KS	Education K-6
Simpson, Dawn	Houston, TX	Christian Leadership
Troyer, Tristin	Phillipsburg, KS	Business Management
Vanderploeg, Nathaniel	Grinnell, IA	Youth Ministry
Vaughan, Ashley	Ponca City, OK	Business Administration

Master of Arts

Blanton, Derek	Colorado Springs, CO	Spiritual Formation
Close, Matthew	Mt. Pleasant, OH	Quaker Studies
Fisher, Nathan	Spokane, WA	Pastoral Ministry
Follette, Brockie	Haviland, KS	Family Ministries
Fuller, Nathaniel	Wichita, KS	Spiritual Formation
Gillingham, Jeff	Prather, CA	Transformational Leadership
Hepner, Daniel	Mechanicsburg, PA	Pastoral Ministry
Hinderliter, Chris	Melba, ID	Family Ministries
Hubbel, Jillian	Turlock, CA	Transformational Leadership
Kelsey, Sarah	Hutchinson, KS	Family Ministries
Kregar, Whitney	Greensburg, KS	Family Ministries
Lujan, Joy	Caldwell, ID	Quaker Studies
McKinley, Kathryn	Indianapolis, IN	Spiritual Formation

Miranda-Troup, Porfirio	Arvada, CO	Transformational Leadership
Penrose, Shawn	Arkansas City, KS	Family Ministries
Penrose, Stacy	Silverton, KS	Family Ministries
Read, Christopher	Haviland, KS	Spiritual Formation
Stander, Morgan	Omaha, NE	Transformational Leadership
Stokes, Aaron	Haviland, KS	Quaker Studies

Graduates 2018

Associate of Arts

Adams, Ryan	Newton, KS	General Studies
Carrasco, Leilani	Forgan, OR	General Studies
Easterwood, Sarah	Rolla, KS	General Studies
Haines, Kathryn	Haviland, KS	General Studies
Maloney, Mykeydran	Wichita, KS	General Studies
Thompson, De'Andrae	Compton, CA	General Studies
Willard, Taylor	Pratt, KS	General Studies
Zuercher, Garrett	Newton, KS	General Studies

Bachelor of Arts

Kellum, Corbin	Burlison, TN	Pastoral Ministry
Skinner, Benjamin	La Center, WA	Pastoral Ministry
Shugart, Scott	Castle Rock, CO	Christian Leadership

Bachelor of Science

Altvater, Aaron	Hutchinson, KS	Missions Bi-vocational
Astleford, Katelyn	Tillamook, OR	Psychology
Barber, Shane	Westminster, CO	Youth Ministry
Burnett, Brandee	Peabody, KS	Business Management
Burnett, Isaac	Peabody, KS	Christian Leadership
Chance, Ethan	Pueblo, CO	Bible Theology
Daniels, Jordan	Pittsburg, KS	Youth Ministry
Donoho, Amber	Kansas City, MO	Psychology and Fam Studies
Hibler, Cole	Miami, OK	Sports Leadership
Ivie, Sarah	Riverton, WY	Business Management
Jacks, Erica	Haviland, KS	Business Administration
Kearns, David	Eudora, KS	Business Administration
King, Kaitlyn	Bend, OR	Biblical Studies
Leach, Thomas	Derby, KS	Business Administration
LeMonds, Nicholas	Newberg, OR	Bible Theology
Lothman, April	Sharon, KS	Bible Theology
Lynch, Akia	Denver, CO	Psychology
Magnuson, Bethany	Haviland, KS	Worship Arts
Maloney, Adrian	Wichita, KS	Sports Leadership
McDonald, Peter	Boston, MA	Business Administration
Milton, Jaqualion	Paris, TX	Business Administration
Morin, Kimberly	Woodland, WA	Psychology
Murphy, Christina	Fort Worth, TX	Christian Leadership
Neal, Terri	Fortville, IN	Christian Leadership

Palmer, Rebekah	Bethlehem, NH	Worship Arts
Stephens, Andrew	Newberg, OR	Psychology and Fam Studies
Stovall, Paul	Bel Aire, KS	Business Administration
Vanderploeg, Katrina	University Park, IA	Education K-6
White, Hannah	Huggins, MO	Education K-6
White, Ossie	Hazard, KY	Psychology

Master of Arts

Beuoy, Deborah	Great Bend, KS	Spiritual Formation
Brinkley, Joelle	St. Louis, MO	Family Ministries
Cochran, Ryan	Raytown, MO	Family Ministries
Dudley, Howard	Spencerville, OH	Spiritual Formation
Harris, Tracy	Parker, CO	Spiritual Formation
May, Joseph	St. Louis, MO	Pastoral Ministry
Mullikin, Alan	LeGrand, IA	Transformational Leadership
Price, Ruth	Hays, KS	Spiritual Formation
Sluder, Charles	Pleasant Garden, NC	Pastoral Ministry
Spiegle, Joseph	Lawrence, KS	Spiritual Formation
Waller, Jesse	Greenleaf, ID	Quaker Studies

Graduates 2019

Associate of Arts

Anderson, Micah	Colorado Springs, CO	General Studies
Barber, Kristina	Belize City, Belize	General Studies
Eltringham, Courtney	Springfield, MO	General Studies
Haines, Ruthanna	Haviland, KS	Biblical Studies
Larson, John	Portland, OR	Biblical Studies
Lucas, Faith	Whittier, CA	General Studies
Tucker, Tanner	Newton, KS	General Studies
Vanderbeek, Taylor	Caldwell, ID	Biblical Studies

Bachelor of Arts

Boudreaux, Lillian	Andover, KS	Missions
Kick, Aaron	Miami, OK	Bible Theology
Kick, Karli	Kearney, NE	Bible Theology
Metcalfe, Bradley	Lake Stevens, WA	Youth Ministry
Muhr, Joshua	Silverton, OR	Missions
Murrell, Charity	Boise, ID	Bible Theology
Newton, Kaitlyn	Friendswood, TX	Bible Theology
Nikolas, Marissa	Kapa'a, HI	Bible Theology
Pfeiffer, Benjamin	Wichita, KS	Pastoral Ministry
Vang, Mason	St. Paul, MN	Bible Theology
Werstler, Jared	Uniontown, OH	Missions

Bachelor of Science

Adams, Nicole	Macksville, KS	Education K-6
Bevan, Bailee	El Dorado, KS	Business Administration
Camp, Noah	Winfield, KS	Youth Ministry

Faulconer, Destiny	Bend, OR	Psychology and Fam Studies
Faulconer, Gideon	Culver, OR	Psychology and Fam Studies
Fruh, Kaylie	Placentia, CA	Business Administration
Gasatura, Deborah	Kigali, Rwanda	Business Administration
Gwin, Samantha	Haviland, KS	Psychology and Fam Studies
Halverstadt, Elaina	Haviland, KS	Biblical Studies
Hays, Jared	Hesperia, CA	Business Administration
Hiser, Kaitlyn	Glenrock, WY	Business Administration
Holguin-Media, Yudit	Kinsley, KS	Psychology and Fam Studies
Jackson, George	Winfield, KS	Business Administration
Kucharek, Ryan	Gaylord, MI	Youth Ministry
Mabry, Taylor	Columbia, OH	Youth Ministry
Maydew, Victorya	Wichita, KS	Education K-6
Nguyen, Jennifer	Placentia, CA	Psychology and Fam Studies
Orieh, Chidera	Houston, TX	Business Administration
Owens, Mycha	Cullison, KS	Business Administration
Potter, Steven	Pratt, KS	Business Management
Richardson, Shawn	Colorado Springs, CO	Business Administration
Sander, Charles	Wichita, KS	Christian Leadership
Skipp, Rune	La Junta, CO	Business Administration
Williams, Jasmine	Derby, KS	Psychology and Fam Studies

Master of Arts

Afanda, Audrey	Raleigh, NC	Spiritual Formation
Bradbury, Mathew	Wellandport, ON	Missional Multiplication
Collick, Marcus	Salisbury, MD	Pastoral Ministry
Dahmer, Justin	Aurora, CO	Transformational Leadership
May, Tamika	Estherville, IA	Missional Multiplication
Mendenhall, Scott	Corona, CA	Transformational Leadership
Perrin, Nathan	Valton, WI	Quaker Studies
Russ, Samuel	New Orleans, LA	Transformational Leadership
Sampson, Aurora	Noorvik, AK	Family Ministries
Simpson, Dawn	Houston, TX	Spiritual Formation
Smith, Beth	Battle Creek, MI	Family Ministries

Graduates 2020

Associate of Arts

Gloude, Alexis	Goodwell, OK	General Studies
Le Shana, Sasha	Haviland, KS	General Studies
Schlichting, Kelsey	Ponca City, OK	General Studies

Bachelor of Arts

Cook, Jonna	Buffalo, OK	Bible Theology
Cox, Issac	Colorado Springs, CO	Bible Theology
Funk, Caleb	Lompoc, CA	Bible Theology
Johnson, Michale	Moran, KS	Youth Ministry & Pastoral Ministry
Norton, William	Rolla, KS	Missions

Pham, Long	Ho Chi Min, Vietnam	Missions
Stewart, Natalie	Haviland, KS	Pastoral Ministry
Taylor, Graham	Haviland, KS	Pastoral Ministry
Weinacht, Ashley	Greenleaf, ID	Worship Arts
White, Ethan	Huggins, MO	Pastoral Ministry

Bachelor of Science

Arnold, Kenneth	Lawton, OK	Sports Leadership
Barnes, Tristan	Osawatomie, KS	Psychology and Fam Studies
Berg, Jennifer Chino	Valley, AZ	Psychology
Brown, Hannah	Haviland, KS	Education K-6
Buehler, Sarah	Camas, WA	Psychology
Collick, Kayla	Georgetown, TX	Youth Ministry & Psychology and Fam Studies
Downing, Richard	Zanesfield, OH	Christian Leadership
Easterwood, Sarah	Rolla, KS	Worship Arts
Fitch, Rebekah	Argonia, KS	Education K-6
Goba, Patrick	Indianapolis, IN	Psychology
Gray-Smith, Hawa	Upper Darby, PA	Business Management
Hall, Justin	Haviland, KS	Worship Arts
Hendershot, Amber	Richmond, TX	Foundations of Education
Lancaster, Kylee	Miltonvale, KS	Psychology
Leemasters, Joshua	Wyandotte, OK	Psychology
Martinez, Cathy	Haviland, KS	Psychology and Fam Studies
Martinez, Kyri	Rolla, KS	Psychology
Mattes, Marissa	Lebanon, MO	Psychology
Moran, Nataly	Indianapolis, IN	Psychology
Nilsen, Eric	Placenta, CA	Business Administration
Nosach, David	Sacramento, CA	Business Administration
Pierce, Jordan	Houston, TX	Business Management
Poindexter, Jacolby	Missouri City, TX	Psychology and Fam Studies
Probst, Ashley	Cape Girardeau, MO	Business Management
Racster-Hall, Dalton	Great Falls, MT	Business Administration
Robinson, Heather	Wood River, IL	Business Administration
Robinson, Magic	New Orleans, LA	Psychology
Sanders, Ceress	Newberg, OR	Business Management (2nd)
Schneider, Madison	Cheney, KS	Worship Arts
Schuck, Mariana	Hugoton, KS	Education K-6
Schuck, Marissa	Hugoton, KS	Psychology and Fam Studies
Singleton, Karalyn	Melba, ID	Education K-6
Singleton, Tyree	Bennett, CO	Psychology and Fam Studies
Smith, Victoria	Freehold, NJ	Christian Leadership
Vestal, Sarah	Ramseur, NC	Psychology and Fam Studies
Watkins, Jessica	Brunswick, GA	Psychology
Widlicka, Kyle	Salem, OH	Youth Ministry
Wright, Kye	Douglass, KS	Worship Arts

Master of Arts

Basebya, Nicodeme	Musanze, Rwanda	Missional Multiplication
Climer, Curtis	Woodburn, OR	Transformational Leadership
Cox, Richard	Hays, KS	Pastoral Ministry
Franklin, Donna	Fishers, IN	Missional Multiplication
Huck, Tanner	Siloam Falls, AR	Sports Outreach
Jones, Roy	Chardon, OH	Spiritual Formation
Kozimor, Steven	Phoenix, AZ	Spiritual Formation
Savage, Rusty	Damascus, OH	Quaker Studies
Williams, Ivy	Upper Marlboro, MD	Family Ministries

Graduates 2021

Associate of Arts

Ballard, Cambrey	Haviland, KS	General Studies
Carter, Mark	Wichita, KS	General Studies
Danner, Brian	Kathleen, GA	Biblical Studies
Franklin, D'andre	Wichita, KS	General Studies
Stewart, Ben	Haviland, KS	General Studies

Bachelor of Arts

Smallbeck, Kaleigh	Tacoma, WA	Bible Theology
Temaat, Elliot	Fishers, IN	Bible Theology
Weber, Trey	Dodge City, KS	Missions

Bachelor of Science

Annen, Ivy	Hesston, KS	Psychology and Fam Studies
Beckem, Tyrone	Chicago, IL	Business Administration
Delagraentiss, Monique	Haviland, KS	Christian Leadership
Hall, Cianna	Haviland, KS	Education K-6
Hoving, William	Bristol, ME	Psychology and Fam Studies
Irvine, Marsena	St. John, KS	Psychology and Fam Studies
Johnson, Serenity	Ulysses, KS	Psychology
Lyon, Olivia	Russiaville, IN	Psychology and Fam Studies
Melton, Summer	Okay, OK	Psychology
Metcalf, Megan	Kinsley, KS	Business Administration
Moody, Amber	Halifax, VA	Psychology
Morin, Jennifer	Vancouver, WA	Psychology (2nd major)
Reynolds, Alexandria	Pelham, AL	Psychology
Smith Jr., Randell	Haynesville, LA	Sports Leadership
West, Taylor	Ordway, CO	Education K-6

Master of Arts

Andermann, Tracy	Lockridge, IA	Family Ministries
Bennett, Bethany	Medicine Lodge, KS	Family Ministries
Burke, Lacey	Ottawa, KS	Family Ministries
Collins, Sarah	Franklin, IN	Family Ministries
Fischer, Brian	Phillipsburg, KS	Transformational Leadership
Howard, Julie	Coyle, OK	Family Ministries

Jackson, Elizabeth	Shreveport, LA	Spiritual formation
Jackson, George	Winfield, KS	Missional Multiplication
Kennedy, Zachary	Farmland, IN	Pastoral Ministry
Kerchner, Diane	San Dimas, CA	Pastoral Ministry
Morton, Molly	Corona, CA	Pastoral Ministry
Muhr, Josiah	Silverton, OR	Missional Multiplication
Snyder, Ben	Farmland, IN	Practical Theology
Street, Gerald	Arvada, CO	Pastoral Ministry
Werstler, Jared	Haviland, KS	Spiritual formation
White, Ossie	Hazard, KY	Family Ministries

Graduates 2022

Associate of Arts

Adhikari, Steve	Wichita, KS	General Studies
Frazier, James	Irving, TX	General Studies
Lee, Hannah	Rose Hill, KS	General Studies
Pack, Ciana	Colorado Springs, CO	General Studies
Robertson, Kia	Humble, TX	General Studies
Savery, Christine	Wheat Ridge, CO	General Studies
Stegman, Kahrie	Pratt, KS	General Studies

Bachelor of Arts

Bogan, Ethan	Hugoton, KS	Pastoral Ministry
O'Brien, Jakob	Alva, KS	Intercultural Studies
Smith, Mason	Maize, KS	Pastoral Ministry
Tuttle, Andrew	Converse, IN	Bible Theology

Bachelor of Science

Andersen, Susan	Kinsley, KS	Business Administration
Bhattarai, Meg	Pittsburg, PA	Psychology and Fam Studies
Castillo, Jacob-Orione	Lathrop, CA	Sports & Recreation Ministry
Catlett, Joseph	Broken Bow, NE	Youth Ministry
Collick, Markeze	Salisbury, MD	Business Administration
Converse, Brittani	Downs, KS	Psychology and Fam Studies & Youth Ministry
Franklin, D'Andre	Wichita, KS	Sports & Recreation Ministry
Gloude, Alexis	Goodwell, OK	Business Administration
Groth, Chase	Sedgwick, KS	Worship Arts
Huck, Kaden	Coldwater, KS	Sports & Recreation Ministry
Huitt, Spencer	Hydro, OK	Business Management
Hutchens, Brian	Shepherd, MO	Christian Leadership
Johnson-Anderson, Beyonsia	Wichita, KS	Psychology and Fam Studies
King, Lydia	Haysville, KS	Education K-6
Meeks, Audra	Colorado Springs, CO	Education K-6
Ross, Kayla	Arlington, TX	Business Management
Stokes, Cassandra	Haviland, KS	Business Management
Street, Mollie	Arvada, CO	Education K-6
Tete, Trina	Wichita, KS	Psychology
Weller, Tresa	Newton, KS	Education K-6
West, Alannah	Leoti, KS	Education K-6

Master of Arts

Cunningham, Steve	Elizabeth City, NC	Biblical Translation
Foster, Mark	Liberty, MO	Biblical Translation
Johnson, Michale	Haviland, KS	Biblical Translation & Spiritual Formation
Marquez, Gloria	Kissimmee, FL	Biblical Translation
Nash, Amy	Chicago, IL	Quaker Studies
Nilsen, Erik	Yorba Linda, CA	Transformational Leadership
Norton, William	Rolla, KS	Quaker Studies
Oxner, Deanna	Pikesville, TN	Biblical Translation
Radcliff, Robert	Mason City, IA	Pastoral Ministry
Shawiak, Stacy	Ormond Beach, FL	Biblical Translation
Smith, C. Chris	Allen, TX	Biblical Translation
Taylor, Graham	Glen Elder, KS	Practical Theology

Graduates 2023

Associate of Arts

Entz, Lucy	Valley Center, KS	General Studies
Hannah, Christopher	Tallahassee, FL	General Studies
Kendall, Neal	Lompoc, CA	General Studies
Pack, Ciara	Colorado Springs, CO	General Studies

Bachelor of Arts

Coleman, Ariel	Greenleaf, ID	Bible Theology
Fitch, Sarah	Swayzee, IN	Bible Theology
Gentry, Clayton	Greenwood, IN	Pastoral Ministry
Halverstadt, Joel	Haviland, KS	Criminal Justice
Holeman, William	Manhattan, KS	Pastoral Ministry & Business Administration
Loewen, John	Meade, KS	Pastoral Ministry
Read, Savannah	Wichita, KS	Bible Theology

Bachelor of Science

Ballard, Cambrey	Haviland, KS	Business Administration
Brown, Chazden	Arlington, TX	Psychology
Danner, Brian	Kathleen, GA	Christian Leadership
Doubrava, McKenzy	Ellsworth, KS	Psychology
Fitch, Hunter	Norwich, KS	Business Administration
Franklin, D'Andre	Wichita, KS	Sports Leadership
Frazier, Cassie	Irving, TX	Education K-6
Gentry, Tayler	Greenwood, IN	Education K-6
Gonzalez, Marcus	Haviland, KS	Christian Leadership
Grande, Brenda	Houston, TX	Worship Arts
Haines, Ruthanna	Haviland, KS	Christian Leadership
Jackson, Ja'mia	Wichita, KS	Education K-6
Johnson, Elizabeth	Moran, KS	Business Administration & Worship Arts
Loewen, Autumn	Homedale, ID	Education K-6

McDonald, Madilyn	Wichita, KS	Education K-6
Nicholson-Marsh, Margaret	Trenton, MI	Bible Theology
Perez, Dillon	San Antonio, TX	Business Administration
Scales, Mauri	Wichita, KS	Education K-6
Thompson, Richie	Burlington, ON	Business Administration
Urban, Megan	Pratt, KS	Business Administration
Vaughn, Courtney	Anthony, KS	Psychology
Vaughn, DeJay	Anthony, KS	Christian Leadership & Pastoral Ministry

Master of Arts

Cunneen, Jennifer	Osteen, FL	Bible Translation
Flood, Cody	Greenfield, IN	Pastoral Ministry
Perry, Kathi	Greystone, Ireland	Practical Theology
Woodard, Robert	Battle Ground, WA	Practical Theology

Index

A Heritage to Remember –
A Future to Claim, 33
Accreditation, 18, 115, 124
Accrediting Commission of
the North Central
Association, 18
Adair, Andy, 144
Adhikari, Bob, 95, 96
ADVANTAGE!, 24, 25, 26,
28, 29, 31, 35, 36, 44, 46,
47, 50, 51, 55, 57, 58, 62,
68, 69, 79, 80
Agbuya, Christianne, 145
All-school Day of Prayer, 15
American Association of
Bible Colleges (AABC), 6
Anders, Lee, 72, 107
Anderson, Chris, 28, 41, 48
Anderson, Jeremy, 41, 46
Anderson, Ray, 73
Arbelaez, Michelle, 35
Aria, 74
Arthur, Ned, 108
Ashlock, Bernard, 55, 77
Associate Dean of External
Studies, 44
Associate degree in Arts and
Sciences, 18
Associate degree in Biblical
Studies, 18
Association for Biblical
Higher Accreditation, 19
Association for Christian
Schools International, 17

Ballard, Traci, 102
Barber, Shelly, 122
Barclay Collee Singers, 13
Barclay College Advantage!, 80
Barclay College Athletic
association, 28
Barclay College Drama
Troupe, 14, 143
Barclay College School of
Graduate Studies, 104, 141
Barclay College Singers, 14,
42, 89, 143
Barclay, Robert, 8, 147
Baseball, 41, 48, 49, 50
Bashford, Kurt, 49
Basketball, 14, 22, 40, 41, 44,
46, 47, 48, 49, 50, 60, 61,
81, 109, 133, 135
Basketball Youth Camp, 133
Batten, Kristen, 46
Bauer, Dusty, 48
Bear's Den, 55, 73, 78
Becker, Bruce, 31
Becker, Chrstine, 29
Beeler, Jim, 36
Bennett, Andrew, 58
Benny Bear, 133
Binford, Allen and May, 99
Board of Trustees, 4, 33, 37,
65, 70, 124, 127
Bond, David, 49
Bontrager, Coleen, 14
Book Mark, 27
Bousman, Tyler, 60

Brandywine Advantage! site, 24, 97
Bridges, Norman, 18
Brodhead, Shandy, 122
Brokar, Amy, 22
Brookman, David, 56, 64
Brown, Dawn, 47, 55
Brown, Dr. Derek, 108, 118, 126, 131, 132, 141, 148, 149, 150
Brown, Stanley, 18
Bryan, DeWayne, 64, 71
Bryan, Paul, 47
Bryan, Royce, 102
Bunce, Josh, 96, 116, 118
Bunce, Marcy, 55
Burns, Michael, 36
Business Manager, 13, 47, 64, 69
Business of the Year Award, 99
Butler, Katelyn, 144

Caldwell, Katrina, 81
Campaign to have 20 million by 2020, 126
Campus of Lights, 89
Candidacy status, 25, 36, 37, 51, 91, 104, 106, 110, 113, 115, 120
Carlson, Amanda, 88
Carlson, Audrey, 60
Carlson, LeAnn, 98
Carlson, Nathaniel, 61, 74
Carnival of Praise, 30, 57
Carpenter, Brad, 61, 95
Carpenter, Jeff, 15, 29, 41, 49

Carpenter, Sheldon, 54
Carswell, Justin, 58, 64
Cavanaugh, Paul, 37
Centennial, 17, 124, 125
Centennial Spectacular, 17
Centro de Estudios Teologicos Latinamericano, 82
Certificate of Excellence in Church Leadership, 75
Chandler & Newville Inc., 33
Chandler, Maurice, 33, 35, 40, 49, 50, 52, 53, 56
Chesnes, Matthew, 102
Chitwood, David, 45
Choate, Brenda, 14, 18
Christian Education major, 13
Christian School Elementary Education (CSEE), 45
Christiansen, Lisa, 140
Christmas Pageant, 109, 118, 125
Church Planting Summit, 81, 83
Chuyma, Diego, 14
Clark, Hank, 57
Clark, Roy, 18
Cloud, Curt, 40
Clubb, Carlotta, 47
Coconis, Madeleine, 29
Coleman, Tim, 144
College 101 classes, 79, 80
College Board, 4, 5, 23, 38, 63, 65, 127, 136
College Hill Apartments, 112, 124

College Level Examination Program, 16
Committee for Assessment and Planning (CAP), 36
Cook, Melba, 47
Cook, Ruth, 47
Cordova, Jesus, 49
Couch, Cheryl, 110, 132
Couch, Michael, 111
Council on Post-secondary Accreditation, 6
COVID, 126, 128
Covington, Del, 13, 14, 15, 21, 143, 144
Covington, Sherry, 13
Cox, Isaac, 145
Crain, Eric, 41, 48, 49
Crowell Trust, 43
Cunningham, Anita, 58
Current statement of mission, 3, 151

Damron, Gary, 79
Daniel, Jarod, 145
Davis, Barbara, 73
Davis, Steve, 50
Deaton, Briley, 60
Decade of Development, 11, 12
December 2007 ice-storm, 90
Derstein, Stacy, 110
Dirrim, Kenn, 116
Doelling, Clarence, 79
Doggett (Unruh), Holly, 79
Drama team, 143, 144
Durham, Debra, 15, 29
Easley, Brian, 110

Easley, Ray, 110
Effective Christian life, service, and leadership, 4
Elementary Education major, 13, 21, 95, 110, 115
Ellis, Robert and Anita, 120
Elmore, Steve, 35, 42, 144
Evangelical Friends (Quaker) college, 4

Face-to-face, 129, 138, 139, 140
Factor, Tony, 30, 31
Family Ministries (MAFM), 140
Ferguson, Willard and Doris, 59, 89
Fiber-optic A+ Interactive Television System, 15
Fine Arts Center, 117
Fitch, Jeanie, 16
Fleener, Amy, 40, 47, 49
Flinkman, Herb, 29
Fly, John, 58
Follette (Harvey), Brockie, 119, 123, 126, 130, 149
Following the Call, 11
Forest (Stewart), Natalie, 145
Foster, Mike, 48
Founded by Friends, 76, 94, 103
Founders Hall, 12, 37, 38, 39
Fowler, Art, 20
Frans, Elkie (Burnside), 30, 36
Frazier, David, 73, 74

Frazier, Dr. Herb, 47, 69, 70, 84, 92, 98, 115
Frazier, Dr. Jeremie, 36, 99
Frazier, Dr. Royce, 13, 70, 77, 91, 98, 101, 102, 104, 105, 108, 113, 117, 120, 125, 139, 149
Frazier, Megan, 74
Free tuition, 84, 88
Friends Bible College, 2, 3, 5, 6, 7, 8
Friends University, 2
Fulbright (Roberts), Pam, 79, 83
Fulbright, Dennis, 79

Garrett, De Ann, 47
Garrett, Tim, 35, 49, 73
Gates, Chad, 21
Gates, Julie, 21
Gere, Jake, 81
Gillingham, Jeff, 21
Ginther, Ron, 13
Go Ye Into All the World campaign, 54, 58
Goering, Katrina, 62
Gonzales, Renee, 98
Grace, Andrea, 144
Great Commission Bike-A-Thon, 49
Great Western Dining, 50
Griffin, Elizabeth, 35, 44, 57

Haase, Ryan, 29, 47, 73, 97, 99, 116, 122, 126
Haley, Jared, 61, 74
Hall, Pat, 102

Hallett, Andrea, 29
Halverstadt, Dr. Adrian, 101, 133, 139
Ham, Bob, 18
Ham, Marilyn, 102
Hanneken, Brian, 79
Hansen, Kim, 128, 131, 133, 134
Harkness (Leppert), Emily, 47, 79, 83, 96, 99
Harkness, Jon, 80, 92
Hart, Rita, 46
Haselwood Phillina, 47
Haviland Housing Corporation, 112
Hawkins, Tim, 95, 126, 132
Healton, Mark, 95
Healy, Tara, 60, 144
Heartland Conference, 77
Hickman, Darby, 49
Hicks, Bruce, 20
Hicks, Dorothy, 13, 21
Hietala, Dr. David, 53, 54, 56, 62, 63, 64, 67
Hinderliter, Chris, 41
Hinderliter, Tom, 29
Hockett Auditorium, 8, 12, 49, 78, 85, 102, 118
Hodges, Jerry, 79
Hodges, Travis, 47, 50
Hodson, Martha, 88, 122
Hoffman, Dr. Paul, 141
Holguin, Andrea, 88
Holliday, Jack, 97
Home College, 26, 44, 82
Hoops, Dr. Marva, 141
Horton, Janet, 58

Houston Graduate School of Theology, 18, 22
Howard, Nicole Ray, 49
Huck, Tanner, 132, 133
Huff, Del, 13, 14

In-service, 16, 19, 36
Institute for Pastoral Leadership Development, 74
Institute of the Blessing, 97

Jackson Hall, 16, 43, 78, 85, 86, 87
Jackson, Sheldon, 4, 13, 18, 27, 39
Jantz, Everett, 29, 73, 89
Jay, Kathy, 13
Johnson, Dr. Fred, 13, 47, 131
Johnson, Elizabeth, 146
Johnson, Kendy, 97
Johnson, Michale, 134
Johnson, Rick, 31, 51
Johnston, Brenda, 29, 47
Johnston, Dr. Robin, 9, 11, 19, 20, 21, 27, 30, 73, 118
Jonah and the German Whale, 27
Jones, Gary, 102
Jones, Kaylan, 59
Jones, Morris, 97
Jubilee Singers, 13
Juniors Global, 114, 116, 118
Kaleo Academy, 119, 123, 127, 129, 130

Kansas Central Bible Training School, 125
Kansas Department of Education, 17, 113, 115
Kavalski, Angelique, 144
Kelley, Jan, 22
Kelley, Mark, 12, 24, 36
Kellum, Kathleen, 21
Kemper, Ruth (Miller), 77
Kendall Justin, 55
Kendall, Hannah, 79, 118
Kendall, Logan, 15
Kendall, Lois, 35, 83, 100
Kendall, Ryan, 50, 60, 61, 73, 79, 96, 114, 117, 123
Kershner, Jon, 110
Kick, Aaron, 121, 149
King, Keith, 21, 22
Kingrey, Dave, 74, 92, 96, 103, 108, 116, 131, 134, 135, 136, 138, 149
Knepper, Dr. Sheila, 28
Kramer, Dan, 141
Kreger, Whitney, 122
Kuffel, Matt, 49
Kunsman, Doug, 13
Kuzak, Lisa, 21

Ladies Auxiliary Auction, 18, 29, 56, 89, 133
Lady Bears, 15, 62, 98, 131
Lawski, Kathryn, 87
Le Shana, Dr. Jim, 110, 114, 126, 139, 150
Le Shana, Jeanine, 110
Leach, Stan, 140

Leadership Education for Adult Professionals (LEAP), 24
Lee, Kevin, 49, 96, 97, 134
Leininger, Chelle, 111, 132, 149
Leininger, Jim, 13
Leininger, Roberta, 13
Lemmons Hall, 38, 43, 99
Lemmons, John, 43
Leppert, Dr. Glenn, 19, 20, 21, 23, 25, 35, 45, 57, 67, 68, 70, 73, 75, 76, 77, 78, 83, 92, 103, 105, 122, 131, 136, 149, 150
Lewis, Jo, 13
Lewis, Larry, 110, 123, 132
Lilly Endowment, 119
Lingafelter, Brad, 47, 50, 61
Lofgren, Josh, 61
Logan, Rick, 49
Longstroth, Heidi, 21, 47
Lund, James, 29
Lyngdoh, Prosperly B., 58

MA in Spiritual Formation (MASF), 139
MA in Transformational Leadership (MATL), 139
Mabee Foundation, 43, 117
Mabry, David, 116, 141
Mann, Steven, 111
Manning, Billy, 29
Mary Poppins, 128
Master of Arts in Biblical Translation (MABT), 141
Master of Arts in Missional Multiplication (MAMM), 140
Master of Arts in Sports Outreach (MASO), 140
Master of Arts in Transformational Leadership (MATL), 104, 138
MATL in Professional Studies, 139, 151
MATL-PS, 139
MCCC Basketball tournament, 15
McCracken, Phyllis, 26
McGilberry, Sean, 144
McKenna, Carol, 48
Meredith, Lora, 116
Merle Roe Preaching Award, 14
Midwest Christian College Conference, 15, 49, 62, 117
Miller, Mark, 122, 132, 135
Mills, Brian, 77
Mini term, 13
Miracle, 69, 71, 72, 73, 93, 97
Miranda-Troup, Pilo, 122
Mission statement, 2, 82, 105
Missions Emphasis Week, 30
Mitchell, Wanda, 18
Mitigation Plan, 129
Moment in Prayer, 129
Momentous, 127
Monaghan, Adam, 95, 102
Monday Study Break, 60

Moody, Dr. Walter, 23, 24, 27, 28, 30, 31, 36
Morley, Sylvia, 28, 77
Mortimer, Kevin, 40, 108, 109, 118, 149, 150
Music Department, 13

National Christian College Athletic Association, 28
National Bible Collegiate Athletic Association, 15
National Friends Church Multiplication Conference, 115
Neifert, Pat, 14
Nessler, Mary, 59
Newton, Katie, 121
Now is the Time Campaign, 64
Nursing, 127, 131, 134, 136

O'Brien, Jakob, 150
Office of External Studies, 44
Ogle, Austin, 122
On Mission With God, 59
Operation John 13, 80, 97
Oren (Leppert), Tricia, 36, 73
Ostrowski, Susan, 59

Parker, Jeanette, 35
Pastoral Ministries (MAPM), 140
Patterson, Sarah, 13, 21
Payette, Dr. Skip, 59, 60, 76, 78, 79, 83
Pedigo, Joel, 145
Pedigo, Marlene, 97
Pedigo, Steve, 97
Pelzl, Louise, 58
Penna, Jesse, 96, 108, 122, 149
Penna, Julie, 88
Pennington, Kim, 64
Pent, Margaret, 35, 41, 144
Performance
  Cinderella, 121
  Fall 1997 Jonah and the German Whale, 143
  Fall 2002 How to Fold a Shirt, 144
  Fall 2002 Oh Lord, 144
  Fall 2009 Harvey, 144
  Fall 2011 Monday Night Live, 144
  Fall 2019 Much Ado About Nothing, 145
  Fall 2021 All Together Now!, 146
  Fall 2022 The Lion, the Witch, and the Wardrobe, 146
  Salt and Light, 42
  Spring 1998 Book Mark, 144
  Spring 1999 The Way He Leads Me, 144
  Spring 2000 Salt and Light, 143
  Spring 2005 Princess Bride, 144
  Spring 2011 Beauty and the Beast, 144
  Spring 2013 Cinderella, 145
  Spring 2018 Joseph and the Amazing Technicolor Dreamcoat, 145
  Spring 2019 Beauty and the Beast, 145
  Spring 2020/Fall 2021 Mary Poppins, 145
  Spring 2021 Newsies, 146

Spring 2022 The Play that Goes Wrong, 146
Spring 2023 Cinderella, 146
Perrin, Nate, 149
Phillips Hall, 12, 28, 37, 38, 39, 43, 46, 59, 86, 97, 99
Pickard, Dr. Gene, 13, 22, 123, 136, 149
Pickard, Jason, 41, 49
Pinkerton, James, 49, 73, 74
Plainfield Advantage! site, 97
Post, Scott, 127, 132, 134
Powell, Roger, 49, 109
Prayer team for admissions, 59
Preliminary Information Form (PIF), 19, 37, 91
Purpose, 2, 3, 6, 8, 9, 102, 103, 104, 105, 147, 151, 152

Quaker Studies (MAQS), 140

Rader, Stephen, 15
Rahenkamp, Jim, 13
Reading day, 15, 27
Re-affirmed accreditation, 82
Re-discovering Your Teenager, 83
Reeser, Keith, 81
Regier, Delbert, 59
Regier, Viola, 59
Reinhart, Laurie, 97
Riggs (Potter), Anissa, 111, 116

Ritschard, Erik, 28, 36, 58, 67
Robert Barclay Institute, 124, 147, 148, 149
Robison, Geoff, 14
Roe, Pam, 13
Roher, Thad, 14, 48
Romosser, Paul, 111
Roseles, Logan, 146
Ross Borchers, Lynne Ann, 48
Ross Ellis Center for Ministry. *See* Ross Ellis Center for the Fine Arts
Ross family, 120
Ross, Jared, 35, 42, 47, 83, 113, 144, 149, 150
Ross, Jeannie, 122, 123, 132
Ross, Paul, 52
Ross-Ellis Center for the Fine Arts, 120, 121, 124, 127
Roundtable talk with faculty and administration, 60
Routon Ken, 49
Run for missions, 95

Sachs, Kim, 73
Saint Mary of the Plains College, 17, 45
Sanders, Arden, 21
Sandstrom, Richard, 46
Sarver, Jon, 13, 26
Sazama, Heather, 55, 73
Schamberger, Justin, 144
Schlichting, Priscilla, 35
Schoonover, Joe, 8

Scott, Dan, 28
Senior Camp on the Prairies, 115
Serve day, 98, 109, 112
Shetley, Randi, 97, 130, 144
Shetley, Shane, 127, 129, 134
Simmons, Dr. Jerry, 95, 110, 123
Sirkel, Tricia, 29
Smelser, Allen, 95
Smith, Maria, 110
Smitherman, Amber, 144
Smitherman, David, 33
Smitherman, Kris, 74
Snyder-Patterson, Linda, 102, 110
Soccer, 14, 15, 29, 40, 41, 44, 48, 50, 60, 61, 74, 89, 109, 116, 122
Sorensen, Kris, 49
Sorensen, Tammy, 15
Southammavong, Tony, 29, 41, 47, 49
South-Central Community Foundation, 43
Spiritual Formation (SF), 138
Staats, Shaleah, 59
Staley, Ben, 116
Starkey, Jeff, 59
Steiner, John, 21
Steiner, Pamela, 21
Stevens, Kayleen, 49, 97
Stewart, Kim, 79, 132
Stimpson, Dr. Donald, 28
Stokes, Aaron, 122, 132, 149, 150

Student Information System, 16
Svoboda, Scott, 28, 35

Tabor College, 17, 45, 115
Talley, Stephen, 29
Temaat, Mike, 96
Teter, Dorothy, 26
Teter, Steve, 96, 109
Tetuan, Isaiah, 48
The John Trent Institute for the Blessing at Barclay College, 107
Thomas, Dr. Debby, 150
Thompson, Marjorie, 69, 76
Thompson, Neil, 28
Thompson, Richard, 134
Thornburg, Heather, 122
Till, Paul, 35
Together We Succeed Campaign, 71
Tornado, May 2007, 84, 85, 86, 87, 98
Towne, Becky, 29
Towne, Jim, 131
Triplett, Mark, 111
Tucker, Annette, 47
Tutoring Center, 111

Unruh, John, 109
Unruh, Kay, 110
Unruh, ohn, 98
Urban, Winona, 29

Van Dame, Tiffany, 90, 122
VandenHoek, Randy, 14
Vanderploeg, Amber, 73
Vanderploeg, Nathan, 121
VanMeter Jessica (Haley), 73
VanMeter, Jason, 73
Velazquez, Carmen, 21
Visioning Community, 147
Volleyball, 15, 44, 47, 48, 49, 50, 60, 74, 98, 109, 117, 132, 135
Volunteers, 26, 43, 55, 78
Volunteers on Wheels, 43, 44, 55, 78

Wachtel, Bryan, 50
Walkemeyer, Dr. Kent, 140
Waller, Jesse, 149
Weber, Brandon, 48
Wedel, Ruth Ann, 35, 55, 67
Weinacht, Alan, 40
Welcome Center, 59, 79
West Hall, 16, 38, 55
West, Judy, 79
Westerhaus, Catherine, 28
Wetmore, Angie, 110, 122, 132
What's in a Name?, 5
What's UP at Barclay e-mail newsletter, 130
Wheeler, Adele, 98
Wheeler, Dr. Tony, 96, 97, 106
Wheeler, Harlan, 48, 59
Wheeler, Stacy, 97
White, Dr. Keith, 110, 131, 136
White, Sheryl, 21, 30
Whiteman (Morley), Nancy, 47
Who's the Oldest Living Alum?, 40
Wilder, Derek, 109
Wiley, Janet, 28
Williams, David, 35, 75, 76, 78, 80, 96, 108, 113, 138, 139, 149
Williams, Josiah, 79
Williams, Sarah, 61, 74, 81
Williams, Shelby, 81, 97
Williamson, Nathan, 48
Windorski, Jessica, 87
Winters, Dr. Clifford T., 141
With Everything, 121
Wolfe, Ton, 47
Wolhlgemuth, Don, 47
Woodall, Joshua, 60
Woods, Carla, 58
Wright, Carol, 12, 97, 109
Wright, Gary, 12, 97, 109
Wright, Mark and Kathy, 97
Writing Center, 92, 111, 112, 116

Year of the Alumni, 40
Year of the Church, 40
YM419 YFC Summer Institute, 36
Youth For Christ certificate, 26

Youth For Christ
  International, 18, 23, 36
Youth Ministry classes, 13

Zapfe, Christa, 79
Zuck, Gail, 47

ABOUT THE AUTHOR

Glenn Leppert holds a B.A. in Secondary Education from Northwest Nazarene University and an M.A. in Religion from George Fox Evangelical Seminary. Glenn also earned an M.A. in History from Fort Hays State University and a Ph.D. in History from Kansas State University. He has served as a teacher and principal in Nigeria, directed an inner-city education program, and pastored in Oregon. A member of Barclay College's faculty since 1985, he has authored several textbooks and has presented at various academic conferences. Glenn and his wife, Sue, reside in Haviland, Kansas.

www.ingramcontent.com/pod-product-compliance
Lightning Source LLC
Chambersburg PA
CBHW060600080526
44585CB00013B/640